JAMES MARTIN

JAMES MARTIN

Essential Writings

Selected with an Introduction by

JAMES T. KEANE

ORBIS BOOKS
Maryknoll, New York 10545

ORBIS  BOOKS

Maryknoll, New York 10545

Fathers and Brothers
MARYKNOLL™

Founded in 1970, Orbis Books endeavors to publish works that enlighten the mind, nourish the spirit, and challenge the conscience. The publishing arm of the Maryknoll Fathers and Brothers, Orbis seeks to explore the global dimensions of the Christian faith and mission, to invite dialogue with diverse cultures and religious traditions, and to serve the cause of reconciliation and peace. The books published reflect the views of their authors and do not represent the official position of the Maryknoll Society. To learn more about Maryknoll and Orbis Books, please visit our website at www.maryknollsociety.org.

Library of Congress Cataloging-in-Publication Data

Names: Martin, James, 1960- author. | Keane, James Thomas, editor.
Title: James Martin : essential writings / selected with an introduction by James T. Keane.
Description: Maryknoll, New York : Orbis Books, 2017. | Series: Modern spiritual masters series
Identifiers: LCCN 2016041667 (print) | LCCN 2016054085 (ebook) | ISBN 9781626982130 (pbk.) | ISBN 9781608336784 (e-book)
Subjects: LCSH: Catholic Church—Doctrines.
Classification: LCC BX1751.3 .M258 2017 (print) | LCC BX1751.3 (ebook) | DDC
   282—dc23
LC record available at https://lccn.loc.gov/2016041667

Contents

Sources and Acknowledgments

The selections in this book are largely drawn from the previously published materials of James Martin, S.J. Grateful acknowledgment is made to the following entities for permission to reprint from copyrighted materials: America Media, the *Huffington Post*, *Portland Magazine*, and the *Wall Street Journal*. In two cases, material has been drawn from unpublished talks given at the Los Angeles Religious Education Congress.

I owe a special debt of gratitude to Joseph McAuley of America Media, whose assistance in organizing James Martin's prolific writings was invaluable in the early stages of the creation of this volume. His colleagues at America Media have also been of great assistance in this project, offering their customary expertise, bonhomie, and encouragement throughout.

Finally, I want to thank James Martin himself, a man who has played many parts in the unfolding of my own life over the past fifteen years: friend, editor, spiritual director, mentor, confidant, occasional confessor, erstwhile brother, and housemate, and a man I am proud to have stood shoulder to shoulder with during times of struggle and times of joy. It has been a privilege to read through the literary fruit of his faithful life of contemplation, action, and diligent service in the name of Jesus to the People of God.

Specific permissions include:

"True Selves and False Ones." *Becoming Who You Are: Insights on the True Self from Thomas Merton and Other Saints*, 19-27. Mahwah, NJ: Hidden Spring, 2006. Copyright © 2006 by James Martin, SJ. Hidden-Spring is an imprint of Paulist Press, Inc. Excerpt reprinted by permission of Paulist Press, Inc. www.paulistpress.com.

"Lourdes Diary." In *Lourdes Diary: Seven Days at the Grotto of Massabieille*, 23-60. Chicago: Loyola Press, 2006. Copyright © 2006 by James Martin, SJ. Excerpt reprinted by permission of Loyola Press. www.loyolapress.com.

Introduction: The Call of the King

The history of Christianity includes many a narrative about a young man or woman who pursues the rewards of a worldly life, seeking fulfilment first in money, power, sex, or the countless other desiderata offered by the culture around him or her, only to experience a powerful conversion to a life of discipleship after that misspent youth. We know some of these stories well because the men and women who lived them became saints and Christian exemplars, such as St. Augustine, St. Ignatius of Loyola, or Dorothy Day, and wrote extensively of their experiences of life before coming to Christ and new life. To the extent their previous life seems empty, so the fruitfulness of their new life seems all the more abundant. Their stories make for some of the most compelling spiritual memoirs of every age, partly because reading their stories allows us to imagine our saints and role models as more human, more like us, and therefore makes us aspire to be more like them. They can quiet the mocking voice that says what is broken cannot be fixed, what is lost cannot be found.

The twentieth century offered up a quintessential example of the genre in the story of Thomas Merton, a privileged young man who eventually forsook his dissolute existence to become a Trappist monk. His 1948 book, *The Seven Storey Mountain*, is still considered a classic of the *conversion memoir* genre. Its pages reveal a man who took to his newfound Catholic faith with all the gusto and rigor with which he had previously worshipped the false idols of materialism and excess. The Brother Louis one encounters in *The Seven Storey Mountain* has no doubts about his new faith and entertains no question that his flight from the world was what saved him from it. "So Brother Matthew locked the gate behind me," he writes of entering the

1

Abbey of Gethsemani, "and I was enclosed in the four walls of my new freedom."

Merton's story didn't end there, however; the archetypal conversion story had many more chapters to come. Though he remained a Trappist monk until his death in 1968, Merton became something rather different from the hermit he imagined he would be for the rest of his life. While still residing in Gethsemani, he found himself opening up more and more to the concerns of the world. In fact, over the last ten years of his life, Merton became perhaps the most influential Catholic in the United States in the worlds of literature, media, and social activism. His correspondents and close friends grew to include some of the major figures of the age, ranging from global intellectuals, writers, and poets to the leaders of the peace and anti–Vietnam War movements, to popular musicians and more. (For example, *Publishers Weekly* announced in August 2016 that Bob Dylan scholar Robert Hudson would be publishing a "book-length study of Dylan's influence on the life and work of Thomas Merton." Not Merton's influence on Dylan; Dylan's influence on Merton) Even if he felt most at home in his hermitage at Gethsemani, Merton also found that flight from the vices of the world needn't mean contempt for that world itself; rather, it could mean participation in that world in a different but still full way—as a commentator, a critic, a guide, a voice of faith and of reason. He found a balance in his life whereby he could, to quote St. Paul, "put off the old man" while still participating in and influencing American culture, and particularly American Catholic culture, in a truly incarnational sense.

It is perhaps no surprise, then, that the figure in American Catholicism whose current role in the American Church most closely corresponds to Merton's outsized role by the end of his life was in fact inspired in his own embrace of his vocation by Merton himself. James Martin, S.J., the Jesuit priest who is perhaps American Catholicism's most prominent public figure, was a lukewarm, nonpracticing Catholic on the fast track to executive riches at General Electric when he happened upon a documentary on Thomas Merton one night while watching television. Thirty years later, Martin is a million miles away from that life as a corporate executive, and yet paradoxically the Jesuit residence in which he lives is literally right around the corner from it in Midtown Manhattan. Though his vows commit him to poverty, chastity, and obedience as a Jesuit priest, he is without question a *Catholic celebrity*, one of the most recognized and trusted religious figures in the United States. Like Merton before him, Martin's abandonment of the trappings of a worldly life has led him not to a life of obscurity and isolation but to his current prominent role in the culture as a commentator, a critic, a guide, a voice of faith and of reason.

Martin's articles are consistently among the most popular printed by *America*, the Jesuit magazine where he is editor at large and has served in roles ranging from television critic to acting publisher to art director over the years. He has also published in countless other magazines and newspapers, including the *New York Times,* the *Washington Post, Commonweal, The Tablet,* and many more. Over the past decade, the online conduits of news and opinion such as *Slate* or *Huffington Post* have also become frequent publishers of Martin's work. These publications have all paralleled his prolific career as a writer and editor of books, many of which have topped the best-seller lists and won awards in (and beyond) the world of religious publishing. Television and social media have provided even broader platforms for Martin's work of evangelization and education, including his use of humor and a light touch to convey the essential truths of the faith. Finally, Martin has proved remarkably adept at taking complex and/or abstruse religious and spiritual concepts and making them accessible and meaningful to the contemporary religious seeker or believer.

PILGRIM JOURNEY

Born in 1960 and raised in Plymouth Meeting, Pennsylvania, a suburb of Philadelphia (a past that has left its mark on his lexicon and pronunciation), Martin was baptized Catholic but not raised in a particularly religious home, and he often admits in his writings that the cultural tropes so familiar to cradle Catholics were often concepts he assimilated and understood only years later in the Jesuits. He attended the University of Pennsylvania from 1978 to 1982, graduating with a bachelor's of science in economics with a concentration in finance from the university's prestigious Wharton School of Business. From 1982 until 1988, he worked in corporate finance at General Electric in New York City and Connecticut, a time he has often described as financially remunerative but personally unsatisfying.

As mentioned above, Martin's conversion narrative truly began one night after work at General Electric, when he chanced upon Paul Wilkes's documentary on Thomas Merton, *Merton: A Film Biography*. Intrigued by the famous monk's life and spirituality, he began to delve deeper into his writings, starting with *The Seven Storey Mountain* and moving on to *No Man Is an Island*. The latter book, Martin later told journalist Krista Tippett, includes the following lines that affected Martin so profoundly he considers them the beginning of the end of his career in finance and the birth of his vocation to religious life:

> *Why do we spend our lives striving to be something that we would never want to be, if only we knew what we wanted? Why do we waste our time doing things which, if we only stopped to think about them, are just the opposite of what we were made for?*

After exploring different options with his parish priest and vacillating between fervor for his newfound vocation and reticence about such a dramatic change in his life (it felt "crazy—like joining the circus," Martin later told a reporter from *USA Today*), he entered the New England Province of the Society of Jesus (the Jesuits) as a novice in the summer of 1988. Years later, he confessed that much of the history and spirituality of the storied order of priests and brothers was a mystery to him at the time.

That two-year novitiate process included several "experiments" (short ministry assignments) working with the poor and the needy, including time spent in a hospice in Jamaica run by Mother Teresa's sisters, the Missionaries of Charity. Most importantly, the novitiate introduced him to the *Spiritual Exercises*, the rigorous and rightly famous method of prayer and discernment crafted by St. Ignatius of Loyola, the founder of the Jesuits. Every Jesuit novice undertakes the full *Long Retreat* (thirty days of silence while being led through the *Spiritual Exercises* by a director) during his first year in the novitiate (then again at the end of his formation before taking final vows), and the retreat is intended as a touchstone to which the retreatant can return for spiritual nourishment and resources throughout one's life. Retreat centers throughout the world offer the full *Spiritual Exercises* as well as eight-day retreats and daily meditation programs with a similar structure to people from all walks of life, and Jesuit and Ignatian institutions throughout the world draw their inspiration from the themes and prayers of the *Spiritual Exercises*. Those same themes, spiritual guidelines, and methods of prayer are prominent in all of Martin's writings.

After taking perpetual vows of poverty, chastity, and obedience in the Jesuits in the summer of 1990, Martin spent three years studying philosophy at Loyola University Chicago. Next, Martin was missioned to Nairobi, Kenya, to work with refugees in East Africa during Regency, the traditional period during a Jesuit's long training when he works for several years before resuming academic study. His experiences there—and the people he encountered during that time—have played a profound role in Martin's life and work since, including inspiring in him a lifelong appreciation for the struggles of those at the margins of church and society. Assigned to work with the Jesuit Refugee Service, Martin helped found the Mikono Centre, a handicraft shop in Nairobi that helps East African refugees who had settled in the city's sprawling slums to achieve some financial independence through the sale of authentic arts and crafts. During that time, he worked with refugees from Ethiopia, Sudan, Somalia,

Rwanda, Uganda, and elsewhere who were hoping to start their own businesses. Writing in *America* of one particular refugee named Benjamin, Martin concluded,

> *When I think of Benjamin, and of the Christian life, I think that whenever I get to heaven, God will not ask how many articles or books I've written, how many degrees I've received or how many times I've appeared on television. I think the first thing God will ask is, "How is my friend Benjamin?"*

Near the end of his second year in Nairobi, Martin began preparing to move back to the United States for his theology studies, the final stage in a Jesuit's training before ordination to the priesthood. However, in a decision that would have far-reaching and unexpected consequences for Martin's vocation as well as for the Jesuits themselves, his superiors decided he needed another year of training before he could begin theology studies. Because Martin had already begun writing (including articles for *America* and what would later become his first book, *This Our Exile: A Spiritual Journey with the Refugees of East Africa*, Martin's 1999 memoir for Orbis Books about his time in East Africa), he was missioned to *America*, the national Jesuit magazine of faith, culture, and the arts, for a third year of regency, working as a writer and editor. Thus began a prolific two-decade ministry of media work that has showed no signs of slowing.

Following his stint at *America*, Martin spent four years of study at Weston Jesuit School of Theology in Cambridge, MA, during which he earned both M.Div. and Th.M. degrees. He was ordained a priest in June 1999 and reassigned to *America* as an editor. In 2009, he took final vows in the Society of Jesus.

BOOKS

Alongside his work at *America* (where his published articles number well over two hundred), Martin has also been an extraordinarily prolific speaker, retreat director, and homilist over the years, including a regular assignment as visiting priest at St. Ignatius Loyola Church in Manhattan. The demand from parishes, retreat houses, and church institutions for Martin as a speaker is so great that his calendar is often full up to two years in advance.

He has also become one of the most popular book authors in the Catholic world. His first book, the aforementioned *This Our Exile: A Spiritual Journey with the Refugees of East Africa*, recounts Martin's experiences working at the Mikono Centre and among the urban refugees of Nairobi. The book also introduces the reader to a style Martin would continue to hone over the coming years: the employment of personal stories and conversations to illustrate and expand on spiritual and theological concepts. Here and throughout his later books, Martin incarnates the theoretical and the abstract in the actual quotidian lives of himself and his readers (Martin's friends have been known to paraphrase David Sedaris: "Never go anywhere with Jim unless you're sure you want to see everything you did in a book"). Orbis Books rereleased *This Our Exile* in 2011.

Martin followed with *In Good Company: The Fast Track from the Corporate World to Poverty, Chastity and Obedience* (Sheed & Ward, 2000), an account of his unlikely journey from the world of corporate finance at General Electric into Jesuit life as a novice and beyond, including the abrupt but ultimately fruitful transitions from a life of wealth and personal freedom to life as a vowed religious—poor, chaste, and obedient. The book, which also offers an introduction into what life in a Jesuit novitiate is like, is still a common gift from Jesuit vocation directors to young men discerning a vocation to the Society of Jesus.

Searching for God at Ground Zero (Sheed & Ward, 2002) was Martin's journal of his time working with first responders after the attacks on the World Trade Center on 9/11. Seeking to offer counsel and comfort to the wounded and the families of victims, Martin found himself just as often counseling the rescue personnel and the police and firemen working in the ruins of the

Twin Towers—and learning powerful lessons from them about hope and God's grace even in the most terrible of circumstances.

Becoming Who You Are: Insights on the True Self from Thomas Merton and Other Saints (Paulist Press, 2006) offers readers Martin's own take on one of his favorite spiritual writers—the aforementioned Thomas Merton—while also exploring the processes of personal transformation and growth toward a more truly authentic self. Martin also delves further into his own vocation story, inspired as it was so strongly by Merton. His reflections on holiness and saintliness prefigure his later writings on the saints and on the quest for sanctity in everyday life.

My Life with the Saints (Loyola Press, 2006) proved to be the *breakout book* for an already-popular speaker and writer, since Martin's unique memoir of his relationship to various saints won numerous awards and climbed the best-seller lists. Avoiding treacly hagiography, Martin instead writes in *My Life with the Saints* of how holy figures—ranging from St. Jude to Pedro Arrupe to St. Peter to St. Aloysius Gonzaga—have inspired him in his own life and pointed him toward more fruitful spiritual paths, and have also helped him through personal struggles and times of spiritual crisis. Cardinal Avery Dulles praised the book for showing "us a new way of living out a devotion that is as old and universal as the Church."

Lourdes Diary: Seven Days at the Grotto of Massabieille (Loyola Press, 2006) followed a similar format to *Searching for God at Ground Zero*, inviting readers into Martin's journal-like account of a week spent with pilgrims and *malades* (those seeking cures) at the shrine of Our Lady of Lourdes in southern France, the location of famous Marian apparitions and historically the site of countless miraculous healings. Martin's account demonstrates the ability of a holy place (or holy people) to strip away the cynicism and hard-heartedness that modern life can feed, replacing it with the simple trust and joy of a pilgrim who knows he or she always needs healing in some way or another.

A Jesuit Off-Broadway: Center Stage with Jesus, Judas, and Life's Big Questions (Loyola Press, 2007) found its genesis in Martin's newfound popularity as a media personality with a powerful gift for explaining church teachings and history in an accessible, comprehensible way (a reputation cemented by his frequent media appearances during the papal transition between John Paul II and Benedict XVI). It tells the tale of Martin's involvement as theological advisor to the cast and crew of *The Last Days of Judas Iscariot*, an off-Broadway play written by Stephen Adly Guirgis and directed by Philip Seymour Hoffman. In retelling his role of parsing tough theological concepts for actors who just as often reflect back to him their own take on theology, the saints, and God, Martin also reflects and comments on the age-old religious questions raised in such conversations, including the problem of theodicy and the difficulty in understanding the unfathomable mercy of God.

The Jesuit Guide to (Almost) Everything: A Spirituality for Real Life (Harper One, 2010) is Martin's extended primer on the history and spirituality of the Society of Jesus, written again as a series of narratives informed by personal stories and conversations with authorities on topics such as Jesuit education, the life of St. Ignatius, the history of the Jesuits in the arts, and more. As much a guide to Ignatian spirituality as an account of all things Jesuit, the book became a *New York Times* bestseller.

Between Heaven and Mirth: Why Joy, Humor, and Laughter Are at the Heart of the Spiritual Life (HarperOne, 2011) employed much the same format in proposing a perhaps-counterintuitive thesis: that holiness entails a good belly laugh more than it requires the dour and humorless personality so often equated with the saints and the saintly in the Catholic imagination. Even Jesus, Martin argues, enjoyed a good joke, poking fun at his disciples and interlocutors or engaging in riddles and wordplay in his teachings. Foraging broadly in Christian history and turning to a wide range of contemporary experts on spirituality, Martin also asserts that our own personal prayer can be enriched by recognizing humor and laughter as spiritual gifts.

Jesus: A Pilgrimage (HarperOne, 2014) is perhaps Martin's most scholarly book, even though it was inspired by a pilgrimage to the Holy Land and is written in the same accessible style as his previous offerings. Relying on the long history of biblical scholarship about Jesus as well as the insights of contemporary scholars from around the world, Martin takes aim at the most common misperceptions about Jesus (that he was not really human; that he was not really God) in explaining and exploring the historical Jesus. At the same time, he attempts to bring Jesus closer to the contemporary reader through his personal narrative of his travels with a fellow Jesuit to the sites of Jesus's life, death, and ministry.

Martin's most recent book was also his first foray into a new genre: the novel. Released in 2015 by HarperOne, *The Abbey* tells the stories of three Philadelphia-area residents—a divorced single mother who has dealt with the staggering loss of her young son, a carpenter who left behind an illustrious career as an architect, and the abbot of the local abbey all interact in different ways as they struggle to make sense of what their lives have become—in all the joys, sorrows, and mysteries of those lives. Novelist Mary Karr (no stranger to conversion narratives herself) has described the book as "a powerfully moving novel about (among other things) how an unbeliever can journey from suffering into spiritual practice. How it happens in an eyeblink."

Martin has also edited several essay collections, including *How Can I Find God: The Famous and Not-So-Famous Consider the Quintessential Question* (Liguori, 1997); *Awake My Soul: Contemporary Catholics on Traditional Devotions* (Loyola Press, 2004); and *Celebrating Good Liturgy: A Guide to the Ministries of the Mass* (Loyola Press, 2005). All of his books have been translated for international audiences and can be found in Spanish, German, Portuguese, Polish, Chinese, Korean, and more.

MEDIA PRIEST

Alongside the printed word, Martin has taken on a similar apostolate on television, where his frequent media appearances on news programs, documentaries, and television talk shows to offer commentary on the church and Christian life have made him one of the most recognizable religious figures in the nation. More than one writer has commented over the years on the disorienting phenomenon that takes place when one accompanies Martin on a quick walk across the exhibit hall at the Los Angeles Religious Education Congress or similar events: he is immediately mobbed by well-wishers, by autograph seekers, by people seeking prayers, and most often by people simply telling him how much of connection they have made with their faith through his work. And, of course, he is mobbed by cell phone–wielding admirers whose sole desire is for the inevitable selfie. Like Archbishop Fulton Sheen so many decades ago, Martin has become the de facto resource for huge numbers of Catholics and other Christians seeking to delve deeper into Christian spirituality, or to understand a theological concept that is beyond their ken or has been misrepresented by the mainstream culture (or, on occasion, by false prophets and pharisees inside the church).

The comparison to Sheen is not as outrageous as it might seem at first glance. Sheen's distillation and delivery of profound religious and spiritual material for a popular audience on *Life Is Worth Living* (1951–58), *The Catholic Hour*, 1930–50) and *The Fulton Sheen Program* (1961–68), as well as in his astonishing seventy-three books (all, to quote *Time*'s somewhat arch commentary, "designed for the middlebrow reader") earned him the following description from *Time* when they put him on the cover of the magazine in 1952: "perhaps the most famous preacher in the U.S., certainly America's best-known Roman Catholic priest, and the newest star of U.S. television." What American Catholic priest fits that description today more than James Martin? Presumably his Jesuit vow never to seek church honors or offices will prevent him from becoming a bishop, but in other ways, the career of this spiritual writer and popular evangelist has paralleled Sheen's in terms of ministry and reach.

That popularity was boosted immeasurably, of course, when Martin turned a 2007 appearance on Stephen Colbert's *The Colbert Report* (to discuss a *New York Times* op-ed on Mother Teresa) into a semiregular guest slot on the comedy program, to the point where Colbert began referring to him as "the official chaplain of *The Colbert Report*."

In the new age of social media, Martin's ministry of evangelization and education takes place online as much as in print or on television, with the result that his Facebook page and Twitter and Instagram accounts have become popular conduits for his brief, careful expositions on faith, morality, spirituality, and the issues of the day. Ironically, a medium condemned by so many for its preference for facile conversations and "hot takes" has become the way many of Martin's followers first come into contact with his ministry. Commenting on this reality, he told *Guernica* magazine:

> *Some Catholics think that social media is beneath them, but these are media through which you can communicate. Jesus used simple media to communicate. That was the media of parables and stories. It wasn't beneath him to use ideas like birds or seeds or wheat, or a woman sweeping her house looking for a coin, or a wayward son coming back to his father. If it was not beneath Jesus to use these simple means and media that people can appreciate, then it should not be beneath us. My joke is, if Jesus could talk about the birds of the air, then we can tweet.*

To give a sense of Martin's reach through these social media outlets, as of August 2016, his Instagram account had 35,000 followers, his Twitter account was followed by 75,000 people, and his official Facebook page was liked by 465,130 fans.

Such popularity inevitably draws detractors as well, and Martin is no exception. Much of the vitriol directed at him (one need simply read the comments on any of his writings online to see it, in spades) is because of his outspoken advocacy on behalf of some of the most persecuted and marginalized voices in the church and in American life, including gays and lesbians, the poor, and refugees and immigrants. Some of the detraction and contempt hurled his way is simply anti-Catholic bigotry, particularly when Martin has pointed out the obvious anti-Catholic tropes present in much of American culture. Some of it comes from (often unintentionally hilarious) attempts by fellow Catholics, even other Catholic priests, to bring the famous Jesuit down a peg or two out of what seems nothing more than sheer jealousy of Martin's success and prominence. Witness the Dominican priest who sniffed on Twitter in early 2016 that he would stop attacking Martin on Twitter because he was "not giving him any more coverage. @JamesMartinSJ has no formal theological education beyond requirements for ordination." And finally, much of the vitriol sent Martin's way is sadly just the cost of doing business in a medium where the coarse, the crude, and the vicious often dominate.

It is in reaction to that last reality that two of the qualities that have made Martin so popular are most clearly in evidence: first, he has an abundant sense of humor about himself; and second, he has the humility to recognize that much of the hatred is aimed not at him, but at some misplaced notion of who he is, what the church is, or what a sense of right conduct in theological dispute dictates. More than simply a thick skin, these two qualities have allowed him to survive and prosper in his ministry.

TOPICS AND THEMES

Martin's career is by no means over, of course; in fact, in priestly terms he is fairly young, fifty-six as of this printing. Already though, he has established a significant corpus of published work; this book focuses on those materials, the bulk of which might be grouped into four major areas.

Martin's primary focus in his articles and books (less so on social media) has always been the spiritual life. Often through the interpretive key of the Ignatian spirituality in which he has been immersed since his entry into the Jesuits almost three decades ago, he has penned hundreds of thousands of words designed to help his readers in their lives of prayer and their discernment of the harmonies that can be found between human desires and God's desires for us. Selections from a number of those books and articles are found in chapter 1 of this volume, "Motions of the Soul: Spirituality and Prayer."

Another typically Jesuit expression of one's relationship to God and the world is the notion from St. Ignatius's *Spiritual Exercises* that God "can be found in all things," that every part of creation can help every creature, each one of us, to grow closer to the divine will. It is a motto that is abused perhaps as often as it is used properly, but in Martin's writings, it points the reader toward the hidden or obscured treasures of daily life, even when that life can seem one of pointless suffering or undeserved struggle. Chapter 2, "God in All Things: The Divine in Daily Life" brings together a number of selections from Martin's writings on the quotidian joys and struggles that, when appreciated in light of God's presence in every event, action, and object, can be seen as prominent figures in the narrative of every believer's faith life and relationship with the Lord.

Such a commitment to finding God in every facet of life necessarily leads (in terms of Ignatian spirituality) to a desire for greater gift of self as well as a deeper compassion for the wounded and the suffering of the world. Selections from Martin's works on suffering in many facets of life appear in chapter 3, "The Care of Souls: Solidarity with the Suffering and the Wounded." These include his spiritual reflections on his own physical and emotional sufferings, his clarion calls for justice for the marginalized of the church and American society (including gays and lesbians, immigrants, refugees, victims of sexual abuse, and victims of violence), and his in-depth reflections on horrific events like 9/11 or the genocidal wars taking place in Africa.

The final category is the one for which Martin is perhaps best known in the larger culture: his reflections on the saints, on saintliness, on what it means to live a holy life in a complex and often contrary world. In chapter 4, "More by Deeds Than by Words: Models of Holiness," selections from Martin's voluminous writings on these topics are gathered together, including some of his most famous reflections on his own lifelong conversations with the saints, on figures such as Mother Teresa and Bernadette Soubirous, on the Holy Family, and on the holiness that each of us can find within us if we can throw away our attachments and our false masks.

CONCLUSION

The unfortunate restrictions on a volume of essential writings from a scribe as prolific as James Martin are necessarily ones of scope and depth. In order to present the writer's *essential* vision, the always-difficult job of pruning becomes a monumental task: what material adequately represents James Martin, and what can be put aside for the inevitable day when Martin's *Collected Works* are published in multivolume format? In the process of pruning for this volume, I do not deny that some healthy branches have been cut away along with the unnecessary ones and that good fruit inevitably had to be cut. Specifically, this often meant favoring Martin's shorter, more journalistic selections over long passages from his books. Oftentimes, it also meant choosing one article or talk to represent Martin's multiple writings on a particular topic or question, as I sought to find a balance between breadth and depth.

James Martin himself would appreciate that pruning metaphor, one of which Jesus himself was fond. At the same time, perhaps Martin (my former spiritual director!) might suggest the selection process for this book be recast in terms of that all-important term in Ignatian spirituality: discernment. Regardless of the terminology, it is my hope that the selections that follow give the reader the broadest and deepest appreciation of James Martin possible and truly present the essential insights of this modern spiritual master.

1

Motions of the Soul:
Spirituality and Prayer

Using the Ignatian spirituality that is the interpretive key to so much of his work, James Martin focuses in many of his writings on the importance of prefacing every action and every decision with prayer and discernment. He stresses the importance of daily structured prayer, of spontaneous colloquies with God, of scriptural reading, of the intercession of the saints, and of a careful parsing of the movements of the spirit in one's individual life on a daily basis. The selections in this chapter range from fairly straightforward introductions to these topics and practices to carefully nuanced treatments of their interplay in Martin's own life and the lives of other seekers.

Martin also includes many elements that might surprise a reader who is more accustomed to more cossetted or traditional treatments of Christian spirituality. For example, Martin often emphasizes the role of humor in one's relationship with God and the church; he is careful to distinguish between spiritual categories like desolation and dryness and their everyday analogues like depression or simply sadness; he recognizes that sometimes the church's teachings and practices can put up spiritual roadblocks to holiness as much as they create pathways to it; and he does not shy away from the role that physical, sensual experiences of sexuality and bodily joy can play in the spiritual life. Finally, Martin treats phenomena like doubt, disbelief, and

*despair not as topics to be dreaded but as realities that confront
many believers at moments in their spiritual quest.*

THE SIX PATHS

In this selection from The Jesuit Guide to (Almost) Everything,
*Martin follows up a brief history of the life of St. Ignatius of
Loyola with a careful parsing of the ways God communicates
to us in daily life.*

As a result of his experience, Ignatius began to understand
things that God wanted to communicate with us. Directly.

This idea would eventually get Ignatius in trouble with the
Inquisition and land him in jail. (Ignatius had his own problems
with "religion" at times!) Some critics suspected that Ignatius
was trying to bypass the institutional church. If God could deal
with humanity directly, what need was there for the church?

Religion enables people to encounter God in profound ways
in their lives: in preaching, in teaching, and in moments like
baptism, confession, marriage. But Ignatius recognized that God
could not be confined to the walls of the church. God was larger
than the church and spoke to people outside of church walls.

Today the Ignatian notion of the Creator dealing directly with
human beings is less controversial. It's assumed by those on the
"spiritual but not religious" journey. The far more controversial
aspect is that God would speak to us through religion!

But the insight that God wanted to communicate with us
directly is as liberating as it was in his time. And it is here that
Ignatian spirituality can help even the doubtful find God.

Some agnostics or atheists await a rational argument or a
philosophical proof to demonstrate the existence of God. Some
will not believe until someone can show them how suffering
can coexist with the belief in God. A few may even hope for an
incontrovertible sign to convince them of God's presence.

There are two problems with this: First, God often speaks in
ways that are beyond our intellect or reason, beyond philosophical proofs. While many believers are brought to God through
the mind, just as many are brought to God through the heart.

Second, God often speaks to us more gently, more quietly. And it is in these moments where God often speaks the clearest.

Let's take some examples of these quiet, heartfelt moments.

- You are holding an infant, maybe your own, who looks at you with wide-open eyes, and you are filled with a surprising sense of gratitude or awe. You wonder: Where do these feelings come from? I've never felt like this before.

- You are walking along the beach during a vacation, and cast your eyes to the horizon and are filled with a sense of peace that is all out of proportion to what you expect. You wonder: Why am I getting so emotional about the ocean?

- You are in the midst of a sexual encounter with your husband or wife, or an intimate moment with your girlfriend or boyfriend, and feel as if you're almost standing outside yourself, and marvel at your capacity for joy. (That's the original meaning of the word, "ecstasy," to stand outside of.) You wonder: How can I be so happy and feel so whole?

- You are out to dinner or at a movie with a friend and feel a sudden sense of contentment, and recognize how lucky you are to be blessed with friendship. You wonder: This is an ordinary night. Where did this deep feeling come from?

- You have finally been able to come to terms with a tragedy in your life, a sickness or death, and find yourself consoled by a friend, and overcome with calm. You wonder: How is it that I am finally at peace in the midst of such sadness?

Gratitude, peace, and joy are ways that God communicates with us. During these times we are feeling a connection with God, though we might not think to express it in that way. The key insight is accepting that these are ways that God is communicating with us. That is, the first step is a bit of *trust.*

—*The Jesuit Guide,* 54–55

Many Catholics were shocked to discover in 2007 that St. Teresa of Calcutta, the founder of the Missionaries of Charity and the modern era's great apostle to the most destitute of society, those in whom she saw Jesus "in the distressing disguise of the poor," had spent much of her life experiencing a profound alienation from God. In this essay and the one that follows it, Martin addresses the troubling notion that even the holiest of persons might experience prayer as a futile or empty exercise for long periods of time and also suggests some reasons for Mother Teresa's plight beyond the facile or sensational media takes at the time. He also makes careful distinctions between many terms that are conflated in discussions of spirituality: darkness, despair, aridity, desolation, disbelief, the "dark night of the soul," and more.

THE LONG DARK NIGHT

Perhaps Catholics should not have been surprised by the revelations in *Mother Teresa: Come Be My Light*, a new collection of letters by the saint of the gutters that show her astonishing battle with spiritual darkness. Reports of her dark night had been circulating since 2003, when Brian Kolodiejchuk, a priest member of the Missionaries of Charity and postulator for her cause for canonization, published on the Catholic Web site Zenit.org a series of articles about her struggles. That same year, in the journal *First Things*, Carol Zaleski wrote an article entitled "Mother Teresa's Dark Night," which quoted selections from her letters. So some information about Mother Teresa's interior struggles with darkness, doubt and despair have been available to the general public for several years.

What is new about *Come Be My Light* is that it gathers together the bulk of letters, which reveals the full measure of her inner turmoil. For the first time readers will learn that Mother Teresa suffered this relentless aridity for roughly 50 years—with one brief respite—until her death in September 1997. "In my soul I feel just that terrible pain of loss—of God not wanting me—of God not being God—of God not really existing," she wrote to a confessor in 1959.

According to Father Kolodiejchuk, these letters were gathered from the files of bishops, priests and spiritual directors to whom Mother Teresa wrote and who had retained them. In a recent interview, Father Kolodiejchuk noted that although Mother Teresa had hoped the letters would be destroyed, the gathering together of such writings is an essential part of the canonization procedure. The letters are also a critical resource for the Missionaries of Charity as they seek to understand more fully the distinctive spirituality, or charism, of their founder.

Early Mysticism and Later Darkness

The posthumous collection is largely an extended cry to God, expressed through candid letters. A recurring syntactical habit—the frequent use of dashes—adds to the breathless urgency of her lamentations. "In my heart there is no faith—no love—no trust—there is so much pain—the pain of longing, of not being wanted—I want God with all the powers of my soul," she writes in the letter of 1959 quoted above.

The feeling of God's absence is not uncommon in the lives of the saints or in the lives of average believers. The Spanish mystic St. John of the Cross called it the "dark night" and posited it as a necessary stage for the ascent to mystical union with God. St. Ignatius of Loyola termed it spiritual desolation in his manual for prayer, *The Spiritual Exercises*. "One is completely listless, tepid and unhappy," he wrote, "and feels separated from our Creator and Lord." During her final illness, St. Thérèse of Lisieux, the French Carmelite nun, experienced a desolation that seemed to reflect doubts over whether or not anything would await her after her death. "If you only knew what darkness I am plunged into!" she once said to the sisters in her convent.

For Mother Teresa, the decades of spiritual darkness, which began not long after she founded the Missionaries of Charity, were all the more acute when she reflected on her earlier relationship with Jesus.

The woman born Gonxha Agnes Bojaxhiu was raised in a devout Catholic family in Skopje, Albania. Her mother, Drana, was a generous woman who used to care for an elderly neighbor who was ravaged by alcoholism and covered with sores. "When you do good," Drana told her daughter, "do it quietly, as if you were throwing a stone in the sea."

A Jesuit priest's talk at her parish stirred within Agnes the desire to do missionary work, and in 1928 at the age of 18 she was overjoyed to be accepted by the Sisters of Loreto in Ireland. Three months after her entrance, Sister Mary Teresa (she took the name to honor Thérèse of Lisieux) was sent on a mission to India to work in a girls' school in Calcutta. In 1937 she pronounced her vows of poverty, chastity and obedience and, as was the custom in her order, was given the title Mother. Five years later she made a private vow to Jesus not to refuse Him anything.

In 1946 on a train ride en route to a retreat (and some rest) in Darjeeling, she was surprised to undergo a series of intense mystical experiences, which included hearing the voice of Jesus, who asked her to begin working with the poorest of the poor. "Wilt thou refuse?" asked Jesus. These experiences, which she would term her "call within a call," convinced her to take the difficult step of leaving the Sisters of Loreto to found a new order.

Her later years of darkness were all the more baffling to her in the wake of the unique graces received early in her religious life. Moreover, since clergy and members of religious orders were (and are) regularly counseled to rely on Jesus as their most intimate friend, his subsequent disappearance from Mother Teresa's inner life was nearly impossible for her to understand.

She also seems to have been slow to recognize that her darkness may have been a kind of answer to her fervent prayers and private vow; in 1951 she wrote of her wish to "drink *only* from His chalice of pain" (her emphasis). For the reader who knows what awaits her, this is among the most difficult passages to read in *Come Be My Light*. The subsequent trials recall the comment of another Teresa, of Avila, who said that more tears are shed over answered prayers than unanswered ones.

I Have Come to Love the Darkness

Ultimately, in 1961 Mother Teresa found some relief from her interior turmoil through the counsel of Joseph Neuner, S.J., who suggested that her dark night might be one way God was inviting her to identify with the abandoned Christ on the cross and with the abandoned poor. He also reminded her that the very longing for God itself came from God. "For the first time in this 11 years," she wrote the Jesuit theologian, "I have come to love the darkness." Indeed, one of the many poignant aspects of *Come Be My Light* is that it makes clear how much someone can suffer without the right spiritual guidance, and how much relief can come with a few words of wise counsel.

Still, while this provided further insight and what one might call intellectual relief, God's absence continued unabated in her prayer. In 1967 she wrote again to Neuner, "Father I want to tell you how—how my soul longs for God—for him alone, how painful it is to be without Him."

Mother Teresa understood how odd her situation was: the woman acclaimed as a living saint struggled with her faith. Though she sometimes admitted feeling like a hypocrite, as she notes in one letter, she decided that a public admission of her struggles would direct focus on herself, rather than on Jesus. Consequently, she suffered her spiritual trials largely alone. One less publicized aspect of her journals lies in this personal act of humility: Had these letters been destroyed, few would ever have known of her trials. As her own mother had counseled, she was trying to do good quietly.

Why?

Most believers who read *Come Be My Light* will at some point ask, "Why would God do this?" Of course one might just as well ask, "Why is there suffering?"

In his *Spiritual Exercises*, St. Ignatius Loyola suggests three possible explanations for spiritual desolation. First, we may be tepid, lazy or negligent in prayer. Clearly this was not the case for Mother Teresa, who was utterly faithful to her daily prayer, to the Mass and to frequent visits to the Blessed Sacrament. Second, it may test how much we are worth and how far we will extend ourselves in the service and praise of God. Again, if Mother Teresa, who worked tirelessly until her death, did not extend herself, who of us has? Third, it may give us true recognition that consolation is a gift and grace from God our Lord. In other words, it reminds us who is in control. But after 10 or 20 years of the darkness, Mother Teresa had grasped this, as her letters to her spiritual directors demonstrate.

Any divine reasons for her trials remain mysterious. But with hindsight certain fruits of her suffering—besides the heightened ability to identify with the poor—may suggest themselves.

For one thing, Mother Teresa, like many saints, had a commanding ego, forceful enough that she argued for the foundation of her order in the face of fierce opposition. A common theme in the early letters is her relentless drive to have the young order approved, a pursuit born of certitude in her mystical experiences. "Why make me wait so long? . . . How long must I wait? May I not write again or straight to Rome?" she wrote to the Archbishop of Calcutta in 1948, when Vatican approval for her order was not immediately forthcoming. Later, when her ministry flourished, she was showered with worldly honors, including perhaps the ultimate secular accolade, the Nobel Peace Prize. Did her spiritual trials temper a natural pride that might have otherwise subtly compromised her mission?

Likewise, one might argue that Mother Teresa's letters, the fruits of her spiritual agony, which she asked to be destroyed, will now help a new group of people. Having ministered to the sick and dying in Calcutta during her lifetime, she will now minister to the doubtful and the doubting as a sort of saint for the skeptics. Could this be a way God will use her sufferings to bring about greater good? Is this the Easter Sunday of Mother Teresa's long Good Friday? Only God, and now Blessed Teresa of Calcutta, knows the answers.

Great Saint, Complicated Seeker

Come Be My Light reveals Mother Teresa to be one of the greatest of all the saints. To that bold statement church historians and theologians will surely respond, "Wait and see." Yet it is difficult to think of anyone who accomplished so much with so little spiritual sustenance. The closest analogues are St. Jane Frances de Chantal, founder of the Congregation of the Visitation, whose turmoil lasted for three decades, and St. Paul of the Cross, founder of the Passionist order, who underwent an even lengthier trial, but was granted relief toward the end of his life.

While every saint has faced spiritual trials, most have felt close to God during their years of active ministry. St. Ignatius Loyola, for example, was frequently overcome with emotion while celebrating Mass, even to the point of tears. Some were even granted unique graces. In his later years St. Francis of Assisi enjoyed mystical experiences at his prayer and, during one retreat, received the stigmata.

In contrast, Mother Teresa felt nothing for 50 years—except for a brief respite—all the way until her death. "[M]y soul is just like [an] ice block," she wrote.

Come Be My Light also provides an unintentional response to those who during her lifetime dismissed Mother Teresa as a sort of well-meaning but unsophisticated believer. Her letters show how, when confronted with a complex spiritual crisis, she questioned with candor, vigor and passion, and ultimately responded with trust, love and works of charity. She is revealed as a complicated and sophisticated seeker.

I Have Never Refused You Anything

The unrelieved spiritual aridity of Blessed Teresa of Calcutta makes her earthly accomplishments all the more remarkable. Her letters also offer some lessons to believers. First, they are a reminder that what could be termed radical Christianity is not simply the province of those called saints. Many imagine that since the saints enjoy privileged access to God in prayer, their work is somehow easier, lighter—a mistaken view that excuses the average believer from striving for sanctity. Instead, Mother Teresa's life reminds us that holiness is a goal for all believers, even those given to doubt. Second, her letters remind us that dryness, darkness and doubt are natural parts of the spiritual life, whether ordinary believer or extraordinary saint. Finally, they remind us that fidelity does not depend solely on feelings or emotions.

Blessed Teresa remained heroically faithful to the original call from the very God who seemed to have withdrawn from her. Shortly before her death, one of her sisters noticed her praying alone before an image of Christ and overheard a phrase that could sum up her life. "Jesus," she prayed, "I have never refused you anything."   —*America*, September 24, 2007

SHADOWS IN PRAYER

One challenge for readers of *Mother Teresa: Come Be My Light,* the collection of Blessed Teresa of Calcutta's letters published last fall, is to distinguish among the terms darkness, dryness, desolation, doubt, disbelief, depression and despair—the "seven D's." On a popular level, some journalists, media analysts and bloggers conflated Mother Teresa's "darkness" with "disbelief." Christopher Hitchens, the atheist author of *God Is Not Great,* was not the only one who asked, after reading selections from the book, whether the "saint of the gutters" was a closet atheist. Even devout Catholics had difficulties grasping how Mother Teresa, considered a paragon of faith, could have suffered from a feeling of abandonment by God. While some Catholics saw her example as one of remarkable fidelity, others were disturbed to read such lines as, "I have no faith." One woman asked me, "How can I expect to pray at all, when even she couldn't believe?"

Such reactions show how easy it is for the media and the public to be addled sometimes by the complexities of the spiritual life and, also, how confused terminology can become, even among those familiar with prayer.

The "seven D's," however, are distinct, and Christian spiritual masters have long used specific terms to refer to distinct experiences. One may experience dryness without depression (for example, during a retreat when one suspects that the period of dryness in prayer is temporary). One may encounter darkness without disbelief (as did St. Thérèse of Lisieux, who continued to believe despite spiritual aridity near the end of her life). Experiences can overlap, too. Darkness can lead to occasional doubt, as in the case of Mother Teresa. And depression can lead, as even atheists and agnostics know, to despair.

Darkness Visible

Darkness has been an important theme in Christian spirituality since St. Gregory of Nyssa in the fourth century. Perhaps the most often quoted source on the topic is St. John of the Cross, a Spanish mystic. Ironically, he may be the most misquoted as well, as illustrated by frequent references to the "dark night of the soul." His original 16th-century poem is called simply *Noche Oscura*, "Dark Night."

"Dark night," however, is only one way of describing a particular state of feeling isolated from God. Around the same time St. John was writing, St. Ignatius Loyola wrote of "desolation" in his *Spiritual Exercises*. So even the most educated Christian can be forgiven for wondering: Are the two saints talking about two phenomena that are the same, or similar or different?

To add to the confusion, where one spiritual director uses "darkness," another might use "dryness" to describe the same experience. "And sometimes directors can be presumptuous, too," says Jane Ferdon, O.P., who has trained spiritual directors in California for 20 years. "People may say that they are in darkness, and we spiritual directors assume we know what they're talking about!"

Perhaps confusion stems not only from an imprecise, overlapping and shifting use of terms but also from a failure to recognize that everyone who prays will at some point encounter many of these states.

What are these states? How do they affect our relationships with God? Lent is a good time to reflect on these categories, not only as a way of taking stock of our spiritual life but also as an invitation to meditate on Jesus' own expression of isolation on the cross, "My God, my God, why have you abandoned me?"

What follows is a brief overview of the seven D's, beginning with some simple definitions, followed by comments from past and present spiritual masters.

Definitions and Descriptions

1. *Darkness* is a feeling of God's absence after having developed a personal relationship with God. For St. John of the Cross, there were two types of "dark nights." The "dark night of the senses" is an experience of one's own limitations and the removal of attachments to the consolation felt in prayer. It is "an inflowing of God into the soul whereby he purges it of its habitual ignorances and imperfections," wrote St. John. At a later stage, some experience the "dark night of the spirit," which is a more profound challenge to faith. But both are steps toward deeper union with God.

Janet Ruffing, R.S.M., professor of spirituality and spiritual direction at Fordham University, describes St. John's dark night as a "mystical experience of God that overwhelms our normal way of apprehending God, and leads not only to an increase in faith, hope and love, but also eventually into a place of light." She believes that while almost everyone who prays seriously will encounter the dark night of the senses, relatively few will experience the dark night of the spirit.

An experience of darkness can be a gateway to finding God in the *nada*, or nothingness, and an entry into the *via negativa*, the negative way. Ruth Burrows, a Carmelite nun, writes in her book *Essence of Prayer* that God "wants us to trust him enough to live with him unafraid, totally defenseless in his presence. We can truly say that John of the Cross's teaching has as its sole aim to bring us to this inner poverty."

A person in darkness feels isolated from God. Yet with patience (whether or not one can identify which "dark night" one is experiencing), one can let go of the need to feel God's presence constantly and gradually move through the darkness to discover greater intimacy with God.

2. *Dryness* is a limited period of feeling emptiness in prayer. "Dryness is more temporary than darkness," says William A. Barry, S.J., author of *God and You: Prayer as a Personal Relationship*. Anyone who prays will at times feel dryness in prayer, when nothing seems to be happening. "There is little in the way of sensible consolation," Father Barry said in an interview.

These natural parts of the spiritual life can increase our appreciation for richer moments. One never knows what kind of inner change occurs during "dry" times, and being with the living God in prayer is always transformative. As a Jesuit novice, I once confessed to my spiritual director that nothing was happening during my prayer. It seemed a waste of time. "Being in the presence of God is a waste of time?" he asked.

Much as even a close friendship goes through some quiet or dull times, so our relationship with God may go through dry patches. But being with a friend in such times is necessary if the friendship is to be sustained and grow in intimacy.

3. *Desolation* is feeling God's absence coupled with a sense of hopelessness. St. Ignatius Loyola describes it as "an obtuseness of soul, turmoil within it, an impulsive motion toward low and earthly things, or a disquiet from various agitations and temptations." It is more than feeling dejected or sad. "Desolation is often confused with simply feeling bad," says Barry. "But it's more accurate to say it is a feeling of estrangement from God."

Margaret Silf, a columnist for *America* and author of *Inner Compass: An Invitation to Ignatian Spirituality*, notes that desolation has a quality of isolation. "Those in desolation are turned

away from the light of God's presence," she told me, "and more
focused on the shadows." Father Barry agrees. "In desolation
it's more about the person than it is about God," he says. "Ultimately this leads to despair."

Desolation is distinct from St. John's dark night. In desolation, writes St. Ignatius, one is moved toward a "lack of faith"
and is left "without hope and love." In the dark night the opposite is happening, as one moves toward complete abandonment
to God. "For the one experiencing this, it may be easier to see
this in retrospect," says Janet Ruffing. "But in the Ignatian worldview, the dark night is actually consolation."

The desolation Ignatius describes may seem far removed from
the lives of average Christians. But it is a common, painful state
experienced by many people, coupled as it is with feelings of
"gnawing anxiety," as Ignatius puts it. He counsels that in these
times one should, among other things, redouble one's efforts
in prayer, remember times when God seemed more present or
remind oneself that it will eventually pass. He also reminds us
that all the fruits of prayer are really gifts from God, which we
cannot control.

4. *Doubt* is an intellectual indecision about God's existence.
Many believers face doubt at some point in their lives. "Most
people are relieved to be able to talk about doubt in spiritual
direction," says Ruffing. "But no one reaches adult faith without doubt. And frequently people encounter doubt and then
move toward a faith that is more complex, paradoxical and,
ultimately, more adult."

Doubt is a supremely human experience, shared by nearly
every Christian since St. Thomas the Apostle. Recently, in John
Patrick Shanley's Pulitzer Prize-winning play, "Doubt," a priest
(who faces his own doubts and the doubts of his parishioners
about his background) points to this universality in a homily:
"When you are lost, you are not alone."

5. *Disbelief* is an intellectual state of not accepting the existence of God. Some commentators concluded that because
Mother Teresa suffered darkness, she did not believe in God.

Once, in her letters, she bluntly wrote, "I have no faith." But, as Father Barry explains, "She was still praying and writing letters to God."

Sometimes disbelief is a way of discarding old images of God that no longer work for an adult believer. Margaret Silf reflects on her own experience: "I've been through times when all the old props have fallen away, and have felt that I just couldn't go on believing. So what to do? Bolster this old system, or let things be and see what happens? For me, this finally enabled me to break through to a deeper level of faith, which I would call trust." Disbelief is a serious challenge in the spiritual life. If the journey ends at that point, there will be little space for God. The key is to continue seeking, even in the midst of disbelief.

6. *Depression* is a profound form of sadness. In the medical and psychological community, it has a more technical definition. "It's a clinical category that is often able to be treated medically," says Barry, who is also a psychologist. "We don't want to spiritualize primarily psychological problems," says Jane Ferdon. "But today," she adds, "we can also psychologize spiritual issues. So it's very important to discern the root causes of depression."

In "The Dark Night and Depression," an essay in Keith J. Egan's book *Carmelite Prayer*, Kevin Culligan, a Carmelite priest, writes that in the dark night there is an acute awareness of one's own incompleteness. However, in this darkness one seldom "utters morbid statements of guilt, self-loathing, worthlessness, and suicidal ideation," as one does during a period of clinical depression.

So one can be in darkness but not be depressed. What about the other way around? Father Barry responds, "Rarely is the clinically depressed person able to experience consolation in prayer."

Therese Borchard, who writes a blog on depression, "Beyond Blue," for the spirituality Web site Beliefnet, has suffered from depression herself. She understands it from both a theoretical and a personal point of view and agrees with Barry. "When you're depressed you feel so angry at God," she told me. "For some people it can lead you closer to God, as you struggle to express your anger and also cling to God as a last hope. For others it can distance you and lead to turning away from God. In general, though, depression usually leads to darkness and dryness in prayer." Clinical depression needs to be treated by medical professionals as well as to be addressed in a spiritual setting.

How do spiritual directors and counselors distinguish between darkness and depression? "When I'm with depressed people, I feel swallowed up by their depression," says Janet Ruffing. "It's the opposite with people going through the dark night. Once, I accompanied one of our sisters, who was dying, through an experience like this, and in her presence I felt God's luminosity—though she couldn't touch it at all."

Sadness is different from depression. As Barry notes, "Sadness over a painful reality in your life can be a sign that you are in touch with God." Jane Ferdon says, "These are some of the people who are the most alive, since they are feeling deeply."

7. *Despair* is a feeling that all is, and will remain, hopeless. The Trappist monk Thomas Merton defined despair in his book *New Seeds of Contemplation* as "the ultimate development of a pride so great and so stiff-necked that it accepts the absolute misery of eternal damnation rather than accept that God is above us and that we are not capable of fulfilling our destinies by ourselves." The form of despair Merton describes implies that we know better than God does, and what we "know" is that things can never get any better. Such pride leads to a spiritual dead end: despair.

This may sound harsh. For those living in grinding poverty, facing a life-threatening illness or confronted with some other tragedy, despair may seem a rational response. It can also stem from depression. "When you are depressed you are often without hope," says Therese Borchard, "and this can lead to despair."

Jane Ferdon thinks that sometimes despair is not a spiritual dead end, but appropriate. She remembers one woman describing her painful circumstances by saying, "I feel like I'm walking among the living dead." Ferdon always asks people if they can find God in this state. "Also, it's important to know if the despair is a reflection of something else, say, aloneness or depression, and what happens when the person brings that despair to prayer. Sometimes the person doesn't want to pray about it, and if not, why not? That may be where Thomas Merton's notion of pride comes in."

Ferdon respectfully disagrees with Merton in definitively identifying despair with pride. "It may be that pride is actually the opposite of what is happening. Despair can be an experience of letting go of our need to control everything, and it can lead to change, revitalization and even consolation." So while a despair that says, "Nothing can change" is perilous in the spiritual life, a despair that says, "I can't do it by myself" could lead to growth.

Distinctions and Deliverance

One need not be a scholar of Christian spirituality, a spiritual director or a person under spiritual direction to see that disentangling these spiritual strands can be encouraging, clarifying, consoling and freeing. Understanding that most of these experiences are common can encourage us by reducing anxiety. "These are stages in everyone's spiritual life," says Janet Ruffing. Knowing that these stages are not identical can be clarifying and help us discern the correct responses to different events in our spiritual lives. (St. Ignatius, for example, prescribes definite steps to take when one is in desolation.) Being able to bring such experiences to prayer can be consoling, since it can deepen our relationship with God, in the same way that speaking about a thorny problem with a friend can strengthen a friendship and lead to greater intimacy.

Finally, knowing that all these experiences can lead us to God can free us from fear, which can cripple our spiritual lives. For the God by whom Jesus felt abandoned on the cross is the same God who delivered Jesus from death, giving him new life. "My God, my God, why have you abandoned me?" is the beginning of Psalm 22. A few lines later, though, the psalmist sings another song. "For he did not hide his face from me, but heard me when I cried to him."   —*America*, March 17, 2008

CONSOLATION

In this selection from his first book, This Our Exile, *Martin treats the spiritual phenomenon of "consolation," perhaps one of the most misunderstood concepts in Ignatian spirituality. Briefly put, consolation is a sudden experience of joy or closeness to God that does not necessarily have an obvious antecedent in one's prayer life or daily routine; Ignatius himself distinguished between real and false consolation, and consolation with and without cause, and stressed the importance of discerning between them. Using narratives from his time working with refugees in East Africa, Martin hints that sometimes what we think is "consolation without cause" is actually consolation that is beyond our understanding, though it may be obvious to our neighbors or outside observers.*

> *If a man leaves his dreamy conceptions aside and focuses on his naked poverty, when the masks fall and the core of his being is revealed, it soon becomes obvious that he is religious by nature. In the midst of his existence there unfolds the bond (re-ligio) which ties him to the infinitely transcendent mystery of God, the insatiable interest in the absolute that captivates him and underlines his poverty.*
> —Johannes B. Metz, *Poverty of Spirit*

After the Mikono Centre had been open for some time, I settled into something resembling a routine. Wake at 6 a.m., thanks to either the dazzling equatorial sunlight that streamed into my room or to a reliable pair of Egyptian ibises who flew over the house at precisely that hour, cawing loudly. Roll over and switch on a short wave radio that a forgetful American visitor had left behind and listen to the BBC World Service. Shower (when there was enough hot water), pray (when I was good enough to remember it), breakfast (tea and a banana) with my Jesuit housemates, glance at the *Daily Nation,* and then drive through Kawangware on the way to Kangemi (if the jeep was working). Usually I'd spot refugees in the slums on their way to visit me; I'd pick them up and we'd start our meeting in the jeep. If I didn't see them, they'd always see me. One day a refugee darted out in front of my jeep. I slammed on the brakes, screeched dramatically, swerved crazily, and barely avoided hitting him. He leaned into the car. "Brother, you are worse than these *matatus!*"

When I arrived at Mikono Centre, the sun already blazing in the clear sky, there were normally a dozen or so refugees waiting for me on the shady porch, mostly women, some nursing children, many bearing crafts they had carried that morning on the *matatu*, others holding letters requesting a small business grant. "*Jambo*, Brother!"

Most of the morning was spent meeting with the refugees. Some needed advice on their projects—keeping the books, dealing with landlords and merchants, resolving arguments, finding new markets—and most requested some financial assistance to help them through a rough time. I met with the refugees in a small room furnished with simple wooden chairs and a low table, where we could talk freely, sometimes in English, sometimes in Swahili, sometimes in French. If a refugee spoke a language that I didn't know, say, Arabic or Luganda or Portuguese, there was usually another refugee willing to translate. In this way, I felt as if we were all working together toward a common goal.

The time we spent together, I soon realized, was one of the most important things I could give the refugees. All of them had been for much of their lives forced to wait and wait and wait in endless lines—in the camps, in the UN offices, in government offices, in jails, in hospitals. And when in those places they were finally ushered in to see this or that official, they were typically treated shabbily and dealt with as quickly as possible. So I was happy to sit with them and listen as carefully as I could to their concerns. Time, not just money, was something that I could easily give them, and it cost nothing.

Most refugees brought goods they hoped to sell and, like Alice Nabwire, would make a good case for why, if I wanted two, I

should buy three instead. Already the shop was doing well financially, so it was easy to accommodate most such requests. Besides,
even if we ended up buying too much merchandise, the money was
going to a good cause. Better to have an overflow of baskets on
our shelves than to allow a family to go hungry.

Often, though, we were visited by refugees who simply wanted
money—a more difficult situation. Though the purpose of our
work was to help the refugees support themselves, there were still
many in need of immediate assistance, mainly to buy food. Usually, I steered them to their local parishes, where JRS had started
a program of providing cash assistance for the emergency needs
of refugees throughout Nairobi. But some needed money immediately. One day a Sudanese woman, carrying a child on her back,
sat down in my office and begged for "some little money." She
had no money for "school fees." The Kenyan public schools were
officially free but demanded exorbitant school fees for spurious
projects, such as building funds for buildings that never material-
ized. What's more, she said, her children had no food.

When I told her she would need to visit her local parish, she
burst into tears. She had, she said, not even enough money for bus
fare. She cried and cried and dried her eyes on her skirt. "Oh,
Brother," she said over and over. Finally I gave her money of my
own. Of course, when she emerged onto the porch her face told
the other refugees that I had given her what she asked for. (It
was also, I discovered, easy for them to hear what was going on
through the open windows.) One Rwandese refugee reminded me
of my breach of procedure. "Brother, you should not give *money*
out," he scolded. "You should be sending her to the parish!"

In between visits from the refugees, I would assist customers
who frequented our shop, showing off our wares and explaining
the mission of JRS. Often, even the briefest descriptions of the lives
of the refugees impelled customers to purchase a good deal more
than they had intended to. And I was not above using the occasional measure of guilt to encourage larger purchases. One day I
noticed an American woman examining a barkcloth bag made by
Jane Tusiime, upon which was embroidered a smiling zebra.

"Could a child use this as a bookbag?" asked our customer as she fingered the rough barkcloth.

"Sure," I replied, having never considered the possibility. "And would it stand up to rain, do you think?"

"I guess so," I offered lamely, desperately trying to figure that out. "I mean it's bark, right?

Trees do pretty well in the rain."

She laughed. "You'd say just about anything to sell these, wouldn't you?"

"Well," I said, "they're wonderful bags, and pretty sturdy . . . but yes, I probably *would* say anything. The woman who makes these is going through a rough time right now. She's just been kicked out of her house." Not surprisingly, the woman bought three. And somewhere in the States is a young boy dragging his books to school in a wet barkcloth bag.

In the afternoon, I visited the refugees in the slums. Some of them were unable to visit Mikono Centre due to their work; on other occasions I wanted to check up on them, to see how well they were working together and if I could offer any advice. Usually, I would be asked to adjudicate a dispute, talk to a truculent landlord, or investigate a broken machine. And so my afternoons usually consisted of long drives through the hot city to discover a woman sitting forlornly in a fish-and-chips stand, where she would shake her head and tell me how very slow business was. Or to a woman's small home where a new sewing machine sat idle, surrounded by scraps of fabric, for lack of business. On these occasions, I would sit with them and simply listen to their frustrations and their problems. For my part, I tried to listen carefully and then offer whatever practical advice I could.

At times I felt overwhelmed by the poverty and misery and sickness that they faced—the seeming lack of hope, the enormity of their problems. But seeing refugee after refugee helped me to feel that I was helping out, even if in a small way. Happily, I quickly rid myself of the idea that I would be able to solve *all* of their problems, as a sort of refugee savior. Ironically, this realization was rather easy to come to, thanks to working in Nairobi.

Whereas in other locales one might imagine oneself able to do everything, the unpredictable and chaotic situation in Nairobi rendered anyone's notions of omnipotence absurd. This realization, I think, enabled me to relax some about my work. I worked hard but tried to leave the rest to God.

After some work, I'd drop off the inevitable passenger and return to Loyola House for Mass in our small house chapel. Following Mass, our community, which numbered a dozen or so Jesuits from around the world—Malta, India, Tanzania, Ireland, Belgium, Canada, and the United States—enjoyed some Fantas, peanuts, and beer. At 6 p.m. promptly a bell rang, and we offered grace in our living room. Dinner was consistently simple. The cooks prepared only enough for those who were expected for dinner, and there were rarely extra portions.

The bishop of the diocese of Garissa visited the Jesuit provincial (the regional superior) one evening and lingered in the living room after grace. The rest of the community proceeded to the dining room and filled their plates with chicken marengo, green beans, and potatoes. After a half an hour the bishop and the provincial strolled into the dining room, only to discover the following victuals awaiting them: three string beans and one potato. No one had thought to leave any leftovers. "Ah," the bishop said to general laughter, "the famous Jesuit hospitality."

After dinner came a traditional Jesuit custom: a "visit" to the chapel to pray before the tabernacle housing the Blessed Sacrament, the bread consecrated during the celebration of Mass. When I arrived at Loyola House and discovered this somewhat outmoded practice, I decided immediately that I wouldn't participate. Visiting the Blessed Sacrament, focusing one's piety exclusively on one *thing,* was not something I felt comfortable with. Didn't that box God in, making God available solely as an object? So for the first few weeks of my stay, when the rest of the Jesuits filed out of the dining room to visit the Blessed Sacrament, I remained behind to clear the plates from the tables.

A few weeks later, the superior of the community asked to see me in his office. Why, he asked gently, was I avoiding the visit after dinner? The priests in the house were wondering why I wasn't participating. Annoyed at even having to explain (wasn't my prayer life *my* business?) I responded simply that this wasn't part of my spirituality. And that, I thought, would be that.

But he suggested that while the visit wasn't part of my spirituality, perhaps it was something I'd like to try. He admitted that it was somewhat outdated, something that younger Jesuits might not appreciate, but could I see my way clear to do it as a way of praying with the community? Grudgingly, I agreed.

The following night after dinner I wandered into the chapel with the rest of the Jesuits. Silently, the men in my community knelt down facing the tabernacle and prayed silently. I knelt, too, resenting every moment of being "forced" to do so. But then, as I looked around the room and saw a dozen men kneeling in prayer together as a community, I was filled with a feeling of quiet, of peace. It was profoundly prayerful. After that I went every night. In the end, I realized that it was not others who were boxing God in: it was me, for refusing to accept the possibility that grace might come to people even in ways that I considered outdated.

Some priests played cribbage after dinner, read the daily papers, perused magazines brought by visitors from the States or Europe, or retired to their rooms to pray. Early on, Jim Corrigan and I discovered a video-rental place in town and hosted video nights for the rest of the community. The videos were obviously pirated and had legends running across the bottom of the screen: "It is forbidden to copy this video," or "For Purposes of the Academy of Motion Picture Arts and Sciences Only. Duplication Forbidden." Which actors were selling their Oscar tapes to Nairobi video pirates? We wondered.

There were two state-owned television networks: KBC, which broadcast low-budget Swahili dramas and news programs; and KTN, whose fare ran heavily to Australian soap operas, Kenyan cricket matches, and reruns of American shows about African Americans, such as *Roc* and *Family Matters*. Friday and Saturday evenings were given over to *Transworld Sports*, a British sports program that summarized, on Fridays, every major soccer match in the UK, and on Saturdays, the world. These shows, though interminable, were required viewing in our community.

More entertaining were the Kenyan commercials, which were evenly divided between ads for wonderfully named soaps (British Imperial Leather, Fa, Lady Gay) and insecticides, known locally as *dawa ya wadudu,* or "bug medicine." Marketing, as it turned out, worked on me in Kenya as well as it did in the States. My choice of bug spray had less to do with its effectiveness, which consisted mostly of drowning the bugs with an overly liberal application, than with its name: Doom.

The evening news in Nairobi began with precisely the same words every night. On KTN: "Today, His Excellency President Daniel arap Moi . . ." Then a litany of the president's day. He had opened a chicken hatchery in the Rift Valley. He had visited a secondary school in Mombasa. He had attended Sunday services in Kiambu. He had spoken to the faithful citizens in Eldoret. On KBC one could hear the same, only in Swahili: "*Leo, Mtukufu Rais Daniel arap Moi . . .*"

At night I liked a snack of boiled milk with honey. The honey jar, which sat on one of the dining room tables, was filled with the dead ants that invaded the jar. They floated on the top of the honey and were exceedingly difficult to extract. After a few times of making a sticky mess of things, I discovered it was more effective to spoon the honey into a cup of boiling milk, let the ants float to the top, and skim them off. This put me in mind of the old saying that there are three stages to missionary life. In the first stage, you separate the rice from the bugs and eat the rice. After a little while, you simply eat the rice and the bugs together. Finally, you separate the rice from the bugs and eat the bugs. Though I still had a ways to go, perhaps I was, in the words of a seasoned missionary friend, "beginning to arrive."

By ten o'clock, I was in bed reading, after a short period of contemplative prayer, called by Jesuits the *examen,* a sort of review of the day in which one tried to see where God could be found. Often, before falling asleep I would hear one of the older Indian Jesuits at prayer. He walked back and forth in the breeze-way, his sandals shuffling across the terrazzo floor; behind his back he held his rosary, the wooden beads clicking quietly as he walked.

I grew to love my work with the refugees and especially enjoyed working in Kangemi. It was the first time I had ever worked in a neighborhood where everyone seemed to know me. (Doubtless my skin color was a big help in that regard.) The refugees I passed on their way to Mikono Centre knew me, to say the least. Greeting them involved a lengthy discussion of their businesses, their health, their families. And then: my business, my health, and—a constant source of surprise no matter how often it happened—my family, a world away in Philadelphia. "Greet your mother and father for us, Brother!"

The vendors and people selling roasted corn and peanuts along Kangemi's dirt paths knew me as well. I took lunches at St. Joseph the Worker parish and grew friendly with the Jesuits and the staff there. It felt good to be imbedded in the community, particularly in such a poor area of the city. I was happy to be there and happy to be there as a Jesuit.

Sometimes my jeep was indisposed—either broken down or lent to a car-less friend. On days without my jeep, after work I would walk across to a bus stop, which lay across a deep valley.

One such afternoon, I began the walk home. The long brown path began at the church, St. Joseph the Worker, which perched on a hill overlooking the Kangemi Valley. From there the bumpy path descended through a thicket of floppy-leaved banana trees, tall, green ficus trees, orange day lilies, long, green cowgrass and maize fields. On the way down into the valley I passed people silently working in their *shambas,* their little plots of land, who looked up and called out to me as I passed. Brilliantly colored, iridescent sunbirds—turquoise, violet, and indigo—alighted on the tips of the tall grasses. At the bottom of the valley ran the Nairobi River, little more than a creek except during the rainy season. Groups of old Kikuyu women laughed and joked as they did their families' laundry on the riverbank. The wet clothes were draped on the dusty bushes, where the hot sun dried them quickly.

Spanning the river was a flimsy bridge constructed of sticks and twigs tied together with twine. When the rains came, the little bridge was promptly washed away, and the people in Kangemi simply built another. The first time I used the bridge I walked over it gingerly, prompting one of the women to laugh and offer advice. "*Wewe ni magari sana, Brother! Hakuna shida!*" You are very thin, Brother! Don't worry!

As I climbed the hill away from the river, I paused. Standing on the hardpacked earth, I turned and looked back at St. Joseph the Worker atop the hill. Though it was four in the afternoon, the sun was near its zenith. It blazed down on the valley, illuminating the reddish brown path, the tiny river, the banana trees, the grasses, the people. Quite suddenly I was overwhelmed by joy. I'm happy to be here, I thought, and happy to be working with the refugees. I was exactly where I was supposed to be. I felt useful and fruitful. And I was quite amazed at my happiness, my contentment, my peace.

Afterward I wondered what it was that made me so happy. The day had been an ordinary one, full of the usual daily problems. Nothing particularly exciting had happened, unless you counted a few successful refugee business stories. There were no major dilemmas solved. No refugee's life had been put back together. I hadn't received any particularly good news. My community was the same community it had been for the past two years. I wasn't looking forward to a special trip or holiday. It wasn't a big liturgical feast day. I wasn't planning to see anyone that night for dinner.

St. Ignatius of Loyola, the founder of the Society of Jesus, wrote about what he called "consolation" in the *Spiritual Exercises,* his manual for spiritual directors. He described consolation as an uplifting of the spirit, a feeling that gives comfort and joy. Such consolation, Ignatius wrote in 1541, gives "genuine happiness and spiritual joy, and thereby banishes any sadness or turmoil. . . ." More precisely, he spoke of "consolation without preceding cause," a feeling that comes over, or passes over, or fills a person quite unexpectedly. This feeling, Ignatius understood from his own experience, was a wonderfully unique gift from God. I've had that type of experience only a few times in my life, but never as intensely as when standing on the hillside that day.

Over the bridge, after passing a few small shacks and more *shambas,* I eventually left Kangemi and arrived in Riruta, though neighborhood boundaries were shifting and evanescent. The path continued past a large church in Riruta, St. John the Baptist, the original foundation parish for the later mission parish of St. Joseph the Worker. The Church of St. John the Baptist was more established and looked more like a traditional European church. Like St. Joseph's, the church in Riruta had a large school attached. Drawing closer I passed Kenyan boys and girls in uniform: pale blue blouses and navy skirts for the girls, white shirts (usually torn) and navy pants for the boys. Most went cheerfully barefoot on the dirt path, holding hands.

The bus stop lay just beyond the church. There the old metal bus shelter was grotesquely twisted, the result of an unfortunate meeting with a *matatu,* and sat in a heap by the side of the road. People sat on what would have been its roof. But most just waited in the shade of a large jacaranda tree that stood by the road. The buses came infrequently, and most of the time they were crowded, with people squeezed on, half-in and half-out, desperate to return home. But I never liked to push on, even though passengers would hold their hands out as the bus pulled away, imploring me to grab on for a ride. It wasn't that I minded the discomforts of the trip, I just didn't mind waiting.

—*This Our Exile,* 109–19

CONTEMPLATION IN ACTION

The election of Pope Francis in March 2013 set off an immediate media frenzy to determine the biographical details of the new pope: who Jorge Maria Bergoglio was, what he stood for, and from whence he had come. Martin's quick sketch of the new pope's likely spiritual sources and practices provides an introduction to some of the basic principles of Ignatian spirituality,

*and also presciently foregrounds many of Francis's actions in the
first four years of his papacy.*

No sooner than the news broke that Cardinal Jorge Mario Bergoglio had been elected Pope, my smartphone started buzzing
with calls and pinging with emails from journalists all asking
the same question: "What's a Jesuit?" In the days following the
election of Pope Francis—the first Jesuit in that office—there
have been more people asking that question than in the past 10
years. So it's fair to ask it here, but more specifically: what is
Jesuit spirituality and how could it influence this new papacy?

A few basics: Jesuit spirituality is based on the life and teachings of St. Ignatius Loyola, the hotheaded-soldier-turned-practi-
cal mystic who founded the Society of Jesus in 1540. Much of
his spirituality flows from his classic text, the *Spiritual Exercises*,
a manual for a four-week retreat that invites a person into imaginative meditations on the life of Christ. In other words, one uses
one's imagination to "enter into" the life of Jesus of Nazareth as
presented in the gospels.

The Exercises mean more than just a reading of the gospels,
or even observing the scenes. As the Jesuit Joseph Tetlow wrote,
one is not even observing from a distance; one is there, "ankle-
deep in the water of the Jordan." Thus, through the Exercises,
one enters into a deeply personal relationship with the person
of Jesus. Each Jesuit makes the Exercises (at least) twice in his
life: during the novitiate and, years later, at the end of his formation. Pope Francis has done this. But there is another aspect
of his training that may go overlooked: during his Jesuit days,
Jorge Mario Bergoglio, S.J., served as the Jesuit novice director
in Argentina, which means he also guided the Argentine novices through the *Spiritual Exercises*. Jesuits often call the novice director the most important job in the province; required to
have both the spiritual depth and a practical mind to help often
confused novices, he is typically both holy and sensible. At the
heart of the Ignatian Exercises is a desire to be freed from anything that might keep one from following Christ.

Now for some important Jesuit lingo: Jesuits are asked to be "detached" from anything that would prevent them from living a full and loving Christian life. We are supposed to be "indifferent," open towards anything, preferring, in Ignatius' famous formulation, neither wealth nor poverty, health nor sickness, a long life or a short one.

Finally, Jesuits are supposed to be *disponible*, a Spanish word meaning "available," ready enough to go wherever God, who works through our superiors, wishes. In all this we aim for the magis, the more, the greater, the better, all "for the greater glory of God."

This helps to explain the accession of Jorge Cardinal Bergoglio to the papacy. Don't Jesuits at the end of their training make promises not to "strive or [have] ambition" for high office in the Church and the Society of Jesus? Yes, Ignatius was adamantly opposed to the clerical careerism that he saw in the Renaissance, and so he built into the final vows a safeguard against that kind of climbing. But there is freedom built into Ignatian spirituality. If we are asked to do something by the Church, we are free, *disponible*, to do so.

Other sources of Ignatian spirituality are found in the saint's terse *Autobiography*; the *Jesuit Constitutions*, written by Ignatius; the lives of the Jesuit saints; and as John W. O'Malley, S.J., points out in his book, *The First Jesuits*, the activities of St. Ignatius and the early Jesuits. It is one thing to know that the Jesuits were available enough to take on any kind of ministry that would "help souls," as Ignatius put it; it's quite another to read that they opened a house for reformed prostitutes in Rome.

But what are the hallmarks of Ignatian spirituality (the broader term used these days, as a complement to "Jesuit spirituality") and how might they affect the Pope? Let me suggest several, and show how they can already be seen in the first few days of his papacy.

First, one of the great shorthand phrases for our spirituality is "finding God in all things." For Ignatius, God cannot be confined within the walls of a church. Besides the Mass and the sacraments and Scripture, God can be found in every moment of the day, in other people, in our work, in our family life, in nature and in music. This provides Pope Francis with a world-embracing spirituality, in which God can be met everywhere. During his first meeting with journalists last Saturday, the Pope offered them a touching blessing: "Since many of you do not belong to the Catholic Church and others are non-believers, from the bottom of my heart I give this silent blessing to each and every one of you, respecting the conscience of each one of you but knowing that each one of you is a child of God." God can be found among non-believing journalists.

Secondly, the Jesuit aims to be the "contemplative in action," a person in a busy world with a listening heart. That characteristic came to the fore in the first few minutes of his papacy. When Francis stepped on to the balcony overlooking St. Peter's Square, he began not with a papal blessing, but with a request for the prayers of the people. He bowed his head and asked for a moment of silent prayer. Quiet in the midst of the crowd: the contemplative in action.

Thirdly, poverty. Like members of all religious orders, Jesuits make a vow of poverty; we make it twice in our lives: at first vows and at final vows. We are, said St. Ignatius, to love poverty "as a mother." There are three reasons for that: first, in imitation of Jesus who himself lived as a poor man; secondly, to free ourselves from the need for possessions; and thirdly, to identify with (as well as help and advocate for) the materially poor. Pope Francis has so far eschewed many trappings of the papacy. Before stepping on to that balcony, he set aside the elaborate mozzetta that popes normally wear, and put on the brocaded stole only when he offered a blessing. He rides on the bus with the rest of the cardinals. He walks rather than taking a limousine. Most Jesuits seeing this would say: "Of course, the simple lifestyle that Ignatius asks of us."

Finally, flexibility. This is sometimes not highlighted in commentaries on Jesuit spirituality. (I could have also added a life of regular prayer, an emphasis on education, a grounding in social justice, a willingness to live in community and, above all, a devotion to the person of Christ.) But over and over in the Constitutions of the Jesuits, flexibility is recommended. And remember that Fr. Bergoglio, before becoming Archbishop of Buenos Aires, was the Jesuit provincial, or regional superior, for the country.

While the Constitutions lay out exacting rules for life in Jesuit communities, Ignatius recognised the need to meet situations as they arise with creativity. After a lengthy description of precisely what was required in a particular aspect of community life, he would add a proviso, knowing that unforeseen circumstances always call for flexibility. "If something else is expedient for an individual," he writes about Jesuits studying a particular course, "the superior will consider the matter with prudence and may grant an exemption." Flexibility is a hallmark of the document, and appears to be with Francis, who has seemed happy to speak off the cuff and adapt himself to the needs of the situation. After his first Sunday Mass at the Church of Sant'Anna, he greeted parishioners one by one on the church steps, and I could imagine him saying to his addled handlers, "Why not?"

Needless to say, I'm delighted with the choice of the conclave (not to mention the Holy Spirit). And obviously, I'm quite biased about our new Jesuit Pope. We don't know what he will do during his papacy. But we do know something about what has informed his interior life. And that in particular fills me with *gaudium magnum.* —*The Tablet*, March 23, 2013

THE MOST INFALLIBLE SIGN

The subject of his book Between Laughter and Mirth, *the theme of humor in the spiritual/religious life, has been a frequent topic of Martin's lectures and media appearances. In this essay from* America, *he treats both the long history of laughter's role in religious practice as well as the reasons why it can be such a healthy element of the spiritual life.*

Joy has a distinguished heritage in the Christian spiritual tradition. It is easy for most Christians to imagine someone like St.

Francis of Assisi smiling. More recently, Pope John Paul II and
Blessed Teresa of Calcutta were often captured by photographers
smiling and even laughing. As Pierre Teilhard de Chardin, S.J.,
said, "Joy is the most infallible sign of the presence of God." Yet
lightheartedness is still an unwelcome guest in some church circles. Many Catholics have met church officials for whom being
a religious leader seems to mean being deadly serious. Catholic
spiritual writing often focuses on finding God through suffering
but far less often on finding God through joy. Some Masses belie
the term "celebration." Are joy, humor and laughter considered
inappropriate for serious Catholics? If so, why?

To understand humor in the Christian spiritual tradition, it
may be helpful to return to the very beginning of that tradition.

Did Jesus Laugh?

While the Gospels show Jesus as clever, especially in his telling
of the parables, few places in the New Testament present him
as humorous. Some scholars suggest that this reflects the predominant Jewish culture, which prized seriousness about God,
a topic not to be taken lightly. Yet if the Evangelists were intent
on painting an appealing portrait of Jesus, why omit his sense
of humor?

Amy-Jill Levine, a New Testament scholar at Vanderbilt University, and author of a new book on the Jewish roots of Jesus,
The Misunderstood Jew, notes that one difficulty with the topic
is that what was considered humorous by people in first-century Palestine might not strike us as funny. For them, the setup
was funnier. "The parables were amusing in their exaggeration
or hyperbole," she said recently. "The idea that a mustard seed
would have sprouted into a big bush that birds would build their
nests in would be humorous."

Daniel J. Harrington, S.J., professor of New Testament at the
Weston Jesuit School of Theology, agreed. "Humor is very cul-
ture-bound," he said. "The Gospels have a lot of stories about
controversy and honor-shame situations. I suspect that the early
readers found these stories hilarious, whereas we, in a very different social setting, miss the point entirely."

There is no way of knowing how much of Jesus' humor was expunged from or left out of the Gospels. But Professor Levine noted that Jesus laughs frequently in some noncanonical Gospels. The church fathers, moreover, intent on combating heresy, would likely not have seen the genre of humor as appropriate.

When asked about humor in the contemporary church, Professor Levine said: "It's undervalued and needs to be recovered. We need to be open to the joys of the proclamation. The good news should put a smile on our face!"

In his book *Man at Play*, published in 1972, Hugo Rahner, S.J., carefully traced the notion of playfulness throughout Greek, Roman and early Christian thought. Rahner noted that while Aristotle encouraged a healthy balance between humor and seriousness, some early Christian writers favored a far more serious approach to life, as they were concerned with facing the dangers of the world and the evils of Satan. St. Paul warned in the Letter to the Ephesians to avoid "smartness in talk." St. Clement of Alexandria inveighed against "humorous and unbecoming words." And St. Ambrose said, "Joking should be avoided even in small talk." St. Augustine, on the other hand, recommended occasional joking, and St. Thomas Aquinas recommended play, opining that there is a virtue in playfulness, since it leads to relaxation.

Father Rahner recognized the need for lightheartedness in the church. In the last chapter of his book, he wrote, "Not everything in our civilization is in the hands of the devil, and thundering from the pulpit is not always in place."

Just a few years earlier, Elton Trueblood, the Quaker theologian, tackled the topic in his book *The Humor of Christ* (1964). His analysis of the paucity of humor in the New Testament took a different tack. First, contemporary Christians are overly familiar with the stories and may overlook their inherent humor. He recounted how his four-year-old son heard the Gospel image of the speck of dust in your neighbor's eye and the log in your own and laughed uproariously.

Trueblood also noted the emphasis the Gospels place on the Passion, with the crucifixion narratives almost overwhelming

the Resurrection. Finally, writes Trueblood, there may be a failure of imagination about Jesus of Nazareth. The fact that Jesus
wept does not mean he never laughed. He must have laughed,
suggests Trueblood, as do most people who tell clever and amusing tales.

Another tantalizing explanation for the dearth of humor and
playfulness in the church is advanced by Barbara Ehrenreich in
her new book, *Dancing in the Streets: A History of Collective
Joy*. Ehrenreich posits that leaders, particularly in European cultures, were frightened by enthusiasm and collective joy, which
they saw as primitive or hedonistic. When the lower classes
assembled to enjoy themselves and strengthen their camarade-
rie and friendship, they often made fun of the ruling class as a
way of asserting their own authority and threatening prevailing
social structures.

Ehrenreich suggests that the church fathers may have set aside
the parts of Jesus' message that embraced what she calls a "sweet
and spontaneous form of socialism" for something more serious.
Spontaneity threatens the status quo. Because of the subversive
nature of humor, many in authority deemed it unacceptable.

Laughing with the Saints

The undervaluing of Christian humor is particularly surprising
in light of Gospel stories in which Jesus evinces playfulness. He
is castigated for not being as serious as John. "The Son of Man
came eating and drinking," says Jesus. "And you say, Look a
glutton and a drunkard" (Matt 11:19). Jesus also approves of
a quick-witted man. When told that the Messiah is from Nazareth, Nathaniel blurts out, "Can anything good come out of
Nazareth?" His mordant joke about the city delights Jesus, who
exclaims, "Here is truly an Israelite in whom there is no deceit!"
Jesus then calls him to join the apostles (John 1:47).

Some residues of humor may still be traceable in the way the
Evangelists wrote and edited the Gospels. But as Professor Levine
notes, we may be so familiar with these stories that we miss the
humor. She points to the story of Eutychus (Acts 20:7–12), who

sits in the window ledge of a room where St. Paul is still talking near midnight. Eutychus dozes, falls out the window, drops to the ground and is presumed dead, until Paul examines him, discovers he is alive and continues talking until dawn.

Many Christian saints and blesseds have celebrated humor and laughter, which run like common threads through their lives, disproving the stereotype of the dour saint. In his biography *God's Fool*, the French novelist Julien Green speaks of the joy of St. Francis of Assisi that "spilled over into the hearts of thousands of men and women."

Stories about the humor of saints reach back to the Roman martyrs. In the third century, St. Lawrence, who was burned to death on a gridiron, is said to have called out to his executioners: "Turn me over. I'm done on this side!" Some saints were known specifically for their sense of humor. St. Philip Neri, called "The Humorous Saint," hung at his door a little sign: The House of Christian Mirth. "Christian joy is a gift from God flowing from a good conscience," Neri said.

St. Teresa of Avila specifically warned her sisters against a deadly serious religiosity. "A sad nun is a bad nun," she said. "I am more afraid of one unhappy sister than a crowd of evil spirits. . . . What would happen if we hid what little sense of humor we had? Let each of us humbly use this to cheer others." A more contemporary example is Blessed Pope John XXIII, whose most famous sally came when a journalist innocently asked, "Your Holiness, how many people work in the Vatican?" John replied, "About half of them."

Why Do Christians Need Humor?

The saints understood the serious uses of joy. Here are 10 reasons for joy, humor and laughter in the church today.

1. *Humor evangelizes.* Joy, humor and laughter manifest one's faith. This essentially positive outlook shows belief in the Resurrection, in the power of life over death and in the power of love over hatred. Bl. Francis Xavier Seelos, a 19th-century

Redemptorist priest, spoke of "holy hilarity" as a tool for spreading the Gospel. In its imitation of Christ, joy draws others to him.

When I was a Jesuit novice, the superior general of the Society of Jesus, Peter-Hans Kolvenbach, visited our novitiate. When asked about the best way to increase vocations, he said unhesitatingly, "Live your own vocation joyfully." Joy attracts others to Christ.

2. *Humor is a tool for humility.* Humor can help one grasp one's essential poverty of spirit. Self-deprecatory jokes deflate our egos and remind us not to take ourselves with deadly seriousness. Pope John XXIII once received a letter from a little boy named Bruno. "Dear Pope," wrote Bruno, "I am undecided. I don't know if I want to be a policeman or a pope. What do you think?" "Dear Bruno," replied Pope John, "If you want my opinion, learn to be a policeman, for that cannot be improvised. Anyone can be pope. The proof is that I have become one. If you are ever in Rome, please stop by and I will be glad to talk this over with you."

Using humor as a tool for humility is a common motif in the lives of the saints. In the 1960's, when the Red Brigade caused sporadic acts of violence in Rome, some people would carry pictures of Padre Pio for protection. One day Padre Pio was going into Rome and one of his friends asked, "Aren't you worried about the Red Brigade?" "No," he said, "I have a picture of Padre Pio."

3. *Humor clarifies.* A witty remark can get to the point faster than a long homily. St. Francis of Assisi once said: "Preach the gospel. Use words when necessary." A clever epigram, but also a profound truth.

St. Anthony Avellino was a 17th-century canon lawyer who entered the Theatine order. One day a pious priest asked him, "Father Avellino, how long should one stay at the bedside of a sick person?" Rather than offer a lengthy explanation, Avellino said, "Always be brief. There are two advantages: if they like you, they'll want you back. If you're boring, their displeasure will be short."

4. *Humor speaks truth to power.* Wit is a time-honored way to challenge the pompous, the puffed-up or the powerful. Jesus used humor in this fashion, exposing and defusing the arrogance of religious authorities. Humor can serve as a weapon in the battle against the arrogance and pride that sometimes infects the church. It is also a gentle weapon that can be wielded by the powerless.

A friend's mother was once in the hospital at the same time as the local bishop. After his operation the bishop went from room to room visiting the patients. When he met my friend's mother, who was recovering from a difficult surgery, he patted her on the head and said, "Dear, I know exactly how you feel." And she said, "Really? When was your hysterectomy?"

5. *Humor shows Christian fortitude.* St. Lawrence's humor was both a pointed challenge to his executioners and a bold profession of faith. Likewise in the 16th century, when St. Thomas More stepped up to the chopping block and said to his executioner, "I pray you, help me on the way up, and I will take care of myself on the way down." This brand of humor says, "I do not fear death."

6. *Humor deepens one's relationship with God.* If prayer can be seen as a personal relationship, then, like any relationship, it requires time, honesty, patience, the ability to listen and moments of silence. And like any relationship, it is leavened by humor. Nonetheless, some Catholics find it difficult to accept the idea that God might want to be playful with them.

While traveling to one of her convents, Teresa of Avila was knocked off her donkey and fell into the mud. "Lord, you couldn't have picked a worse time for this to happen. Why would you let this happen?" And the response in prayer that she heard was, "That is how I treat my friends." Teresa said, "And that is why you have so few of them!" This is a playful way of addressing God that assumes God's own playfulness.

Humor invites Christians to consider God's playfulness. As the Book of Isaiah says, "The Lord takes delight in you." Christians may not be used to the image of God delighting in them, or to thinking of the unexpected as a sign of God's playfulness. But if one thinks of God as parent, it is easy to see how much a parent enjoys being playful with a child. Imagining God's delight may mean considering God not simply loving you, but as the theologian James Alison says, liking you. Or, as Anthony deMello, S.J., wrote: "Look at God looking at you. And smiling."

7. *Humor welcomes.* Hospitality is an important virtue in both the Old and New Testaments. In the New Testament, the act of welcoming Jesus into one's home signaled acceptance. And if a town did not welcome the disciples, Jesus told them to wipe the dust of that town off their feet (Mark 6:11). Jesus himself welcomed outsiders into the community, by healing them and by casting out demons. He manifested God's hospitality.

Humor is a subtle way of showing hospitality. Perhaps the easiest way to make someone comfortable is to prompt laughter. Only when people feel at home can they laugh.

A few years ago I worked in Nairobi, Kenya. At the end of my first year there I signed up for an eight-day retreat at the Jesuit retreat house. On the final day the staff hosted a celebratory dinner, at which participants were asked to speak about their retreat. Looking around, I realized that the few other men on retreat had already left; present were dozens of African sisters. Feeling uncomfortable, I worried that I would say the wrong thing. So I blurted out, "I see that I'm the only man here." From across the room an African sister called out, "And blessed are you among women!" Everyone laughed, and I instantly felt at home and could talk honestly about my retreat. Laughter had welcomed me.

8. *Humor heals.* Physicians, psychologists and psychiatrists believe that humor helps the healing process in the physical body. If we take seriously the Pauline image of the body of Christ, we might ask if the same holds true for the Christian community. In the midst of some of the worst times in the church, the people of God could use some laughter. This is not to say that one laughs

over the considerable pain in the church. Rather, humor gives us a much-needed break and can help heal.

9. *Humor fosters good work relations.* In her recently published biography, *Team of Rivals,* Doris Kearns Goodwin tells how Abraham Lincoln gathered together a contentious group of men around him in his cabinet. Often they disagreed with one another, quarreled and even worked against one another. One way Lincoln lightened the atmosphere or made a point without offending anyone was to tell a good joke or a little country story. Laughter, say neuroscientists, also releases endorphins, which help people relax and, perhaps, listen better. Humor makes for easier social relations, something important in the church.

Shortly before the Second Vatican Council, John XXIII picked up a preparatory document, took one look at all the people that the document condemned and found it too harsh. Rather than arguing with the men who wrote it or discussing his theological objections, the pope simply picked up a ruler, measured a page and said: "Look. There are 30 centimeters of condemnations here!"

10. *Humor is fun.* There may be no better reason for humor than fun. Fun—a word not often heard in church circles—is a foretaste of the heavenly banquet, when "every tear will be wiped away."

Joy is a vital part of the Christian spiritual life. Humor and laughter are divine gifts that help us enjoy creation. They are also neglected virtues we need to recover for the health of the church. The saints understood this, and I would wager that the man whose first miracle was to turn water into wine also understood the need for some high spirits in life.

—*America*, April 2, 2007

THE BUSINESS OF BELIEF

A detail of Martin's life history that always fascinates audiences is that he attended the Wharton School of Business and worked

for six years in corporate finance, not the typical route to the
priesthood or the usual background of a writer of spirituality.
Here he uses his experiences in corporate life to inform a sketch
of the challenges and possibilities for living a spiritual life in the
business world.

You've probably noticed the *S.J.* that follows my name and may
have already concluded that a Jesuit couldn't possibly know
anything about life in the corporate world. And in part, that's
true; most members of religious orders don't worry much about
salary increases, downsizing, employee benefit plans or climbing
the corporate ladder.

But bear with me, because before entering the Jesuits, I
studied business as an undergraduate and worked for six years
in corporate finance and human resources with what I'll call
a Fortune 10 corporation. Like the vast majority of those in
the business world, I struggled with being a good person in the
office, doing the right thing on the job and wondering whether
I was in the right place. Today most of my friends (those who
aren't Jesuits, that is) work in a variety of businesses, so I try
to keep up with the difficulties of working in the corporate
world.

And if anything, it seems that despite the stunning economic
prosperity that many in this country enjoy, living a spiritual life
in corporate America has only grown more challenging. So after
four years of business school, six years of work, 12 years of
reflection and almost 20 years of hearing stories from friends,
here are what appear to be the main challenges of living a spiritual life from 9 to 5.

Finding Time for God

Nine to 5? More like 24/7. Quite obviously, time is at a premium
for anyone working in a corporate environment. Indeed, despite
vaunted increases in prosperity and technology (remember how
PC's were going to lead to four-day workweeks?) the amount of
time demanded by corporations from their employees has only

increased. Round-the-clock markets, round-the-clock financial news and round-the-clock access with e-mail, cell phones and beepers, translates for many into round-the-clock work. Moreover, decreasing job security and increasing numbers of dual-career households have led to more stress and less time for married couples and parents. And yet, in the midst of these pressures, the believer desires to live a spiritual life, one that is rooted and grounded in God's love. Hence the first challenge: How is it possible to find time for a life of prayer and worship?

A few friends with whom I spoke recently suggested that the only way to do this is by carving out time from work. "It's a conscious choice," one remarked, noting that while he found it difficult at times, he could avoid what he called "the trap of constant work" only by sacrificing some upward mobility and choosing to spend time with his family and in pursuit of a spiritual life. Otherwise, he said, life inevitably becomes informed solely by work and, without the nourishment of either individual or communal prayer, one's spiritual life slowly atrophies.

But while my friend is a busy man with a growing family, he is also a successful investment banker and can perhaps afford to forgo a rung on the corporate ladder. More difficult challenges attend the lives of people struggling to make ends meet: the single mother working two jobs or the underpaid father desperate to earn a better living for his family. Here the challenge of finding God *at* work takes on greater import and meaning.

But that challenge is, after all, a universal one. Indeed, one of the pitfalls of trying to live a spiritual life is overlooking the possibility of encountering God in the workplace. There is often a tendency to "compartmentalize" one's spiritual life, by looking for God only on Sundays or during prayer. Find God in all things, as St. Ignatius Loyola counseled, and that includes work. For some, this means finding a job that offers not only personal satisfaction but also a chance to contribute to the common good. Or it could mean recognizing the opportunity to enjoy deep friendships with co-workers as a way of experiencing God's love. Nevertheless, the ability to appreciate the presence of God at work comes more readily when one is willing to set aside time for prayer and worship.

Finding Time for Solitude

Whether at home or on the road, growing numbers of business-men and women are never far from e-mail, courtesy of Palm organizers or laptops, and are never without their cell phones, beepers, voice mail or fax machines. The sight of a woman striding down a city street with a cell phone nervously pressed against her ear is a common one, as is that of a traveler desperately checking e-mail on a laptop while waiting for the next flight home. But while these high-tech gadgets are terrific for keeping us in touch with work, they also serve to pare away the few moments of solitary time we have left—time for silence and reflection. Where is the time for even a few minutes of solitude, the opportunity for "recollection," as spiritual writers say?

The second challenge, then, can be framed as follows: How can the working man or woman balance the desire to be "connected" with the need for solitude, a requirement of the spiritual life?

Sometimes, in fact, it seems that we can no longer stand to be "out of touch," or, more to the point, to be alone. Thomas Merton wrote about this phenomenon in *No Man Is an Island*. "The person who fears to be alone will never be anything else but lonely, no matter how much he may surround himself with people."

Paradoxically, as Merton noted with his usual acuity, a mea-sure of solitude and silence is precisely what enables us to con-nect on a deeper level with others, for in solitude we connect with the deepest part of ourselves—God. And in coming to know God, we are better able to find God in others and are ulti-mately freed of our loneliness and anomie.

Working (and Living) Ethically

When I studied business ethics as an undergraduate, most of our textbook cases were of the black-and-white variety, solved with obvious, simplistic answers. Would you give a bribe to an unscrupulous businessman who demanded one? (No.) Would you pollute the environment with nasty chemicals? (No.) When I entered the working world, however, I was surprised to learn how much subtler most ethical dilemmas are, and how rarely they are framed in black-and-white terms.

This is not to say that black-and-white dilemmas never arise. A lawyer friend, well into her career, described for me the dilemma she faced when asked to defend a doctor in a malpractice case. An obstetrician who regularly performed abortions, he had seriously injured a woman during an abortion procedure. "I didn't want to make a big deal of it," she explained, "but I felt uncomfortable taking his case. It felt as if I would be defending the act." She quietly told her manager that she would rather not, and as a result faced persistent questioning from her boss and withering criticism from her peers.

But subtler problems are far more common. Despite rosy reports of companies offering Bible study and prayer groups for employees, the corporate environment can still present formidable challenges for the believer. What do you do, for example, when you discover that you work in a corporation where religious values are not paramount? During my time working in human resources, I had to confront a manager who was planning to fire one of his employees. The employee had just received an incentive award for outstanding performance on the job. Finding it bizarre that we would suddenly fire one of our top employees, I told the manager it was a bad idea. "I don't care," he said. "I don't *like* him!" Then I reminded him that this middle-aged employee had been with the company for 20 years, had consistently done an excellent job and that not liking someone was not a valid reason for dismissal. None of that mattered, he snapped. Finally I said, "Have some compassion. The guy's got a family." His answer was short and memorable: "To hell with compassion!" he shouted. (Only he used a one-word substitute for "to hell with.") For me the episode neatly encapsulated the ethos of the company and ultimately led to a decision to leave.

So the third challenge is: How can one stay true to one's values on the job? For many in business, this means searching for a company whose values are congruent with their own religious values. A friend who manages investments for a multinational corporation told me he was glad that the values he prized—integrity, honesty, rectitude—were precisely the ones valued in his world of long-term investing. "If you're dishonest, your reputation and therefore effectiveness will suffer," he explained. So he felt at home in his company.

But what happens when you work in an environment where the value of, say, compassion is held in low regard or, worse, is ignored? One response might be to strive to change the work environment by your own actions, serving as a sort of leaven at work. Another path might be to maintain a degree of what spiritual writers call "detachment" from the prevailing ethos of the corporation. If you work for a corporation that stresses aggressive or downright mean behavior, you need not always be mean or aggressive yourself. Sometimes superior job performance can overcome the perceived need to participate in activities that go against your moral grain. That is, talent trumps aggression and meanness.

But is there ever a need to sacrifice some upward mobility in exchange for a clear conscience? One friend put it bluntly, "I don't expect to make partner, because I don't play the games that others play, but I don't really want that; it's not good for me." For if you work in a corporation that prizes offensive behavior you might find it necessary to choose between advancement in the company and your own ethical standards.

Remembering the Poor

In this era of dot-com zillionaires, 10,000 Dows, I.P.O. instant millions, day-traders and Bill Gates, it is easy to forget the poor not only in this country but around the world. As many commentators have noted, it is in times of prosperity that the poor are more easily forgotten. In lean times, when the public is more concerned with the causes of economic distress, our thoughts naturally turn to the poor; in fat times the poor somehow embarrass us.

It is also tempting to conclude that this current wave of prosperity is the best situation imaginable. Isn't everyone getting rich? And if there are only a few people who are poor, well, it's about the best we can hope for, right? Implicit in this line of thinking, of course, is the unwillingness to criticize any aspect of capitalism. Last year the Harvard theologian Harvey Cox wrote a trenchant article in *The Atlantic Monthly* slyly suggesting that "The Market" was our new God. Think about it: It has its own "priests," who alone understand its mysteries (including the high priest Alan Greenspan); it moves in mysterious, awe-inspiring and ultimately perfect ways; like the ancient gods, it must occasionally be placated with sacrifices (for example, with what economists call the "transitional unemployed"); it rewards those who follow its rules, and so on. It is supreme.

But if the market is infallible, then it is also above criticism. "Such is the grip of current orthodoxy," wrote Mr. Cox, "that to question the omniscience of The Market is to question the inscrutable wisdom of Providence." Indeed, faulting American capitalism, circa 2000, can seem heretical in the corporate world. And this, in particular, only encourages us to ignore the situation and the needs of those whom capitalism has failed: the poor.

Hence the fourth challenge: How can one remember the need to care for the poor and marginalized? One friend, a successful accountant, said that she finds three things helpful: first, being grateful for what she has; second, helping out in a church community; and third, stretching herself when she gives charitably.

I would suggest an additional help: to spend time with the poor and underprivileged, to get to know these persons as individuals, rather than simply as objects of charity. And it is not just the poor who benefit from such personal contact. The wealthy too learn one of the secrets of the kingdom of God: that the poor are uniquely able to evangelize the more affluent. As Jon Sobrino, S.J., wrote in *The True Church and the Poor*: "The poor are accepted as constituting the primary recipients of the

Good News and, therefore, as having an inherent capacity of understanding it better than anyone else."

Overall, you might say that living a spiritual life in the corporate world requires, among other things: carving out some time for both prayer and solitude; being willing to search for God at work; practicing detachment from some of the values of corporate America; and remembering the need for solidarity with God's poor, even in prosperous times.

It's a tall order, of course, but no one, least of all Jesus, ever said the Christian life was going to be easy. Or, as my father is fond of saying, "Why do you think they call it *work?*"

—*America*, July 1, 2000

HOLY DIRT

Though perhaps more properly an essay about the saints, this selection is included here because of Martin's emphasis on the value of sacramentals (in this case, the "holy dirt" of Chimayo) as aids for a fruitful and imaginative prayer life as well as for their importance in connecting the faith of each person to a larger culture of believers.

So what do you want to see in New Mexico?" asked my friend. For two days last October, I had been speaking at a meeting of Catholic foundation directors in Santa Fe. Now, for the first time in a few months, I had a free day. I would spend it with my friend Bill, a priest who works in New Mexico. Bill is stationed at a parish outside Taos, roughly 50 miles from the center of Santa Fe, where we stood.

"Well, we saw the cathedral yesterday morning," I said. "After his morning Mass, the archbishop gave us a tour." The impressive Romanesque structure was built in 1884 by the first bishop of Santa Fe, Bishop Jean-Baptiste Lamy, the redoubtable French cleric on whom Willa Cather based her novel *Death Comes for the Archbishop*.

"What about St. Joseph's staircase?" asked Bill.

Much of what I knew of the famous structure, I was embarrassed to admit, came from a cheesy television movie called *The Staircase*. As the story goes, in the late 19th century the Sisters of Loretto were searching for someone to build a staircase in their chapel. (The tricky spot had defeated the best efforts of two previous carpenters.) The sisters decided to make a novena to St. Joseph, the patron saint of carpenters. On the final day of their novena, a gray-haired man riding a burro and carrying a toolbox visited them. He was looking for work. With only a few tools the carpenter constructed a gracefully winding staircase that makes two 360-degree turns. He completed a structure that stands without nails or any visible means of support. Before the sisters could pay the carpenter, he left. The nuns concluded that none other than St. Joseph could have done such fine carpentry. (As an added mystery, the wood used is not native to New Mexico.)

Bill and I made our way to the chapel of Our Lady of Light, now a museum near the center of Santa Fe. At 2:35 in the afternoon, as the sun blazed above us, we found a sign announcing that the chapel had closed at 2:30. "I've come all the way from New York," I said to the guard, who stood silently beside the sign. "Uh-huh," he said. "It's still closed."

"What about Chimayo?" said Bill. "It's on the way to Taos."

The Story

El Santuario de Chimayo, nestled in the Sangre de Cristo Mountains, is often called the Lourdes of America. As with a visit to Lourdes, another town set in hill country, a pilgrimage to Chimayo makes little sense without some understanding of its history.

When Archbishop Michael Sheehan gave us a tour of the cathedral the day before, he showed us an impressive reredos (the wall behind the altar) in a side chapel. Some of the statues on the reredos, he said, were linked with the history of a still-active lay Catholic group called the Penitentes. The story of

Chimayo springs from the experience of one of these 19th-century Penitentes, Don Bernardo Abeyta.

On the evening of Good Friday in 1810, as he prayed in the hills, Don Bernardo saw a strange sight: a light coming from the valley below. Though there was no moon out, the ground seemed to glow. He decided to investigate. Digging at the spot, like Bernadette Soubirous digging at Lourdes, he unearthed an elaborate wooden crucifix, five feet high. Don Bernardo and his fellow Penitentes alerted the local pastor in nearby Santa Cruz. Together the group carried the crucifix in procession back to their church.

The next day, however, they awoke to find that the crucifix had disappeared. Retracing their steps, they discovered that it had returned to the original site. Don Bernardo and his friends carried it away again, but the crucifix returned. After the third effort, they concluded that God wanted the crucifix to remain where it was, at Chimayo.

When I heard this story, I thought of what the British writer Anne Wroe had written about the tradition of relics. In the Middle Ages, she wrote in an essay in *Awake My Soul*, relics were not merely commodities, but expressed something of the "will" of the saint: "The saint expressed himself through his body, in that when [the relic] was being carried by devotees from its original place of repose, it would indicate where it wished to rest. And it usually did so by becoming impossibly heavy to carry further when it had reached its desired home."

The Penitentes and local families built a chapel on the spot where the object was discovered. In time, pilgrims began to come to rub their hands in the soil that held the crucifix. Miraculous healing properties were attributed to the shrine. It was like Lourdes, but instead of water, the faithful at Chimayo rubbed dirt from the hole on their bodies, daubed it on photographs of family members, took it away in small portions and even ate it.

Today the site attracts 300,000 visitors each year, including, according to the custodian of the chapel, 30,000 pilgrims on Good Friday, some of whom walk from as far away as Albuquerque.

The Pilgrimage

I first heard about Chimayo from a Jewish friend named Ned. He and three other Jewish friends were touring the American southwest. They met two Catholic sisters on their trip and visited the shrine with them. According to Ned, you had to duck in order to enter the room where the dirt was. "The hole miraculously fills up with dirt every night," said Ned. "Or at least that's what we heard."

The way from Santa Fe to Chimayo passed through some of the most beautiful countryside I have ever seen. In his dusty pickup truck, Bill and I rattled through a mountainous region dotted with greenish-gray sagebrush, blue cornflowers and cottonwood trees that were golden yellow against a brilliant blue sky. After an hour, we turned off onto a narrow road, passing small adobe houses. Bill said that one house always made him stop. A few minutes later he pulled over next to a small pink adobe house with a rusting car parked out front.

On the side of the house was a vividly colored portrait, perhaps three feet tall, of the head of a suffering Christ, gazing skyward. A lurid crown of thorns encircled his head. "To me, that's New Mexico," Bill said. We sat for some time before the painting.

Though my friend Ned had told me that Chimayo was small, I wasn't prepared for how small. We turned onto a dusty road, passed a few shops selling santos, and there in the middle of a compact plaza was a yellow adobe structure with two small towers topped with wooden roofs. It looked as if it were about to collapse.

Inside we met a friend of Bill's, the custodian of El Santuario, Father Julio, a Spanish-born priest who is a member of the Society of the Holy Family. Father Julio told us something of the history of the chapel. Several decades after its construction the chapel fell into disrepair. John Meem, an architect who had heard of the site, was passing through New Mexico. Surprised by its deterioration, Meem, an Episcopalian, began to restore the chapel along with the help of a local preservation society. In 1929, after completing the restoration, Meem purchased the site from its original owners and turned it over to the archdiocese. So we have an Episcopalian to thank for this Catholic shrine.

In the interior, its wooden pews nicked and its walls covered with paintings of dozens of saints, were a few pilgrims. On a far wall, in the center of an impressive reredos, was the mysterious cross that Don Bernardo had found. As Father Julio mentioned, it was not of a style one would expect to find in the area. Even the wood was foreign. How had it gotten to Chimayo?

The Prayer

For the last 12 years I have suffered from carpal-tunnel syndrome, which is sometimes painful and always makes typing a challenge. Each year when I am invited to accompany the Order of Malta on their trip to Lourdes, I pray for healing. Yet each year I find that my hands have gotten no better. (On the other hand, they've gotten no worse.)

During my first visit to Lourdes I visited the baths twice. The next day a Jesuit friend with whom I was traveling said, "Are you cured?" I shook my head. "I guess Mary said no," he said. "Maybe next year!"

When it comes to places like Chimayo, I try to give the story the benefit of the doubt. (Lourdes is of a different order, however. Cures there have been authenticated by the church and by medical doctors, who have attested to 67 miraculous healings since 1858.) My faith does not depend on these traditions. On the other hand, I figure that if God can create the world out of nothing and raise his son from the dead, then moving a crucifix from one place to another is simple by comparison.

The Room of Miracles, also called El Pocito (literally, Little Well), is near the main chapel, connected by an anteroom where one finds an explosion of paintings of dozens of saints, holy cards, letters of gratitude and crutches hung on the wall in testimony to the healings received. As Ned had told me, you have to duck to enter El Pocito. Once inside you see even more prints of the saints and letters tacked to the walls. In the middle of the earthen floor is a small hole, about the right size for planting some flowers. Somewhat incongruously, into the hole were stuck three brightly colored plastic shovels, like those a child would use at the seashore.

Saying a prayer, I bent down and rubbed my hands in the dirt. Would I be healed here? Was Chimayo where God wanted me to be freed of my little ailment? The dirt was cool and silky.

On the way out, I gingerly asked Father Julio about my friend's tale of the miraculously refilling dirt. "Oh no!" he said cheerfully. "Some people believe that, but it's no secret: we refill it every morning, and during Holy Week and the summertime several times a day. We take the dirt from a nearby hillside, so it's the same earth in which the crucifix was discovered."

The Return

The next day, Bill and I woke up early and drove to San Francisco de Asís Church in Ranchos de Taos. At 6 a.m. the morning star was still visible in the inky sky. Bill's pink adobe church is best known as the subject of several moody Georgia O'Keeffe paintings, in which the church becomes a mass of shapes looming against a cloudy sky. "I can't believe I have a key to this work of art," he said as we walked in. It was the feast of St. Jude, one of my favorite saints. The Mass, celebrated in Spanish and punctuated with songs accompanied by a guitar and an accordion, was deeply moving.

After a colossal breakfast of huevos rancheros, which we shared with a few parishioners, Bill drove me to the Albuquerque airport, where the customs inspector asked me to open my bag. Inside was a small tin canister I had bought from one of the santos stores in Chimayo with an image of another local devotion, the Infant of Atocha.

"What's inside?" he asked suspiciously.

All I could think to say was, "It's holy dirt."

"Ah sí!" said the inspector, and I noticed for the first time his Hispanic features. "Chimayo!" he said.

My hands have not improved much. But then again, I have been able to write this article, so I will credit the pilgrimage to El Santuario of Chimayo for a little healing. Maybe just the amount that I needed.   —*America*, February 25, 2008

A PRAYER FOR FRUSTRATED CATHOLICS

This prose-poem reflects some of Martin's own frustrations with the church, including sharp divisions between Catholics and denunciations of leading progressive Catholics as heretics during the papacy of Benedict XVI, particularly those seeking to implement the reforms of Vatican II. However, it also indicates where Martin believes healing is possible and movement beyond impasse most likely: in a focus on Christ, on the saints, on the long arc of history.

Dear God, sometimes I get so frustrated with your church.

I know that I'm not alone. So many people who love your church feel frustrated with the Body of Christ on earth. Priests and deacons, and brothers and sisters, can feel frustrated, too. And I'll bet that even bishops and popes feel frustrated. We grow worried and concerned and bothered and angry and sometimes scandalized because your divine institution, our home, is filled with human beings who are sinful. Just like me.

But I get frustrated most of all when I feel that there are things that need to be changed and I don't have the power to change them.

So I need your help, God.

Help me to remember that Jesus promised that he would be with us until the end of time, and that your church is always guided by the Holy Spirit, even if it's hard for me to see. Sometimes change happens suddenly, and the Spirit astonishes us, but often in the church it happens slowly. In your time, not mine. Help me know that the seeds that I plant with love in the ground of your church will one day bloom. So give me patience.

Help me to understand that there was never a time when there were not arguments or disputes within your church. Arguments go all the way back to Peter and Paul debating one another. And there was never a time when there wasn't sin among the members of your church. That kind of sin goes back to Peter denying Jesus during his Passion. Why would today's church be any different than it was for people who knew Jesus on earth? Give me wisdom.

Help me to trust in the Resurrection. The Risen Christ reminds us that there is always the hope of something new. Death is never the last word for us. Neither is despair. And help me remember that when the Risen Christ appeared to his disciples, he bore the wounds of his Crucifixion. Like Christ, the church is always wounded, but always a carrier of grace. Give me hope.

Help me to believe that your Spirit can do anything: raise up saints when we need them most, soften hearts when they seem hardened, open minds when they seem closed, inspire confidence when all seems lost, help us do what had seemed impossible until it was done. This is the same Spirit that converted Paul, inspired Augustine, called Francis of Assisi, emboldened Catherine of Siena, consoled Ignatius of Loyola, comforted Thérèse of Lisieux, enlivened John XXIII, accompanied Teresa of Calcutta, strengthened Dorothy Day and encouraged John Paul II. It is the same Spirit that it with us today, and your Spirit has lost none of its power. Give me faith.

Help me to remember all your saints. Most of them had it a lot worse than I do. They were frustrated with your church at times, struggled with it, and were occasionally persecuted by it. Joan of Arc was burned at the stake by church authorities. Ignatius of Loyola was thrown into jail by the Inquisition. Mary MacKillop was excommunicated. If they can trust in your church in the midst of those difficulties, so can I. Give me courage.

Help me to be peaceful when people tell me that I don't belong in the church, that I'm a heretic for trying to make things better, or that I'm not a good Catholic. I know that I was baptized. You called me by name to be in your church, God. As long as I draw breath, help me remember how the holy waters of baptism welcomed me into your holy family of sinners and saints. Let the voice that called me into your church be what I hear when other voices tell me that I'm not welcome in the church. Give me peace.

Most of all, help me to place all of my hope in your Son. My faith is in Jesus Christ. Give me only his love and his grace. That's enough for me.

Help me God, and help your church.

Amen.

—*America*, June 6, 2012

2

God in All Things:
The Divine in Daily Life

Perhaps the greatest temptation in every expression of Christian spirituality is the attempt to establish a demarcation between, on the one hand, a God who is all good and, on the other hand, the world of created things, which the truly holy person must disdain and from which he or she must flee in order to achieve true union with God. This temptation can be found as a constant thread throughout thousands of years of Christian spiritual writings and practices, despite the fact that some of the very first lines of the Book of Genesis state that God found creation to be very good. It has parallels in most major world religions, and can easily be buttressed by proof-texts from Scripture or by evidence from the fallen world around us. However, it also denies the reality of the Incarnation, God's choice to enter creation directly so as to redeem it fully. Modern spiritual writers, as much as their ancient counterparts, struggle with this tension, alternately fleeing the world for the monastery or the cloister and yet always returning, in some sense, to the little revelations of the divine in the everyday.

A typically Ignatian expression of one's relationship to God and the world is the notion from St. Ignatius's Spiritual Exercises *that God "can be found in all things," that every part of creation can help every creature, each one of us, to grow closer to the divine will. It is a motto that is abused almost as often as it is used properly, but in James Martin's writings, it points the reader toward the hidden or obscured treasures of daily life, even when that life can seem one of pointless suffering or undeserved struggle. This chapter brings together a number of selections from Martin's writings on the quotidian joys and struggles that, when appreciated in light of God's presence in every event, action, and object, can be seen as prominent figures in the narrative of every believer's faith life and relationship with the Lord.*

SIX STUPID THINGS I NEVER WANT TO DO AGAIN

Two months ago I turned 51. That feels pretty old to me. But at least I'm a bit more experienced and, I hope, a little wiser than I was at 21. With that in mind, here are six stupid things I have done that I never want to do again. Maybe you've done some of them too. But I'll bet we'd both be happier if we don't ever again . . .

1. *Compare.* Ever heard the saying "Compare and despair"? Comparing yourself to someone else usually means that you imagine the other person is better off, more satisfied—in a word, happier.

But here's the problem: We end up comparing what we know about our life, which is a mixed bag of good and bad, with a fantasy of someone else's supposedly "perfect" life. Why do we do this? Because we know all about our own problems, but other people's problems are harder to see. As a result, our real life always loses out. That leads to despair. Besides, there's probably someone comparing his or her life to your supposedly perfect one—which shows you how ridiculous it all is.

2. *"Should" on yourself.* It's easy to imagine yourself making a choice that would have taken you to a different place in your life. I should have married this person; I should have taken that job; I should have moved. This is called "shoulding all over yourself." (Say it aloud and the negative meaning becomes clearer.) Reflecting on our choices is an important way to grow, but you cannot

live your real life if you're busy living in your "should have" life. Jesus of Nazareth once said you cannot serve two masters. You can't live two lives either.

3. *Get people to like you.* I spent all of my teens, most of my 20s, a great deal of my 30s and too much of my 40s trying to get people to like me. But forcing people's affection never works. Besides, it takes too much energy to tailor yourself to what you think people will like. Your true friends like you already. Be open to change and growth by all means, but treasure friends who love you for who you are. St. Francis de Sales, the gentle and lighthearted 17th-century saint, once said: "Be who you are and be that perfectly well."

4. *Be a jerk.* You're tired. You're rushed. You've got a cold. You're late. You're angry about something your boss said. Yes, you are miserable. That doesn't mean you have to be a jerk to everyone else. It really doesn't. Sure, share your frustrations and struggles with close friends, but don't make everyone else's life more miserable by passing on your misery. Once I joked to a friend, "Boy, my life is such a cross!" "Yes," he said, "But for you or others?"

5. *Make fun of people.* Nothing brings me lower than a few minutes of mocking another person. (Particularly if the person is not present.) But the snappy putdown has a high value in our culture, and famous snubs are often repeated approvingly. Much of our current political climate consists in politicians mocking their opponents. (That's been a big help, hasn't it?) Malicious speech is an easy way to wound. If you feel powerless to resist badmouthing someone, ask yourself three questions: Is it kind? Is it necessary? Is it true?

6. *Be hard on yourself.* One of my Jesuit mentors used to say, "Be easy with yourself, Jim." If you're reading this list and taking it at all seriously, you may be beating yourself up about stupid things that you've done in the past. (Believe me, my list is just as long as yours.) But you also want to change yourself,

which is good. So be careful to "trust in the slow work of God," as the Jesuit Pierre Teilhard de Chardin used to say. (He was also a paleontologist, so he knew about things moving really slowly.)

If you ever get discouraged about your rate of change, just think about trees—yes, trees. In the summer they're green. In the fall they're red. And no one sees them change.

—*America*, February 13, 2012

NOW I GET IT

Now I get it. Or at least part of it. The prospect of not raising children was not a big deal for me when I entered the Jesuits. It wasn't a deal at all, really. And, over time, while I calculated (almost daily) the difficulty of going through life without one special person to stand by my side, I rarely thought about forgoing the blessings of children in my life. Not that I didn't like children, à la W. C. Fields. Rather, never having spent much time around them as an adult, I liked them more in the abstract.

But with my sister and brother-in-law now the parents of two small children—one 7 years old and one 13 months—I am beginning to see something of what I gave up, and what it is that parents may experience.

For one thing, I am amazed at how much I love my nephews. When my father died a few years ago, I remember thinking, "I never knew that one could be so sad." When I am around my nephews I think, "I never knew that one could love so much."

Last summer I spent a Saturday with my sister's family and her oldest son, Charles, a person whom I had already told he was "my favorite person in the world." After passing a sunny afternoon with my nephew doing his favorite things—battling each other with his plastic "Star Wars" light sabers, reading surprisingly detailed books about dinosaurs and playing with anything remotely connected with water (water pistols, water guns, water balloons), I poured myself onto a local commuter train for the ride home.

Suddenly a wave of emotions swept over me: a deep love for my nephew, for my sister and brother-in-law; gratitude for God's creative love; and then—oddly—fear. I felt how much I cared for Charles and how ardently I hoped that nothing terrible would ever befall him.

Then, with a start, I realized that this must be one one-hundredth of what parents must feel every day about their children.

But fear only rarely raises its head. After all, my primary job as an uncle is to have fun with my nephews (and to make sure the sacraments are taken care of). Most of the time I spend with Charles and Matthew, his baby brother, is a lark. That's another significant benefit of being a priest: no dirty diapers, no late-night feedings and no dealing with tantrums. At 7, my nephew has grown into a bright, funny and kind little boy, who sometimes amazes me with his comments and asides. On Easter Sunday this year we all watched the movie *Jesus of Nazareth*. (He endured this only because I told him we couldn't play with his stuffed animals before Jesus rose from the dead.)

When Charles saw the image of Jesus on the cross, silhouetted against the overcast sky in Zeffirelli's film, he said, "That's beautiful." I asked what he meant and he said, "Well, I know it's sad, but it's sort of beautiful, too."

Spending time with my nephew also has heightened my appreciation for childhood non sequiturs, especially when it comes to organized religion. One of my sister's friends, for example, who is married to a Jewish man, recently took their young son to Mass.

During the exceedingly boring homily, the child wailed, "Can we go home now?"

The mother said, "No, the Mass is only half over."

The son answered, "Well, I'm only half Catholic. Let's go home."

Seeing things through a child's perspective is a healthy spiritual practice, especially if we ever hope to enter the reign of God. So I never miss an opportunity to find out how Charles sees the world. Last year, I asked how his infant brother passed his time. "He eats and he sleeps and he cries and he poops," he said. I took this as a reasonable summary of Matthew's life and started to move to another topic, when Charles said excitedly: "Uncle Jim, I almost forgot! He throws up, too!"

My nephew really is my favorite person in the world. (Recently, though, I have realized that now that he has a younger brother, I'm either going to have to do some quick thinking or hope that Charles won't mind my having two favorite people.) Of course, even his parents and grandmother would admit that Charles is not a perfect child. But he is a beautiful soul. And seven years ago he did not even exist.

My little nephew's presence in the world makes me grateful to be alive, astonished at the goodness of the Creator, conscious of what I have forgone as a Jesuit and, as an added benefit, more able to laugh at life.

And I'm getting pretty good with those light sabers, too.

—*America*, August 14, 2006

TRUE SELVES AND FALSE ONES

In this long excerpt from his book Becoming Who You Are, *Martin treats a subject that was always close to Thomas Merton's heart: the true self hidden behind all the masks and entanglements each of us wraps around it. By Merton's non-uncontroversial reckoning, once one peeled away all those layers and obstacles, the path to holiness became clear: simply be who you are.*

In his book *New Seeds of Contemplation,* Thomas Merton wrote, "Every one of us is shadowed by an illusory person: the false self." With his typical insight, Merton identifies the false self as the person that we wish to present to the world, and the person we want the whole world to revolve around:

> *Thus I use up my life in the desire for pleasures and the thirst for experiences, for power, honor, knowledge and love, to clothe this false self and construct its nothingness into something objectively real. And I wind experiences around myself and cover myself with pleasures and*

> *glory like bandages in order to make myself perceptible*
> *to myself and to the world, as if I were an invisible body*
> *that could only become visible when something visible*
> *covered its surface.*

This notion of being "clothed" with the bandages of the false self, like the Invisible Man being wrapped, mummy-like, in long, winding strips of cloths, struck a deep chord within me. The self that I had long presented to others—the person interested in climbing the corporate ladder, in always being clever and hip, in knowing how to order the best wines, in attending the hottest parties, and in getting into the hippest clubs, in never doubting my place in the world, in always being, in a word, *cool*—that person was unreal. That person was nothing more than a mask I wore. And I knew it.

I had known it for some time, too.

One warm day in spring, during senior year in college, I was walking jauntily across campus to a job interview dressed in a new suit and tie. On one level, I felt confident. Assured. Certain. Just about to finish up my degree at Wharton, I had a full slate of job interviews lined up with some of the world's biggest companies. In a few months I would be making lots of money, possibly have my own office, and be set for life. Over my arm I was carrying an expensive new khaki raincoat that I had just bought for interviewing season.

On my way, I passed a good friend. She took one look at me and said, "Wow, you look like you're carrying a prop." I felt unmasked.

Of course, almost any college student would probably feel strange in that situation; everyone I knew felt as if they were doing a bit of playacting when it came to interviews. But my friend's words struck at a deeper level: I felt as if those bandages that I had wrapped around me had suddenly been stripped away. My heart knew that as much as I *wanted* to want this, I wasn't made for the life that I was supposed to want.

Now, I should note that business is a fine vocation for a great many people—many of my friends, in fact. The point is not that business is somehow bad, but rather that this life was pretty much the opposite of what I wanted to be doing. Yet I had created, over many years, this persona, this other self, which I thought would be pleasing to everyone: to my family, my friends, my professors. And this "false self," separated from my true desires, was sure that a life in corporate America was the right path. This false self was sure about everything.

I love what Richard Rohr, the Franciscan priest, says about this in his book *Adam's Return:* "Our false self is who we *think* we are. It is our mental self-image and social agreement, which most people spend their whole lives living up to—or down to."

Keeping this false self alive requires a good deal of work. And for me, it was an almost all-consuming effort. It took work to convince people that I was all the things I wanted them to think I was: "Of course I can't wait to start my job!" It took work to make sure that no one saw me as uncertain about anything in life, especially in my professional life. "Of course I love reading *The Wall Street Journal!*" It took work to run away from my true desires, my true feelings, and my true vocation in life: "Of course I love my job!"

The "clothing" of yourself with these bandages, in Merton's phrase, also means that if you are not ever vigilant, those bandages may occasionally slip, and reveal your underlying true self to others. A few years after beginning my work at General Electric, I used to doodle on my desk this note, over and over, in small letters: "I hate my life." How sad it is to remember that. But it felt that this was the only way I could express myself.

One friend, sitting at my desk one evening, noticed these scribblings. It was around 10 at night, and we were horsing around, laughing and throwing wadded-up pieces of paper at each other. Letting off steam after a tiring day. He glanced down at my desk. In an instant, his face dropped and a wave of pity crossed his face. "Do you really hate your life?" he said quietly.

How strange it felt to sit across from my friend. How strange it felt for my false self to be revealed, to have the bandages slip and show my real feelings. I longed to be honest with him. There were two choices: to be honest and share myself with another person, or to lie and conceal myself from my friend. I chose the second option. "What?" I said.

He pointed to the words I had written. Looking over his shoulder, I pretended to read them for the first time. "Oh," I said, carefully rearranging the bandages of my false self, "I was just having a bad day, you know?" The false self had reasserted itself. Those bandages would not fall away for many years.

The trajectory of Merton's own life clearly shows his own steady movement away from the false self. This is perhaps most evident in his gradual acceptance and understanding of his vocation as a Trappist monk.

Merton's early journals and letters are filled with a confidence that unsuccessfully masks a deep longing for a place to belong. These feelings continue unabated until the day he enters the monastery, when he finally finds the home he has long been searching for. But even then, during his years at the abbey, even after he has become a monk, Merton continues to meditate on what *kind* of monk he is intended to be, as he moves closer toward being the person God intended him to be. His spiritual journey was far from complete when he entered the doors of the abbey. In many ways it had just begun.

But it was not a solitary journey. Indeed, Merton speaks of this journey as "discovering myself in discovering God." Ultimately, he says, "If I find Him I will find myself, and if I find my true self I will find Him." In other words, God desires for us to be the persons we were created to be: to be simply and purely ourselves, and in this state to love God and to let ourselves be loved by God. It is a double journey, really: finding God means allowing ourselves to be found by God. And finding our true selves means allowing God to find and reveal our true selves to us.

Those spiritual phrases may sound overly abstract and overly pious, and maybe even a little hollow and hokey. What does this mean on a practical level? And how does one put that insight into action?

Simply put, one attempts to move *away* from those parts of ourselves that prevent us from being closer to God: selfishness, pride, fear, and so on. And one also tries, as far as possible, to move *toward* those parts of ourselves that draw us nearer to God. In the process, one gradually finds oneself growing more loving and more generous. One also trusts that the very *desire* to do this comes from God. That is, the desire for our true selves to be revealed, and for us to move nearer to God, is a desire planted within us by God.

At the same time, one's own individuality, one's own brand of holiness is gradually revealed. Our personalities are not eradicated as much as they are made fuller, more real, and finally more holy. In his collection of essays entitled *Karl Rahner: Spiritual Writings,* the esteemed Catholic theologian wrote, "Christianity's sense of the human relationship to God is *not* one that says that the more a person grows closer to God, the more that person's existence vanishes into a puff of smoke."

In the quest for the true self, one therefore begins to appreciate and accept one's personality and one's life as an essential way that God calls us to be ourselves. Everyone is called to sanctity in different ways—in often *very* different ways. The path to sanctity for a young mother is different from that of an elderly priest. Moreover, the path to sanctity for an extroverted young man who loves nothing more than spending time with his friends cheering on their favorite baseball team over a few beers is probably very different from that of the introspective middle-aged woman who likes nothing better than to sit at home on her favorite chair with a good book and a pot of chamomile tea. One's personal brand of holiness becomes clearer the more the true self is revealed.

And as we move closer to becoming our true selves, the selves we are meant to be, the selves that God created, the more loving parts of us are naturally magnified, and the more sinful parts are naturally diminished. As are so many other blocks to true freedom. As Richard Rohr writes, "Once you learn to live as your true self, you can never be satisfied with this charade again: it then feels so silly and superficial."

By the way, this may anticipate an important critique of the notion of the true self. Just recently, when I told another Jesuit about this book, he asked, "Well, that's fine, but what happens if your true self is a horrible, lying, mean-spirited person?"

My answer was that this would not be the person God created. In other words, to find his true self, the horrible, lying, mean-spirited person would have to uncover his true self—the good self that God created—from underneath all those layers of sinfulness. And I would suspect that the longer he had been living as a selfish person, the longer it might take for him to uncover his true self.

Over the course of his life, Merton, for example, became a more expansive and generous person, and, likewise, his intolerance of others diminished over time. This was an outgrowth of his quest to be himself and to move closer to God. And it is evident in his writings.

In *The Secular Journal,* for example, the collection of journals from the 1930s and 1940s that immediately preceded Thomas Merton's entrance into the Trappists, the reader meets a clever young man full of enthusiasm and strongly held beliefs on literature, art, politics, people, and, in time, religion. The reader also meets a young man who is sometimes insufferably smug. (It is a testimony to Merton's humility that he allowed some of the smuggest passages to remain in his manuscript.)

There is, for example, a cringe-inducing entry detailing his visit to the New York World's Fair in 1939. In his journal, he recounts his reactions as he observes the crowds observing some notable paintings that have been sent over for exhibition at the Fair. It is a merciless portrait of Merton's fellow human beings, who are depicted as far less sophisticated than the writer. He even mocks some of them for not being able to correctly pronounce the name of the Flemish artist Peter Bruegel, who painted in the sixteenth century.

There were a lot of people who just read the name: "Broo-gul," and walked on unabashed. . . . They came across with the usual reaction of people who don't know pictures are there to be enjoyed, but think they are things that have to be learned by heart to impress the bourgeoisie: so they tried to remember the name.

The possibility that among those crowds were people who appreciated what they were seeing is entirely lost on the young Merton. The idea that he might give them the benefit of the doubt is likewise absent.

A few years later, in *The Seven Storey Mountain,* Merton reveals more of his youthful and occasionally patronizing attitudes, particularly when it comes to other religions. Though one could find some "sincere charity" among Quakers, the Society of Friends is summed up in a few dismissive lines: "But when I read the works of William Penn and found them to be as supernatural as the Montgomery Ward catalog, I lost interest in the Quakers." Ironically, Eastern spirituality, which would play a great role in Merton's later life, is similarly dismissed. After a discussion about his attempts at self-hypnosis, he writes, "Ultimately, I suppose all Oriental mysticism can be reduced to techniques that do the same thing, but in a far more subtle and advanced fashion: and if that is true it is not mysticism at all." So much for *that* spiritual tradition! But Merton grants them this: "That does not make it evil *per se* . . ." How generous of him!

Still, unlike his earlier writings, buried within *The Seven Storey Mountain* is Merton's awareness that his arrogance is not motivated by love. He begins to realize how much his responses to people stem from his own shortcomings. After he criticizes the services at the Zion Church near his grandparents' house in Douglaston, Long Island, he recognizes that his own pride "increased the irritation and complicated it."

How different all of this is from the later Merton! After several years in the monastery, he began to soften to other people, to other viewpoints, and even to "the world," which had previously stood for all that was bad in life. Merton's true self, the loving person buried under his arrogance and his hurt, began to be revealed, so that even people that he did not know were seen in the light of their relationship to God. The more time he spent with God, the more generous he became. His true self was a generous self.

Compare his experience with those museumgoers in 1939 with his famous epiphany in Louisville in 1958. He writes about this in his book *Conjectures of a Guilty Bystander*. Merton has just been into town to see a doctor. Standing on a busy intersection he finds this:

> *In Louisville, at the corner of Fourth and Walnut, in the center of the shopping district, I was suddenly over-whelmed with the realization that I loved all those people, that they were mine and I theirs, that we could not be alien to one another even though we were total strangers. It was like awaking from a dream of separateness, of spurious self-isolation in a special world, the world of renunciation and supposed holiness.*

It is no wonder that in later life Thomas Merton said that he no longer knew the man who wrote *The Seven Storey Mountain*. The person who years before had stood apart from the crowds is now firmly in their midst, loving them. The true self can now contemplate the false self with some distance, some wisdom, and even some compassion.   —*Becoming Who You Are*, 19–27

In this essay and the three following it, Martin treats some of the negatives of our day-to-day experience of Catholicism in the United States: not only our own griefs and gripes but the misper-ceptions and bigotries of many non-Catholics and the American media. As is typical in much of his writing, he does not flinch from hard truths but also seeks to find elements of (and evidence for) the divine in every moment and act.

DON'T BE A JERK

"Coarsened" is a word you've probably heard more and more frequently in the past few years. It's most often applied to the state of public discourse in our country, particularly in the polit-ical sphere.

Lately, some of our political candidates have been calling one another names, using schoolyard taunts and shouting over one another during televised debates. There have even been articles written that used insights from child psychologists to aid parents hoping to teach their children that this is not how adults should behave. On top of that, your social media feeds (Facebook, Twitter and the like) may be filled with increasing levels of invective. Even in our own church many Catholics seem ready to call another person a "bad Catholic" at the drop of a biretta.

You can be excused for feeling that having a conversation on a controversial topic might prove dangerous for your emotional, psychological, spiritual and maybe even physical health. You might get slugged.

All this reminds me of some great advice I once heard from the Jesuit historian John W. O'Malley, author of several books, including *The First Jesuits* and *What Happened at Vatican II?* But it isn't an *aperçu* from St. Ignatius Loyola or one of the early Jesuits. Rather, this wisdom came from an older Jesuit whom John had once known. They were three rules for getting along in Jesuit community: (1) You're not God; (2) This isn't heaven; (3) Don't be a jerk. That last one was originally in saltier language—using a synonym for a kind of donkey—but it still works.

The first two are essential for life in general. "You're not God" has multiple implications. First, you can't change most things, so stop trying. Second, you're not in charge, so stop acting as if you were. And third, you don't know everything, so stop acting as if you do. It brings calm, perspective and humility.

The second dictum, "This isn't heaven" can help to reduce the complaining you do. For example, if you live in a Jesuit community where the roof leaks (as ours once did, in my room, for several months) or where the elevator apparently runs up and down on a stream of molasses (as ours has always done), you are reminded to complain less because, well, this isn't heaven.

But it's that last apothegm that I wish more people remembered when they enter into public discussions: "Don't be a jerk." Now, I'm the first to admit that I break that rule from time to time (probably more than I know, since I may not notice it). But today a surprising number of people think nothing of attacking people anonymously on Twitter, calling fellow politicians terrible names and maligning their integrity during debates, posting mean comments on Facebook and shouting over one another on talk shows—basically, being a jerk. And jerkiness is contagious, I think. Seeing public figures shouting on television probably encourages people to do it in their private lives. At the very least, it does not encourage charitable behavior.

How does one avoid that contagion? Here's where some other traditional bits of wisdom can help. First, always give people the benefit of the doubt. Believe it or not, St. Ignatius placed that simple maxim at the beginning of his *Spiritual Exercises*, where he called it a "Presupposition." "Every good Christian," he wrote, "ought to be more eager to put a good interpretation on a neighbor's statement than to condemn it." Amen.

Second, avoid ad hominem arguments—that is, attacks on the person. The difference here is between "I think your argument is incorrect because . . ." and "You're a bad Catholic." Avoiding that will ratchet down emotion significantly and help all interactions go more smoothly.

Finally, an overtly spiritual approach: Ask God to help you see others the way God sees them. The old adage that everyone is fighting a battle (or carrying a cross) is helpful. In the *Spiritual Exercises*, St. Ignatius invites us to imagine the Trinity looking down on all of humanity with love. The next time you're angry with someone, think of the Trinity gazing down on the person you're about to flame.

None of this should prevent people from discussing things, whether one-on-one, online, in public, on television, even on debate nights. You can always disagree. You can even disagree vehemently.

Just don't be a jerk.   —*America*, April 18, 2016

THE LAST ACCEPTABLE PREJUDICE?

The advertisement for a student-loan company features a picture of a nun in a veil with the legend "If you're a nun, then you're probably not a student." The movie *Jeffrey* includes a trash-talking priest sexually propositioning a man in a church sacristy. One can readily venture into novelty stores and buy a "Boxing Nun" hand-puppet or, if that's out of stock, perhaps a "Nunzilla" windup doll. *Late-Nite Catechism*, a play that features a sadistic sister in the classroom, has become a favorite of local theaters across the country. Since last fall nine Catholic churches in Brooklyn, N.Y., have been vandalized; statues have been decapitated and defaced. In some instances hate mail was sent as well. The playwright Tony Kushner, writing in *The Nation*, calls the pope a "a homicidal liar" who "endorses murder." During one Holy Week *The New Yorker* displays a picture of the crucifixion on its cover; but in place of the corpus, a traditional Catholic icon, appears the Easter Bunny. On PBS's *NewsHour with Jim Lehrer* a commentator discussing mandatory DNA testing for criminals identifies the following groups as "at risk" for criminal behavior: "teenagers, homeless people, Catholic priests." A Catholic priest highly recommended by a bipartisan committee that spent "literally hundreds of hours" in their search for a chaplain for the U.S. House of Representatives is rejected with no adequate explanation. And the leaders of Bob Jones University, where Gov. George W. Bush appeared during his presidential campaign, call Pope John Paul II the "Anti-Christ," and the Catholic Church "satanic" and the "Mother of Harlots."

Examples of anti-Catholicism in the United States are surprisingly easy to find. Moreover, Catholics themselves seem to be increasingly aware of the specter of anti-Catholic bias. In the past, a largely immigrant church would have quietly borne the sting of prejudice, but today American Catholics seem less willing to tolerate slander and malicious behavior. In addition, the question of anti-Catholic bias has recently been brought to the fore by the Catholic League for Religious and Civil Rights. Emboldened by its public-relations successes, with attacks on television shows like *Nothing Sacred*, Broadway offerings like *Corpus Christi* and last year's exhibit Sensation at the Brooklyn Museum of Art, this organization has made anti-Catholicism a hot political issue.

But this raises a critical question: How prevalent is anti-Catholicism in American culture? Is it, as some have termed it, "the last acceptable prejudice?" Is it as serious an issue as racism or anti-Semitism or homophobia? Or are rising complaints about anti-Catholic bias simply an unfortunate overstatement, another manifestation of the current "victim culture," in which every interest group is quick to claim victimhood?

In short, is anti-Catholicism a real problem in the United States?

Historical Roots

It is, of course, impossible to summarize 400 years of history in a few paragraphs. But even a brief overview serves to expose the thread of anti-Catholic bias that runs through American history and to explain why the eminent historian Arthur Schlesinger Sr. called anti-Catholicism "the deepest-held bias in the history of the American people."

To understand the roots of American anti-Catholicism one needs to go back to the Reformation, whose ideas about Rome and the papacy traveled to the New World with the earliest settlers. These settlers were, of course, predominantly Protestant. For better or worse, a large part of American culture is a legacy of Great Britain, and an enormous part of its religious culture a legacy of the English Reformation. Monsignor John Tracy Ellis, in his landmark book *American Catholicism,* first published in 1956, wrote bluntly that a "universal anti-Catholic bias was brought to Jamestown in 1607 and vigorously cultivated in all the thirteen colonies from Massachusetts to Georgia." Proscriptions against Catholics were included in colonial charters and laws, and, as Monsignor Ellis noted wryly, nothing could bring together warring Anglican ministers and Puritan divines faster than their common hatred of the church of Rome. Such antipathy continued throughout the 18th century. Indeed, the virtual penal status of the Catholics in the colonies made even the appointment of bishops unthinkable in the early years of the Republic.

In 1834, lurid tales of sexual slavery and infanticide in convents prompted the burning of an Ursuline convent in Charlestown, Mass., setting off nearly two decades of violence against Catholics. The resulting anti-Catholic riots (which included the burning of churches), were largely centered in the major urban centers of the country and led to the creation of the nativist Know-Nothing Party in 1854, whose platform included a straightforward condemnation of the Catholic Church.

By 1850 Catholics had become the country's largest single religious denomination. And between 1860 and 1890 the population of Catholics in the United States tripled through immigration; by the end of the decade it would reach seven million. This influx, largely Irish, which would eventually bring increased political power for the Catholic Church and a greater cultural presence, led at the same time to a growing fear of the Catholic "menace." The American Protective Association, for example, formed in Iowa in 1887, sponsored popular countrywide tours of supposed ex-priests and "escaped" nuns, who concocted horrific tales of mistreatment and abuse.

By the beginning of the 20th century fully one-sixth of the population of the United States was Catholic. Nevertheless, the powerful influence of groups like the Ku Klux Klan and other nativist organizations were typical of still-potent anti-Catholic sentiments. In 1928 the presidential candidacy of Al Smith was greeted with a fresh wave of anti-Catholic hysteria that contributed to his defeat. (It was widely rumored at the time that with the election of Mr. Smith the pope would take up residence in the White House and Protestants would find themselves stripped of their citizenship.)

As Charles R. Morris noted in his recent book *American Catholic,* the real mainstreaming of the church did not occur until the 1950's and 1960's, when educated Catholic sons and daughters of immigrants were finally assimilated into the larger culture. Still, John F. Kennedy, in his 1960 presidential run, was confronted with old anti-Catholic biases, and was eventually compelled to address explicitly concerns of his supposed "allegiance" to the pope. (Many Protestant leaders, such as Norman Vincent Peale, publicly opposed the candidacy because of Kennedy's religion.) And after the election, survey research by political scientists found that Kennedy had indeed lost votes because of his religion. The old prejudices had lessened but not disappeared.

Contemporary Prejudices

But why today? In a "multicultural" society shouldn't anti-Catholicism be a dead issue? After all, Catholics have been successfully integrated into a social order that places an enormous emphasis on tolerance. Moreover, the great strides made in dialogue among the Christian denominations should make the kind of rhetoric used in the past outmoded if not politically incorrect.

But besides the lingering influence of our colonial past, and the fact that many Americans disagree with the Catholic hierarchy on political matters, there are a number of other reasons for anti-Catholic sentiments. Most of these reasons are not overtly theological. (However, as the recent flap at Bob Jones University demonstrated, strong theological opposition to the church still exists among small groups of Baptists and evangelicals in the South.) Rather, these sentiments stem mainly from the inherent tensions between the nature of the church and the nature of the United States.

First, in any democracy there is a natural distrust of organizations run along hierarchical lines, as the Catholic Church surely is. The church's model of governance can strike many as almost "anti-American." (Many Americans, for example, view the church's ban on women's ordination largely in terms of democratic principles, or "rights" and "representation.")

Second, the church's emphasis on community, as well as what St. Ignatius Loyola famously called "thinking with the church," is often seen as at odds with the American ideal of rugged individualism. This attitude manifests itself whenever the institutional church is criticized but personal faith is celebrated. This is also the philosophy represented in such movies as *Dogma* and

Stigmata. The implicit message is that while organized religion is bad, "spirituality" (especially in a highly personalized form) is good. Similarly, in a pluralistic society the church's emphasis on the one, eternal truth can strike some as difficult to comprehend.

Third, in a rational, post-Enlightenment society the church's emphasis on the transcendent seems at best old-fashioned, and at worst dangerously superstitious. The church teaches a transcendent God, embraces mystery, seeks to explain the nature of grace, and believes in the sacramental presence of God. The rational response: How can an intelligent person believe in such things?

Fourth, in a culture obsessed by the new—whether in technology, entertainment, lifestyle or ideas—the church reaches back into ancient practices and beliefs. This creates another obvious tension.

Fifth, especially for intellectuals in a postmodern world, where the notions of "truth" and "texts" are suspect, the church proclaims its belief in eternal truths and—as if to make matters worse—truths that can be found by meditating on texts.

Sixth, the church's tendency to regulate belief, according to the rules of canon law and practices of the magisterium, often strikes many Americans—especially journalists and writers—as "censorship." As Avery Dulles, S.J., has noted (*Am.*, 10/1/94), this sentiment provides journalists with a built-in bias against the teachings of popes and bishops and organizations like the Vatican's Congregation for the Doctrine of the Faith.

Anti-Catholic bias in the United States is therefore something more than simply a historical legacy. It is the result of inherent tensions between aspects of the Roman Catholic worldview and a democratic, post-Enlightenment, postmodern American culture. And while all religions labor under this postmodern critique, Catholicism has been singled out as a highly visible, seemingly powerful and therefore consistently tempting target.

The Political Arena

Anti-Catholicism today is arguably less a political matter (manifesting itself in political venues and overt political action) and more a cultural one (expressing itself in various cultural arenas, most notably entertainment and advertising.)

This is not to deny its still-potent power in the political world. The recent furor over the rejection of a Catholic priest as chaplain in the U.S. House of Representatives is a case in point. Similarly, when church spokespersons offer commentary, for example on abortion, they are frequently dismissed as simply "parroting" Rome's line. In a 1995 interview with *America* (7/1), the U.S. bishop's spokesperson for pro-life issues neatly summed up this line of thought: "The Catholic part of you has disabled the thinking part of you," said Helen Alvaré.

The media also have a tendency to reduce the church's positions to a single issue. In 1993, during the national health care reform debate, the U.S. bishops issued a thoughtful letter calling for universal coverage, strongly criticizing a "two-tiered" system that favored care for the rich over the poor, and opposing abortion. The media, however, focused only on abortion—the one area where the bishops were out of step with liberal Democrats. Still, this may simply represent myopic reporting, not anti-Catholicism.

The anti-Catholicism that one might deduce from observing the political world may stem less from deeply rooted prejudices than from disagreements with positions set forth by the hierarchy. In other words, not everyone who disagrees with the church is biased or malicious. So what may initially appear as antipathy toward the church may simply be political rhetoric that has exceeded the boundaries of civility. Occasionally, however, such disagreements can lead to genuine antipathy toward the church and constitute a real prejudice—just as strong disagreements with the political agenda of gays and blacks are sometimes expressed in gay bashing and racism. And when such rhetoric does cross the line, complaints of "anti-Catholicism" may be justified.

Indeed, it is groups that are most opposed to the church's stance in the political arena that most often lapse into prejudices and stereotypes in their public rhetoric. The pro-choice organization Catholics for a Free Choice, for example, can be counted on to disagree with the church on almost any topic. Similarly, many vocal members of the gay community, who have found themselves—not surprisingly—at odds with a magisterium that labels them "objectively disordered" are often virulent in their criticism. In an article in *The New York Times Magazine* (9/26/99), Andrew Sullivan recounted how, in the 1980's, the "mainly gay" activist group Act Up desecrated Communion hosts at a Mass in St. Patrick's Cathedral. "Some of the most anti-Catholic bigots in America are gay," Mr. Sullivan opined.

Still, in the political sphere it is difficult to gauge whether criticism of the church represents an honest critique or is indicative of prejudice. Here, therefore, one should use the words "anti-Catholic" sparingly if at all. Where anti-Catholic tendencies seem to be stronger—or at least more obvious—is in the fields of entertainment and advertising.

Advertising and Entertainment

It is difficult to know where to begin a discussion of anti-Catholicism in advertising, so ingrained is it in the industry. Perhaps two quick examples will suffice. Last year *Details* magazine featured an advertisement for Diesel jeans showing a quintet of buxom nuns, hands folded primly, wearing Diesel jeans while, in the background, a polychromed statue of the Blessed Mother peers down at them from on high. And in an advertisement for Grateful Palate, a food and wine wholesaler, a nun named Sister Mary Lemon Curd is featured (in full habit) with the following quote: "I love Grateful Palate products, especially Burton & Co. curds . . . Sometimes I just rub it all over my . . . oops. Never mind. . . . I'd rather eat curd than anything else, except the holy sacrament."

What is the purpose of this kind of advertising? The answer is contained in the very goal of advertising—that is, to sell, to make money. Anything that sells the product—anything—is useful. So, for example, if Diesel Jeans wants to convince people that their products are daring or fashionable, their ads must convey this impression of daring. It doesn't matter that sending up Catholic symbols is a hackneyed device; for certain consumers who decide to buy jeans on the basis of a magazine ad, a tired attack can still elicit the desired *frisson* of shock. And since there is almost nothing advertisers can do to shock anymore (sex? been there; nudity? done that) advertisers are desperately looking for new sacred cows to gore.

The entertainment industry, however, is of two minds about the Catholic Church. On the one hand, film and television producers seem to find Catholicism irresistible. There are a number of reasons for this. First, more than any other Christian denomination, the Catholic Church is supremely visual, and therefore attractive to producers and directors concerned with the visual image. Vestments, monstrances, statues, crucifixes—to say nothing of the symbols of the sacraments—are all things that more "word-oriented" Christian denominations have foregone. The Catholic Church, therefore, lends itself perfectly to the *visual* media of film and television. You can be sure that any movie about the Second Coming or Satan or demonic possession or, for that matter, any sort of irruption of the transcendent into everyday life, will choose the Catholic Church as its venue. (See, for example, *End of Days*, *Dogma* or *Stigmata*.)

Second, the Catholic Church is still seen as profoundly "other" in modern culture and is therefore an object of continuing fascination. As already noted, it is ancient in a culture that celebrates the new, professes truths in a postmodern culture that looks skeptically on any claim to truth and speaks of mystery in a rational, post-Enlightenment world. It is therefore the perfect context for scriptwriters searching for the "conflict" required in any story.

Yet, paradoxically, the entertainment industry is where one finds the most obvious contempt for the Catholic Church. It is as if producers, directors, playwrights and filmmakers feel obliged to establish their intellectual *bona fides* by trumpeting their differences with the institution that holds them in such thrall. Chief among the laugh-getting scenes in the trailer for

last year's lowbrow movie *Superstar*, about a Catholic school-
girl, is a scene where a nun gets kicked in the face during a
kickline. The 1995 movie *Jeffrey*, as mentioned, featured a
scene in a sacristy where the priest gropes a male parishioner.
When the parishioner expresses surprise, the priest exclaims,
"Maybe you didn't hear me. I'm a *Catholic* priest! Historically,
that falls between being a florist and a chorus boy." The movie
Stigmata featured a plot line implying that the corrupt Catholic Church is sitting on a secret Gospel. And last year's offering by the director Kevin Smith, the theology-obsessed *Dogma*,
displays its occasional anti-Catholic jibes as badges of intellec-
tualism: Nuns are addled, cardinals nutty, the Mass irrelevant
and so on.

But it is television that has proven the most fertile ground for
anti-Catholic writing. Priests, when they appear on television
shows, usually appear as pedophiles or idiots, and are rarely
seen to be doing their jobs. (When was the last time, for example, that you saw a hospital chaplain on *E.R.*?) On Fox-TV's
Ally McBeal, a show which also featured a sexually active nun,
the show's writer David Kelley (who also gave viewers a foot-fe-
tishist priest in *Picket Fences*) featured a Protestant minister who
is being prosecuted for having an affair with a church worker. "I
realize that doesn't make me an altar boy," he says to one of the
lawyers. "If you were an altar boy," the lawyer responds, "you'd
be with a priest."

Of course, the purpose of television entertainment is not to
inform but to increase network revenues; so it is misguided to
expect sitcoms to be documentaries. *Ally McBeal*, after all, is
not *Frontline*. And—as in advertising—with few taboo subjects left, TV producers and writers are desperate for anything
that will titillate, shock or amuse. So the Catholic Church is a
particularly tempting target. We are at once in the mainstream
(and therefore familiar enough to the average viewer) and out of
the mainstream (and therefore an object of some suspicion and
contempt). But the maliciousness of the humor can be startling,
focusing as it does on the Catholic Church.

The Catholic League

The group that has had the most to do recently with bringing the question of anti-Catholicism to the fore is the Catholic League for Religious and Civil Rights, a previously quiescent organization founded in 1975 by Virgil Blum, S.J. It is a lay organization with no official ties to the Catholic Church. However, the location of its current offices in the New York Archdiocesan chancery building suggests it has at least the tacit approval of the archdiocese.

Under the leadership of Mr. William Donohue, a sociologist by trade and now a frequent commentator in the media, the Catholic League has experienced a series of stunning public relations successes, organizing protests over such entertainment offerings as *Nothing Sacred*, *Priest*, *Dogma* and *Corpus Christi*. And they are obviously doing well financially: In October 1999 they purchased a full-page advertisement (at $35,000) in *The New York Times* denouncing *Vanity Fair* magazine for its alleged anti-Catholic slant.

By focusing attention on instances of anti-Catholic bias, the Catholic League serves an important function. Many of its critiques have been timely, accurate and on target. And the league's methods of publicizing its grievances have been successful in raising awareness of the issues surrounding anti-Catholic bias. It is doubtful, for example, that the recent controversies over the Congressional chaplain and Bob Jones University would have received much media attention without the efforts of the Catholic League. But some important questions remain about its methods, questions about how the church operates in a particular culture, in this case the media culture.

In order to gain media attention today, one must be two things: *first* and *loud*. Indeed, the person or organization that is first to comment on a particular topic instantly becomes the resource for every succeeding news story on that topic. Unfortunately, being first frequently means that there is inadequate time for reflection on the issue. Even more unfortunately, the

Catholic League, in its rush to issue press releases, sometimes doesn't take the time to study or even to see what it is condemning. Its critique of *Dogma*, issued weeks before the show opened, included condemnations of lines of dialogue that did not appear in the final print. So while being first may be an effective way to increase one's chances of attracting media attention, there is a danger that the Catholic League reinforces the stereotype that the Catholic Church is at best unreflective and at worst unfairly biased and paranoid. And in the long run, this may do more damage to the church's reputation than a short-lived movie or play.

Similarly, the media today favor the loudest, that is, those best able to furnish controversy and argument. So rather than a measured, considerate and nuanced response to issues, many denunciations issued by the Catholic League are phrased in overheated and strident terms. (This was particularly the case with the recent exhibit "Sensation," which featured a painting entitled *Blessed Virgin Mary* decorated with elephant dung and cutouts of pornographic photos.) The problem with this approach is twofold. First, more moderate and conciliatory voices are perforce passed over in favor of the more controversial ones. Second, the church may be seen, by association, as strident and reactionary.

When asked to respond to these critiques, the president of the Catholic League pointed to results. "Have we been loud and confrontational? Yes," said Mr. Donohue in an interview with *America*. "But when I took over this organization I was absolutely determined to get results and get them fast. So I was tough, but got the results: Anti-Catholicism is now an issue. Maybe down the road, when things are up and running, I'll change my style. But for now I am adamant about making anti-Catholicism an issue."

The Catholic League's insistence on claiming that other groups would not tolerate such prejudice is also a two-edged sword. On the one hand, it helps to focus needed attention on issues that might otherwise be ignored. The method of imagining how other groups would respond in a similar situation is a helpful mental exercise that can clarify the issues. Imagine, for example, the reaction that might greet a play called *Late-Nite Hebrew School*, and you get the idea.

On the other hand, anti-Catholicism is clearly not as virulent or violent as the prejudice directed against blacks, Jews and gays. One does not find many Catholics facing difficulties in this country in obtaining jobs and promotions because of who they are, as do many blacks. Nor, like Matthew Shepard, the gay Wyoming teenager, are American Catholics today tortured, pistol-whipped and killed because of who they are. Attempts to claim parity with such groups leads inevitably to a misunderstanding of persecution, as well as to embarrassing public statements. In 1997 one archbishop publicly compared the critiques leveled against the church in *Nothing Sacred* to the persecution of Jews in the Holocaust. This is solipsism at its worst and most dangerous.

So while the Catholic League provides a useful service by focusing attention on a real problem, its sometimes ill-considered methods may ultimately prove damaging to the church at large.

Reason and Charity

Anti-Catholicism exists. As the Catholic League's annual report ably testifies, it manifests itself in a number of spheres in the culture, most notably in entertainment and advertising. Commentators who deny its presence ignore the historical record and perhaps succumb to a sort of creeping secularism that sees all aspects of the church as inherently risible.

On the other hand, anti-Catholicism in the United States is simply not the scourge it once was, nor is it today as virulent as anti-Semitism, homophobia or racism. Ignoring this fact only leads to misunderstandings. In a *New York Times* (11/2/99) article on the Catholic League, one of its benefactors remarked, "There aren't attacks on Jews." Really? What country does this person live in?

So what is called for? Overall, the best way for the church to respond to real or perceived anti-Catholicism is with an approach of reason and charity. It should be a stance based on an understanding of the history of anti-Catholic bias as well as the history of deeper-seated prejudices held against other groups. It must also be an approach that gives other persons or groups the benefit of the doubt, and is exceedingly careful in labeling others as "anti-Catholic" or as purveyors of "blasphemy." A response to anti-Catholicism needs to be measured, tolerant and considerate, and must be a response that reflects well on the church. It cannot be an approach of invective and suspicion, of overheated pronouncements and wholesale condemnations—all tactics that poorly reflect the charism of the church. It must be, in short, an approach of reason and charity: the approach of the thoughtful Christian and hopeful American Catholic.

—*America*, March 25, 2000

REASONS TO GO TO CHURCH

A few weeks ago, Andrew Sullivan, a senior editor of *The New Republic*, wrote an impassioned article that appeared in the op-ed section of *The New York Times*, entitled "Losing a Church, Keeping the Faith." In his article, Mr. Sullivan discussed his ardent desire to reconcile his homosexuality with his Catholicism. In the end, however, he finds himself unable to reconcile the two and also finds himself, for the first time in his life, unable to attend Mass. Among the reasons he offers are his longstanding opposition to the Vatican's labelling of homosexual activity as intrinsically disordered and his categorical disagreement with the recent document on same-sex unions. His article manifests the intense pain and anger that many gay and lesbian Catholics have expressed over the past several years.

Though the Vatican's opposition to homosexual activity and same-sex unions is exceptionally strong, gays and lesbians are not alone in their struggles in the church. The past few years have been painful ones for Catholics, especially in this country. If you are divorced and remarried, you may feel unwelcome in your parish. If you are a woman, you may feel anger over the

Vatican's stance on ordination. If you are married, you may find yourself at odds with the church's teaching on contraception.

But it is not just liberal Catholics who struggle. You may feel that the beauty of the Mass has been watered down, and that the mystery that you treasured has been taken away. You may think that too often the spirit of Vatican II is taken to mean that anything goes. You may lament that so many Catholics seem to disregard church teaching and tradition without bothering to learn or understand it. You may have been angered by the hierarchy's increasingly strong opposition to capital punishment, or by the Vatican's opposition to the war in Iraq and its support of the United Nations.

Finally, no matter what your theological bent, you may feel angered, confused, saddened or disgusted over the sexual abuse scandal. If you are a layperson, you may be angry at your pastor, your bishop, the bishops' conference or the clergy in general. If you are a priest, you may feel tarred with the brush of scandal. And if you are a victim, or a relative of a victim, you may feel particularly hurt.

In his best-selling book *The Holy Longing,* Ronald Rolheiser, O.M.I., offers nine reasons why one should go to church. They are: because it is not good to be alone; to take my place within the family of humanity; because God calls me there; to dispel my fantasies about myself; because the saints have told me so; to help others with their pathologies and to let them help me with mine; to dream with others; to practice for heaven; and for the pure joy of it.

In these times, I think, it is particularly important to focus on the third reason—because God calls me there.

The church in this country needs help. It needs single and married Catholics, and it needs divorced and remarried Catholics. It needs Catholics who protest at the former School of the Americas, and it needs Catholics who pray at Medjugorge. It needs Call to Action and it needs Opus Dei. It needs *Commonweal* and it needs *Crisis.* It needs conservatives and liberals, men and women, gays and straights.

As St. Paul wrote, "the body of Christ does not consist of one member, but of many." And in order to be healthy the church needs all of its members—especially those who feel in any way marginalized. "The eye cannot say to the hand, 'I have no need of you' . . . On the contrary, the members of the body that seem to be weaker are indispensable" (1 Cor 12:14, 21–22).

How do we know this? Because in baptism all of us were called by God to be active members of the body of Christ. So while it may be difficult at times to believe that the church wants you, never stop believing that church needs you.

—*America*, November 10, 2003

In this excerpt from his book Lourdes Diary *and the essay that follows it, Martin gives the reader blow-by-blow accounts of two of his pilgrim experiences, emphasizing the importance of the happenstance conversations and small moments in each day. To quote many a pilgrim before him, the journey is often more important than the destination.*

LOURDES DIARY

Several years after the novitiate, when I was doing my theology studies, a professor of church history recommended Ruth Harris's book on Lourdes. Except on Bernadette's feast day, I had hardly thought about her at all since the novitiate, and I remembered her story only dimly. But when I began Harris's book, I was as captivated as I had been when I first saw *The Song of Bernadette*.

Around the same time, I received a phone call from a man in Washington, DC, who had read an article I had written and wanted to take me to lunch. Always happy for a free meal, I agreed to meet him during his next trip to New York. Rob, as it turned out, was not only a dedicated Catholic, a good father, and an avid reader, but also a knight of Malta.

"Do you know much about the Order of Malta?" he asked me.

Again, my ignorance of Catholic culture came to the fore. I shook my head no, and Rob gave me a precis of the history of the worldwide Catholic charitable organization—officially titled the Sovereign Military Hospitaller Order of St. John of Jerusalem of Rhodes and of Malta—which dates back to at least the eleventh century. The group boasts a colorful history of work in hospices and even military exploits on behalf of pilgrims traveling to the Holy Land. Technically, the august order is a sovereign state: it enjoys diplomatic relationships with other countries and even is afforded "permanent observer" status at the United Nations, much like the Vatican.

Today the international group concentrates not only on fostering the spiritual life of its members, but also on performing a great many charitable works, especially in its support of Catholic hospitals. The order consists of men and women (knights and dames), priests, brothers, bishops, and the occasional cardinal. Among its members are those who, like men and women of other religious orders, pronounce solemn vows to the order. And like other religious orders, it is governed by a superior (in this case called the Grand Master), who lives in the group's headquarters in Rome. The Order of Malta has a special connection with another location, too.

"One of our biggest works is an annual trip to Lourdes," Rob told me. "We stay for seven days. And it's just an amazing experience. Would you ever think about coming along as a chaplain?"

I told Rob how surprising his offer was: I was right in the middle of Harris's book about Lourdes. But, though flattered, I turned down his kind invitation. "Too busy," I said. Rob smiled and told me that he would persist in asking me until I finally agreed to come.

He kept his promise. The following summer he called me while I was directing a retreat—a time when one naturally feels more open and free—and invited me again in earnest to work as a chaplain on the next trip. And would I like to bring along two other Jesuits to work with me?

"Sure," I said. "Sign us up."

Finding Jesuits was easy: two friends—Brian, a young priest working at a retreat house, and George, a prison chaplain who would be ordained a month after our trip—signed on with alacrity.

As the time approached for our departure, I bought a little spiral-bound notebook to keep as a journal of our pilgrimage to Bernadette's city.

Wednesday, April 28

The Order of Malta has asked us to arrive at Baltimore/Washington International Airport three hours before our 7:00 p.m. charter flight direct to Tarbes-Lourdes-Pyrenees International Airport, which is located a few kilometers from Lourdes. We are greeted by a sea of people, mostly middle-aged or elderly, some wearing silver medals dangling from red ribbons denoting the number of pilgrimages made. Many in the group seem to know one another. Rob makes a beeline for George, Brian, and me and welcomes us to the group.

Scattered in the crowd are men and women seated in wheelchairs or looking painfully thin. Couples cradle children obviously suffering from illness or birth defects. These are, as I already know from Ruth Harris's book, the malades, or the sick, the main reason for the journey. Their trips have been paid for by the order—a wonderful act of charity. Everyone, including the malades, boards the plane cheerfully.

The flight begins unlike any I've been on, with a bishop leading us in the rosary. The in-flight movie, not surprisingly, is *The Song of Bernadette*, which I have not seen for many years. It corresponds reasonably well to the original story of the apparitions at Lourdes, though it doesn't show enough of Bernadette's natural toughness—which to me makes her a more convincing saint than the film's softer version.

Thursday, April 29

We land after a long flight, and a sleepless one for me. The bus ride from the airport through a rainy countryside studded with tall poplars is full of lively conversation, and we quickly arrive at our lodgings, the Hotel Saint Sauveur. Seemingly all the hotels and shops at Lourdes have religious names, and it is startling to see a shop selling tacky souvenirs that is named after Charles de Foucauld, who lived in extreme poverty in the desert, or, worse, a knickknack shop under a sign proclaiming L'Immaculee Conception.

After lunch, our group (there are perhaps 250 of us) processes to Mass in what will become our usual style: the malades seated in small hand-pulled carts in front, accompanied by friends or family, followed by the rest of us.

A letter I received before our departure said, unexpectedly, "Your cassock can be worn anywhere at any time. It will be useful for the Mass in the grotto if the weather is cold, and of course during all the processions." Jesuits haven't worn cassocks since the Second Vatican Council ended in the mid-1960s. But rather than risk giving offense, Brian, George, and I scrounged up some Jesuit cassocks before we left, and we have decided to wear them today.

Far from being an embarrassment, as I had expected, the black cassock feels right in Lourdes. As we cross the square in front of the basilica, I notice brown-robed Franciscans, white-robed Dominicans, and even a black and-white-robed Trappist. While the plain Roman collar makes me feel priestly, the cassock helps me feel very Jesuit. And the cassock is still recognized here. A few days later, a pilgrim greets us with "Ah, les jesuites!"

After Mass in the ornate basilica, someone suggests a visit to the grotto, which I had assumed was far-off. But the church is built directly atop the rocky outcropping, and when I go around the corner and pass huge racks of tall white candles for sale, I am shocked to come upon it.

Now, under the massive bulk of the gray church is the site familiar from holy cards and reproductions in churches around the world: sinuous gray rocks hover over a plain altar before which stands a huge iron candelabrum. In a small niche, where the apparitions occurred, a statue of the Virgin is surrounded by the words spoken to Bernadette on March 25, 1858: "*Que soy era Immaculada Concepcion*."

The area before the grotto is marked off by signs requesting silence, and as I approach I am drawn to the obvious peace of the place: serenity seems to radiate from Massabieille. Hundreds of people are gathered before the space—malades in their blue carts, a Polish priest with a group of pilgrims praying the rosary, a young backpacker in jeans kneeling on the ground.

Many stand in line to walk through the grotto. Joining them, I run my hand over the smooth wet rock and am astonished to spy the spring uncovered by Bernadette. I am filled with wonder at being here.

As I pass beneath the Virgin's statue, I notice a host of tiny flowering plants of marvelous variety under her feet, and I think of medieval tapestries.

Here at the grotto I am also reminded of the importance of pilgrimage in the spiritual life.

In a brief essay entitled "Pilgrimage," Kevin White, a Jesuit priest, points out that many stories in both the Old and the New Testaments show how believers have often sought God by traveling to a holy site. After the Jewish people had settled in Israel, for example, the holy city of Jerusalem, whose great temple contained the Ark of the Covenant, became a pilgrimage destination for devout Jews. In fact, several of the psalms—120 through 134—were sung by Jewish pilgrims in their long and arduous travels to Jerusalem. "I was glad when they said to me," says Psalm 122, "`Let us go to the house of the LORD!"`

The Gospel of Luke tells us that it was during one of these journeys that the young Jesus was separated from Mary and Joseph. "Now every year," writes Luke, "his parents went to Jerusalem for the festival of the Passover." Later in his life, Jesus would often journey with his disciples to the holy city. In a wonderful aside in his journals, the Trappist monk Thomas Merton describes how his abbot encouraged him to think of these travelers whenever his spirits flagged during the monastery's common prayers.

"He said," wrote Merton in 1948, "I should think of Jesus going up to Jerusalem with all the pilgrims roaring psalms out of their dusty throats."

The disciples were, in so many ways, pilgrims. And, of course, Jesus himself would die in Jerusalem during a time of pilgrimage.

The subsequent history of Christian pilgrimage is extraordinarily rich, dating from the earliest periods of the church. In the first few centuries of the church, Christian pilgrims began visiting the tombs of martyrs to venerate the relics of the saints. Then, starting around the fourth century, journeys to the Holy Land, where the devout would visit shrines associated with the life of Christ, also became popular.

The Middle Ages was the golden age of pilgrimage, with believers traveling to the Holy Land, to local shrines, and to ones more far-flung. The shrine of Santiago de Compostela, located in Galicia, Spain, is said to be the resting place of the relics of St. James the Great, who is supposed to have traveled to Spain to evangelize the region. The great cathedral there became a major focus for pilgrims in the Middle Ages. Today millions of believers still stream to places like Jerusalem, Rome, and Santiago de Compostela, as well as the Marian shrines scattered across the world, including Lourdes.

Pilgrimages are time-honored ways of fostering reliance on God, so dependent are pilgrims on the grace of God, which manifests itself in the charity and kindness of fellow pilgrims and in those we meet along the way. The time of travel is also what one of my spiritual directors called a liminal time—a transitional moment, or an in-between space. We find ourselves caught between one place and another, and during these times we can be especially aware of God. Removed from our comfortable routines, we are naturally more aware of our fundamental reliance on God, and are therefore often more open to grace.

We are sometimes more attentive to God when our normal routines are set aside, and when our defenses are down. It is then that we more easily recognize our own "spiritual poverty," that is, our basic need for God.

As the German theologian Johannes Baptist Metz wrote in his book *Poverty of Spirit*: "When the mask falls and the core of our Being is revealed, it soon becomes obvious that we are religious 'by nature,' that religion is the secret dowry of our Being."

Pilgrimages are times when the mask often falls.

Friday, April 30

A few hours later, I cross the street to my former hotel for a huge breakfast with George and Brian. As I walk over, the night clerk at the Hotel Moderne spies me through the plate-glass window. He smiles slyly and playfully waggles his finger at me as if to say, "I know all about your revelry last night, Father."

By now, Brian, George, and I have met many members of the order, as well as many of the malades. The term is not pejorative here. "We're all malades in one way or another," says a bishop on pilgrimage with us. The range of illnesses they live with is stunning: cancer, AIDS, Lyme disease, dementia, birth defects.

At lunch I sit with a couple from Philadelphia. She suffers from a disease I have never heard of, and that has left her, in her late thirties, unable to walk easily and prone to a host of painful physical ailments.

She and her husband are aware of the seriousness of her condition, but they are consistently friendly, happy, and solicitous, and I like them immediately. "Oh, I'm fine," she says. "I've been laughing since I got here. So many funny things have happened!" As we process to Mass, Brian and George quietly explain the conditions faced by other malades they have met.

Lourdes, of course, is famous for its healing waters, though nothing in the words of Mary to Bernadette suggests that the waters can heal. (She merely said, "Go drink of the waters and bathe yourself there.") The short guide we receive from the Order of Malta wisely counsels against expecting physical healings. Spiritual healing is more common for pilgrims. But I pray for actual physical healing for the malades anyway, especially the ones I know, here and at home.

In the afternoon, our group goes to the stations of the cross, located on the side of a steep hill. The life-size figures are painted a lurid gold. The knights and dames of the order assist many of the malades along the rocky terrain in a cold drizzle. We are handed a small booklet called *Everyone's Way of the Cross*, and I groan inwardly, expecting banal sentiments.

But I am wrong. If the writing is simple, the prayers are powerful, particularly as I notice a frail man being helped over the slippery ground by his companion.

"Lord, I know what you are telling me," says the text for the fourth station. "To watch the pain of those we love is harder than to bear our own."

The afternoon is a good chance to spend some time in prayer at the grotto, even in the chilly rain. In the weeks before my departure, I started asking friends and family members if they had any intentions that they might like me to remember at Lourdes. I was astonished by the response. Even my agnostic friends had heard of Lourdes and asked for prayers. The requests grew so numerous that I began to write them down on a little note card, to guard against forgetting anyone's intentions. (And almost everyone, no matter what his or her beliefs, asked if I could bring back some Lourdes water.)

Now I take from my wallet that folded note card covered with almost fifty prayer requests: for the conception of a child from a childless couple, for the remission of cancer from a friend's sister, for good luck in finding a job from another friend. As I stand under an umbrella, I imagine myself standing before Mary and Bernadette, presenting each petitioner to them and asking them to bring our prayers to God. It takes almost an hour to go through the list, but when I am finished I feel as if I have completed an important assignment.

Tonight's rosary procession is, if possible, as moving as last night's. Somehow, in the midst of this huge crowd, Brian, George, and I are spotted by one of the officials of the Domaine, that is, the sprawling area surrounding the grotto and the basilica. "*Vous etes pretres?*" he asks. "Are you priests?" When I nod, he pulls us through the crowd to the steps of the basilica. There we join other priests, who gaze out at the enormous throng, just then raising their voices in the *Lourdes Hymn* in the damp night air. An English priest turns to me and says, "The universal church looks well tonight, doesn't it?"

Saturday, May 1

This morning I am waiting for a turn at the baths. On long wooden benches under a stone portico sit the malades, along with their companions and other pilgrims. Flanking me are two men from our pilgrimage with the Order of Malta. One, a fortyish red-haired man, is strangely quiet: later I learn that he is suffering from a form of dementia brought on by Lyme disease. His caring wife suffers greatly. Carved in the stone wall are the Virgin's words to Bernadette: "Go drink of the waters and bathe yourself there." Every few minutes an *Ave Maria* is sung in another language.

After an hour, the three of us are called into a small room surrounded by blue and white striped curtains. Once inside we strip to our undershorts and wait patiently on plastic chairs. From the other side of another curtain I hear the splashing of someone entering the bath, and in a few seconds he emerges with a wide grin.

As I wonder if the legend that Lourdes water dries off "miraculously" is true, another curtain parts. A smiling attendant invites me inside: "*Mon Pere, s'il vous plait.*"

Inside a small chamber three men stand around a sunken stone bath. My high school French comes in handy and we chat amiably. One volunteer points to a wooden peg, and after I hang up my undershorts, he quickly wraps a cold wet towel around my waist. ("I think they kept it in the freezer for us!" says one of the malades at lunch.) Another volunteer carefully guides me to the lip of the bath and asks me to pray for the healing I need. When I cross myself, they bow their heads and pray along with me. Two of them gently take my arms and lead me down the steps into the bath, where the water is cold, but no colder than a swimming pool.

"*Asseyez-vous,*" one says, and I sit down as they hold my arms. Here, praying in this dimly lit room, in this spring water, held by two kind people, I feel entirely separated from the rest of my life. It's a kind of mini-retreat, removed from the rest of the world but somehow very much part of it.

And then-whoosh-they stand me up and point to a small statue of Mary, whose feet I kiss.

Then I'm handed a quick drink of water from a pitcher.

As I emerge from the bath, a volunteer asks me to bless him and the others. Wearing only a towel, I bless the men, who kneel on the wet stone floor and cross themselves. "The first time you've blessed without your clothes?" asks one, and we laugh.

After the bath, I rush over to the Grotto of Massabieille, where our group is celebrating Mass. And, yes, the water dries from my skin immediately.

At the end of the Mass, the presider asks the congregation to pass up any petitions that we have brought. I'm happy that I still have my little note card full of prayer requests in my wallet, and I hand it to a man collecting scraps of paper and envelopes from people in the crowd. The pieces of paper are all stuffed in a small gray box that stands near the spring in the grotto, and I briefly wonder how God will be able to sort them all out, but I trust that God will, somehow.

At five o'clock, Brian and I walk through a light drizzle to a nearby Carmelite monastery. The plain white chapel, with low wooden benches for pews and a carved Crucifixion scene on the sanctuary wall, is utterly quiet and a welcome break from the crowds. We sit for a few minutes until a bell rings loudly. A dozen nuns silently file in for Vespers. They sit behind a tall iron grate to the left side of the altar, separating them from the rest of the chapel.

Seeing their brown and white habits reminds me of the nineteenth-century French saint Therese of Lisieux, whose own Carmelite community is located in the north of the country. Therese is

one of my favorite saints. Raised in a tightknit family, almost smoth-
ered with affection by her father and her sisters, Therese entered
a Carmelite convent in the town of Lisieux at the age of fifteen.
Protesting that in the garden of life, she could never hope to be a
great rose or an impressive lily, she instead decided to be content
as a "little flower," concentrating on doing small things with great
love. Therese believed that God blesses each of us individually:

> *Just as the sun shines simultaneously on the tall cedars
> and on each little flower as though it were alone on the
> earth, so Our Lord is occupied particularly with each
> soul, as though there were no others. And just as in
> nature all the seasons are arranged in such a way as to
> make the humblest daisy bloom on a set day, in the same
> way, everything works out for the good of each soul.*

This spirituality, often called the Little Way, is most clearly
described in her famous autobiography, *The Story of a Soul*, published shortly after her death, in 1897, at age twenty-four.

The chanting of the Carmelite sisters is beautiful—done in
high, clear, girlish voices—and it dawns on me that their songs are
probably close to the words and tunes that Therese heard each
day of her life in the monastery at Lisieux. As plainchant fills the
chapel, I feel very near to Therese and overwhelmed with a sense
of the holiness of her life, and I find myself filled with emotion.

Sunday, May 2

A gargantuan church, called the Basilica of St. Pius X, was built
underground in 1958 near the Grotto of Massabieille. It seats,
unbelievably, twenty thousand people. The concrete structure
would resemble an enormous oval parking lot were it not for
the huge portraits of saints, perhaps ten feet high, that line the
walls. One banner, portraying Pope John XXIII, reads "*Bienheu-
reux Jean XXIII.*" The French word for "blessed" means, literally, "well-happy" and seems a far better one than our own. In
the morning our group processes to the underground church for
a solemn Mass for the Order of Malta.

There are scores of priests in the sacristy, dozens of bishops, and even three cardinals. The entrance procession, with tens of thousands of malades, their companions, knights, dames, pilgrims, students, and everybody else, is almost alarmingly joyful. High above the floor, mammoth screens show the words of the verses of the *Lourdes Hymn*, which, now in English, now in French, now in Italian, now in Spanish, now in German, is taken up by the throng.

At communion I am handed a gold ciborium brimming with Hosts and am pointed to a young Italian guard who carries a yellow flag. He has a girlfriend in America, he explains, and maybe she could call me if she needs to talk? With his flag aloft, he leads me into a sea of people, who engulf me and reach their hands out for communion as if it's the most important thing in the world. Which, of course, it is.

Later on, as I am walking in front of the basilica with a Franciscan friend, a French pilgrim asks me to hear a confession. We sit on a stone bench in the sun, and when we have finished, I look up. A little line has formed, and I call my Franciscan friend over to help.

An Italian man sits down next to me. "*Italiano?*" he says, and I nod. But my Italian is very poor, and after a few minutes I am utterly lost. Before giving him absolution, I tell him that while I might not have understood everything he has said, God has.

In the afternoon I wander through town searching for little gifts for friends at home. Before I left the States I heard some Jesuits lament the tackiness of the shops here, but I'm not bothered by them. Most shoppers, I imagine, are thinking of people at home, and so buying souvenirs is just another way of remembering people while at Lourdes.

Looking at a rack of rosary beads, I see an exact copy of the rosary I bought twenty years ago at the Cathedral of Notre Dame in Paris, right after graduating from college.

The rosary is everywhere in Lourdes. It is present not simply during the grand rosary processions in the evenings, but in quieter ways as well. You see people kneeling on the cold stone ground of the grotto and fingering the beads of their rosaries, wandering around the Domaine with them clutched behind their backs, and even furtively taking them from their pockets in the hotels to pass what little free time they have in prayer.

Whenever I see the pilgrims with their rosaries, I wonder when they first received them. Perhaps their mother and father gave them their rosary on the day of their first Holy Communion, as my parents did for me. Perhaps the rosary was a gift from a beloved aunt or uncle or priest or sister. Or perhaps they purchased their rosary themselves at another Marian shrine far from here: at Fatima, in Portugal; or Knock, in Ireland; or Medjugorje, in Bosnia and Herzegovina.

The rosary that I'm looking at in the little souvenir shop has a tiny metal disk attached to the chain with a portrait of Mary on one side and the word *indecrochable* on the other. When I returned from Paris all those years ago, I looked up the word in a French–English dictionary, which defined it as "strong or unable to be defiled." And I thought that was a good title to apply to Mary: *Indecrochable.*

The shopkeeper comes over. "*Ah oui*," says madame. "*C'est indecrochable.*" Then in English she says, "That means these beads are unbreakable." She gives them a tug. "See how strong they are?"

I laugh and tell her that I thought the word applied to Mary, not to the beads. That it was sort of a theological title—*Immaculee, Indecrochable.* The shopkeeper laughs heartily and quickly tells her assistant, who smiles indulgently. "No," the shopkeeper says in English. "This is not a theological title. This is a marketing title!"

Monday, May 3

At six-thirty this morning, some thirty of us leave in a tour bus for the house of Bernadette Soubirous. On the way over, we pass dozens of souvenir shops, and George leans over to me. "Bernadette was lucky, wasn't she?" he whispers. "On the way back from the grotto she could stop off and buy some souvenirs for herself." Two women, malades, sitting in front of us hear his comment and giggle.

Bernadette's small house, the *cachot*, is located on a narrow side street. Astonishingly, it is even smaller than the horrible room depicted in *The Song of Bernadette*. In Rene Laurentin's biography *Bernadette of Lourdes*, he notes that in this dank hovel, two beds served six people.

I think of the incongruity of it all: we are here because of a poor fourteen-year-old girl who came from the simplest of backgrounds and then returned to her hidden life. Robert Ellsberg remarks on this in his book *Blessed among All Women*:

> *In traditional stories of the saints it is common to remark on the many ways, even as children, that they stood out among their neighbors. But even the most zealous admirers of St. Bernadette, try as they might, could find little to distinguish her. She was good, honest, and devout; on this much everyone agrees. Otherwise she was quite ordinary. She considered herself of no importance, simply a poor vehicle of God's grace, who was content to withdraw into obscurity once her mission was complete.*

During the rainy afternoon I spend a few hours in a vaguely Gothic building with a white and blue sign out front that reads "Confessions." In front of the building is a stone statue of a kneeling St. John Vianney, the nineteenth-century French priest known for his compassion in the confessional. It was said that St. John, known as the Cure d'Ars, or the curate of Ars, spent upwards of eighteen hours a day hearing confessions.

In a narrow hallway, people sit placidly on benches outside doors that announce confessions in English, Spanish, French, Dutch, German, and Italian. There seem to be far more Germans than anyone else. Every few minutes someone pops into my English cubicle and asks hopefully, "*Deutsch?*"

Tuesday, May 4

Tomorrow we will return to the States, so I decide to return to the baths today. By now I have gotten to know a few of the attendants

who help the pilgrims seated on the benches under the stone portico. I ask one how he likes his job. "Oh, it's not a job!" he says
cheerfully. "I'm a volunteer, like everyone else here! If it were just
a job, then I would be thinking, One euro for each person I help.
Or, maybe, One euro for each kilo that the person weighs!" He
laughs. "But this way I look at everybody like a person, not a
number."

He says that many pilgrims are nervous and worried when they
come for the first time. "*C'est naturel*," he says. "People might be
sick, or they might be cold, or they might be afraid of slipping
inside." But his first experience, he says, was transforming. He
struggles to find the words in English and then switches back to
French. "I felt as if a door had opened in my heart." He flings his
hands away from his chest to demonstrate. "After that, nothing
was the same."

Once inside, I see a gregarious attendant I have met before, and
with a broad smile he shouts out, "*Mon ami!*" The other volunteer
notices my cassock and says, "You are a Jesuit? Then you know
my family." When I look confused, he says, "I am Polish and my
name is Kostka." So I am helped into the bath by *mon ami* and
a member of the family of St. Stanislaus Kostka, one of my Jesuit
heroes.

In the afternoon, after filling a few plastic bottles with water
from the taps near the grotto, I return to my hotel. Brushing my
teeth in my bathroom, I think that if Mary were to appear today,
it would probably be in a place as unlikely as a bathroom. After
all, the original apparitions occurred at Massabieille, a filthy
place where pigs came to forage.

A few minutes later, when I enter the hotel lobby, an elderly
man from our group asks to speak with me about something
that happened to him in the baths this morning.

This rational and sensible Catholic has come to Lourdes after
a long illness. (I've changed some of the details here, but not the
essentials.) Through tears, he says that after the bath, he was in the
men's bathroom and heard a woman's voice say in a few words
that his sins were forgiven. The bathroom was entirely empty, and

there are, obviously, no women anywhere near the men's baths at Lourdes.

Before coming to Lourdes, he had prayed for this grace: despite a recent confession he still felt the weight of his sins. In response, I tell him that God communicates with us in many ways, and that while people rarely report this type of experience, it is not unheard of. Something similar represented a pivotal event in Mother Teresa's life.

He is surprised when I tell him that I was just thinking that a bathroom wouldn't be such a bad place for a religious experience. And though his experience was unexpected, it makes sense: a grace received in a clear and distinct way while on pilgrimage. Besides, I say, your sins really are forgiven.

"What did the voice sound like?" I ask. "Oh," he says. "Very peaceful."

Our conversation reminds me that God can communicate with us in any way God wishes to. Most of us will probably never experience God's communication the same way that my friend did in that little bathroom in Lourdes.

But there are other, no less important ways that God can communicate with us. God can speak to us through our emotions—in the happiness we feel for a bit of good news, in the love we feel for our family and friends, in the awe we feel before a beautiful sunset, in the gratitude we feel during "peak" events in our lives, like the birth of a child. God can speak to us through other people in our lives—a spouse or family member, a friend or coworker, even a homeless person we meet on the street. God can speak to us through the Scriptures, as we are able to connect a particular passage or story with our own experience. God can speak to us in our prayer, as we gain insight into the life of Christ and the invitation that God offers to anyone seeking meaning in life.

In essence, God speaks to us in as many ways as there are believers. The key is being aware and attentive enough to recognize this.

The story recounted by Bernadette Soubirous is difficult for even some devout Catholics to accept. Of course, it's not essential that a Catholic believe in this story or in the apparitions at Lourdes, as one needs to believe in, say, the Resurrection. And the church's tradition on this is clear, as explained in the Catechism of the Catholic Church, in a passage on "private" revelations.

Throughout the ages, there have been so-called "private" revelations, some of which have been recognized by the authority of the Church. They do not belong, however, to the deposit of faith. It is not their role to improve or complete Christ's definitive Revelation, but to help live more fully by it in a certain period of history. Guided by the Magisterium of the Church, the sensus fidelium *[sense of the faithful] knows how to discern and welcome in these revelations whatever constitutes an authentic call of Christ or his saints to the Church.*

The Virgin's message was simple and sensible: penance, prayer, pilgrimage. And it is this, not simply the many well attested healings at Lourdes over the years, that has made Bernadette's visions one of the few private revelations officially accepted by the Catholic Church.

Still, many have their doubts.

But the natural beauty of the story and Bernadette's personal character have made it easy for me to accept. I am reminded of a passage from one of my favorite novels, *Brideshead Revisited*, by the English novelist Evelyn Waugh. Early in the book, set in 1920s England, a young Catholic named Sebastian is being pestered by the narrator over his belief in the story of the birth of Jesus, as recounted in the Bible. The narrator is also mocking his friend for his belief in Catholicism in general:

> "But, my dear Sebastian, you can't seriously believe it all."
> "Can't I?"
> "I mean about Christmas and the star and the three kings and the ox and the ass."
> "Oh yes, I believe that. It's a lovely idea."
> "But you can't believe things because they're a lovely idea."
> "But I do. That's how I believe."

Of course, even before traveling to Lourdes, I knew that Bernadette's tale was much more than just a lovely idea. And somehow, after visiting Lourdes, I have become even more convinced of the truth of her story, thanks to the place itself and the people I have met here.

Early on my last morning here, before our flight, I make a final visit to the grotto. Even before dawn, a Mass is being celebrated, and pilgrims are already here, kneeling before the space, running their hands over the rock, praying the rosary, and hoping for healing, as they have been since 1858.

The sun rises over the basilica, and the bells chime the first clear notes of the *Lourdes Hymn* as I cross the square.

—Lourdes Diary, 23–60

HERE'S HOW GOD WORKS

Here are two ways God works. First, God seems to clear a path so obviously that you can't doubt God's activity. As St. Paul wrote, All things work together for good for those who love God. Second, God seems to make achieving something so difficult that you realize that the struggle is part of the journey. And here I like to quote St. Catherine of Siena: Nothing great is ever achieved without much enduring. Most of my life consists in proving the second observation. Just walking around Manhattan can be trying. Not long ago I was on my way to hear confessions, the day after appearing on a few television stations to comment on the recent papal conclave. A few blocks from the church, someone shouted, "Are you Father Martin?" When I nodded, he ran up to me, poked his finger in my chest and said, "The next time you're on television, you should just shut up!"

As St. Catherine said, much of life is about enduring.

But there are moments when everything works out with almost alarming grace. In April I was invited for a return trip to Lourdes with a Jesuit friend named George. We were part of a pilgrimage organized by the Order of Malta, an international Catholic group that sponsors an annual trip for the sick and their companions (and their chaplains) to the famous shrine in southern France.

This year George and I decided to make a side visit to Loyola, the Spanish town and birthplace of St. Ignatius, founder of the Jesuits. So after a few days at Lourdes celebrating Masses, walking in eucharistic processions, visiting the baths, hearing many confessions and singing Immaculate Mary about a zillion times, we rented a car for our pilgrimage within a pilgrimage. Secretly I wondered whether we would get lost. Plus I wondered if we would be able to procure any Loyola water, which supposedly helps women get pregnant, and which had been requested by some of our fellow pilgrims.

Our trip took us along the coast of southern France, past Biarritz, the fabled resort where I imagined the moneyed gentry still living in Cole Porter–like style. To my surprise, George and I arrived in Loyola in just three hours, and here is where it became obvious, at least to me, how God can make things easy.

When we walked into the ornate basilica in the center of town, we discovered that a Mass in Basque (St. Ignatius' mother tongue) was to begin in just a few minutes. After the Mass (which George said might as well have been in Navajo, for all we understood) we toured Loyola Castle, located within the basilica complex. On the uppermost floor, we stumbled on the room in which St. Ignatius experienced his first conversion, while recuperating from battle injuries in 1521. In that room a French priest was just about to celebrate Mass before an ornate wooden altar. Waving us in, he invited us to join a group of pilgrims just starting a pilgrimage to Compostela. We celebrated Mass with them and proclaimed the readings in our high-school French. Afterward the priest asked us what we did back home. I'm a writer, I said, and George is a prison chaplain.

He put his arms around us and smiled broadly. "*Ces deux vocations ont commencé dans cette chambre,*" he said to the pilgrims. These two vocations began in this room.

Immediately afterward, in the gift shop, George and I met a cheerful Jesuit brother, who invited us to the Jesuit residence for lunch, which was just about to begin. Using what Spanish we remembered from summer classes as novices, we asked about the history of the complex of buildings at Loyola and the work of the Jesuits in the community. The meal was all the more delightful, as I was down to my very last euro.

Afterward, one of our lunchtime partners gave us an extensive tour of their main apostolate, which was, appropriately enough, a colossal retreat house located on immaculately kept grounds, called the Centro de Espiritualidad, or, more accurately in Basque, the Gogarte Extea. Each of the five floors boasted its own chapel, each appealing to a different style of prayer: one ornate, one spare and so on. One even looked very Zen, though I knew neither the Spanish nor the French for that word (and certainly not the Basque). We left the retreat house with just enough time to return to Lourdes.

All things worked together for good, and at just the right time, too. On the other hand, we failed miserably in our attempt to get Loyola water. (The sacristan shrugged eloquently when we asked whether they had it in the house.) But no matter. George filled a bottle of water from a fountain outside the basilica and said triumphantly, "Loyola water!" When I looked doubtful, he said, "Well, it's from Loyola, and it's water." We returned to Lourdes just in time for dinner with our friends. When I described how perfectly our trip to Loyola had gone, a fellow pilgrim said, "Like a confirmation of your Jesuit vocation!"

The day after returning to New York, I received a letter from someone who had seen me on television. He called me an idiot.

Oh well, I thought, back to enduring.

—*America*, August 29, 2005

In the following two essays Martin uses the important days of the Lenten season and their commemoration in the liturgical calendar as teaching moments, reminding the reader that they make sense only in the context of Easter Sunday and, further, that they are neither commercial holidays nor hopeless narratives of sadness and suffering.

THE FIVE LESSONS OF GOOD FRIDAY

The sufferings and death of Jesus, which Christians commemorate on Good Friday, may seem far removed from our everyday lives. After all, it is almost impossible to imagine that anyone reading this essay will ever be crucified. (On the other hand, persecution of Christians continues in many parts of the world even today.) So what can the story of Jesus's crucifixion, as recorded in the Gospels almost 2,000 years ago, teach us about our own lives?

One. Physical suffering is part of life.
Unlike philosophies or belief systems that suggest that suffering is more or less an illusion, Jesus says this from the cross: suffering is real. As a fully human person, Jesus suffered. On Good Friday, he was beaten, tortured and then nailed to a cross, the most agonizing way the Roman authorities had devised for capital punishment. There, according to the Gospels, he hung for three hours. Victims of crucifixion died either from loss of blood or, more commonly, asphyxiation, as the weight of their bodies pulled on their wrists, compressed their lungs and made breathing impossible. Jesus's life, like any human life, included physical suffering, and an immense amount of it on Good Friday.

But even before Good Friday, Jesus suffered physically, because he had a human body like yours and mine. Growing up in the tiny town of Nazareth, and later as an adult traveling throughout Galilee and Judea, Jesus likely had headaches, got the flu, sprained an ankle or two, and perhaps even broke a bone—in an era of lousy sanitation and only the most primitive of "medical" knowledge. As a fully human person with a fully human body, he suffered physical aches and pains. Good Friday was not the only day he suffered physically.

Two. Emotional suffering is part of life.
When Christians speak of Jesus's suffering on Good Friday, they tend to focus on his physical trials. Many Early Renaissance artists, for example, depicted that agony in gruesome detail, as a

way of reminding Christians of what their Savior underwent. But Jesus's "Agony on the Cross" included emotional sufferings as well. In these emotions we can see further intersections with our lives.

To begin with, Jesus of Nazareth felt a deep sense of abandonment. How could he not? All of his disciples had abandoned him before the crucifixion, save for a few faithful women and the Apostle John. Peter, his closest friend, denied even knowing him. Moreover, Jesus felt the suffering of betrayal: another close friend, Judas, betrayed him outright. How that must have weighed on his heart as he hung on the cross.

Finally, Jesus likely knew the crushing disappointment of seeing his great work seemingly come to an end. That is, he may have felt like a failure. While it's almost impossible to know what was going on in Jesus's mind on Good Friday (save for the few words he utters before Pontius Pilate and while on the cross) it's not unreasonable to think that he lamented the end of his public ministry.

Now, here we enter some complicated theological terrain. On the one hand, since Jesus had a human consciousness, he would not have known what was going to happen. On the other hand, since he had a fully divine consciousness he would have.

So, on the one hand, it is possible that Jesus knew that the Resurrection was coming. (By the way, for anyone who thinks that this "lessens" his suffering, think of being in a dentist's chair: knowing it will be over soon does not remove the pain.) In fact, Jesus predicts the Resurrection at various points in the Gospel. But it is also possible that Jesus the fully human one may have been surprised on Easter Sunday, when he was raised from the dead.

Thus, as he hung on the cross, Jesus might have mourned the end of his great project—into which he had poured his heart and soul—the end to his hopes for all his followers, the end to all that he tried to do for humanity. And so he says, "It is finished."

Three. Suffering is not the result of sin.

Sometimes it is. If we do something sinful or make immoral decisions that lead to our suffering, we could say that this suffering
comes as the result of sin. But most of the time, particularly
when it comes to illness and other tragedies, it is assuredly not.
If you still harbor any doubts about that, think about this: Jesus,
the sinless one, suffered a great deal. He was not being "punished for his sins."

This idea was more or less common in Jesus's time. In the
Gospel of John, when Jesus meets a man who was born blind,
his disciples ask, "Rabbi, who sinned, this man or his parents,
that he was born blind?" Jesus answered bluntly. "Neither this
man nor his parents sinned."

Sadly, this attitude is still common today. Recently, a friend
living with inoperable cancer received a visit from friends she
knew from her church. They callously told her that they felt her
illness was the work of "Satan." In other words, sin had entered
her life and she was being punished. When she told me this, I
reminded her not only of the Gospel of John, but Jesus's own
suffering.

Four. Jesus is fully human.
Christians believe that Jesus Christ is fully human and fully
divine. Now this is, as theologians like to say, a mystery, something that we will never be able to fully comprehend. But belief
in this is essential for Christian belief. Besides, attempts to paint
Jesus as either only human or only divine simply don't square
with the Jesus we encounter in the Gospels. We read of him both
weeping at the death of his friend Lazarus (hardly something
that the classic Aristotelian or Platonic God would do), and we
also see him heal the sick, still storms, and raise people from the
dead (hardly something that people expected of religious figures in first-century Galilee and Judea, or modern-day anywhere
today).

In the events of his Passion, we see Jesus's humanity on display. On Holy Thursday, in the Garden of Gethsemane Jesus
says, "Remove this cup." In other words, I don't want to die.
Only when he realizes that it is his Father's will that he undergo

death, does he assent. But initially the human one expresses, in the bluntest language possible, that he does not wish to die. Later, also revealing his humanity, he utters a great cry from the Cross, "My God, my God, why have you abandoned me?" I don't think Jesus ever despaired—to my mind, someone in union with the Father would not be able to do that—but he clearly struggled and, at that moment, felt a profound sense of God's absence. Here is his humanity on full display.

This is often a consolation to people who pray to Jesus, the risen one in heaven. Why? Because he understands their humanity. He gets it. Christians do not have a God who cannot understand them, because God endured all the things that we do.

Five. Suffering is not the last word.
The message of Good Friday is incomplete without Easter. The story of the passion is not simply of a man being brutally tortured, nailed to a cross and executed by the Romans. It is the story of a man who turns himself fully over to the Father's will, trusts that something new will come out of this offering, and receives the astonishing gift of new life. The message of Easter is not only that Christ is risen, not only that suffering is not the last word, not only that God gives new life, but this: Nothing is impossible with God.

So may you have a prayerful Good Friday, but, more important, may you have a happy Easter.
—*Huffington Post*, April 17, 2014

A SORROWFUL JOY

The Gospel reading for Ash Wednesday, taken from the Gospel of Matthew (6:1–6, 16–18), includes these lines: "When you fast, see to it that you groom your hair and wash your face. In that way no one can see you are fasting but your Father, who is hidden. . . ."

What do Catholics do every year in response? They approach the altar to have their foreheads dirtied with a black smudge, more or less guaranteeing that everyone "can see." Non-Catholic observers may find this paradoxical. But this is only one of several paradoxes surrounding the day that marks the beginning of Lent, which this year falls on Feb. 25.

The celebration (*Dies Cinerum*, "Day of Ashes") appears in the earliest existing copies of the Gregorian Sacramentary, dating from the eighth century. But the Christian practice of applying ashes is much older; fourth-century penitents donned sackcloth and were publicly dusted with ashes to show their repentance, as sanctioned by the Old Testament.

Traditionally, the ashes distributed are made by burning the leftover palms from Palm Sunday of the previous year. The remains are then pulverized to make the dense, slightly oily powder that even the most lapsed of Catholics readily associate with Lent.

Paradoxically, many disparage rather than celebrate some Catholics who attend Mass or receive ashes on the day. "CAPE Catholics" is a term for those who appear in churches only on Christmas, Ash Wednesday, Palm Sunday and Easter. "A&P Catholics" attend on Ash Wednesday and Palm Sunday. Both terms are humorous but faintly derisive.

The long lines outside churches show that sacramentals speak to many people in ways that it would be foolish to ignore. Rather than looking askance at CAPE Catholics, one might ask: What calls so clearly to those whose regular practice of the faith has waned? Is it the earthy symbolism of ashes? Is it the public identification with the church? More simply, is the desire for conversion something to be revered, not mocked, and something upon which parishes can build creatively?

Ash Wednesday, then, is a day with a surprising Gospel reading and a controverted reputation. It highlights the paradoxes not only of our faith (we die to live; in weakness we are strong) but also of the season that we are about to enter.

Lent is a time of penance, but not just penance. The Second Vatican Council's "Constitution on the Sacred Liturgy" spoke of the twofold character of this liturgical season: it "recalls baptism or prepares for it," and it "stresses a penitential spirit." Catechumens, preparing for baptism, joyfully anticipate the Easter

Triduum, as do the rest of us. Paradoxically, this sorrowful season is also about desire and hope.

Another paradox is that the approach to this season of traditions has recently moved in some refreshingly untraditional directions. Whereas in the past many Catholics were encouraged to "give something up," more common today are invitations to "do something positive." And while many past exhortations focused on individual sin, Vatican II underlined the idea of "social sin." Where, for example, do you participate in structures that perpetuate sinful practices? Perhaps instead of giving up chocolate, you could help your company pay a fairer wage.

A final paradox of Lent: Christ is risen. As with Advent, when it can seem odd to pretend that baby Jesus has not yet arrived (Keep him out of that crèche!), it may be disconcerting to hear homilies that make it seem as though Jesus has not yet been crucified, died and risen from the dead.

Nonetheless, it is important to enter into his story once again. While Jesus Christ has undergone his passion, death and resurrection, his story takes place in our lives every day. We are called to take up our crosses, to die to ourselves, to search for signs of the resurrection in our lives and, paradoxically, to remember the story that we are still living.

—*America*, February 23, 2009

A SIMPLE CHRISTMAS

One benefit of taking a vow of poverty is that it greatly simplifies Christmas shopping. I realized this during my first year as a Jesuit novice, when our monthly stipend (or *personalia*, in Jesuit lingo) was set at $35. That year my family and friends, who had long been used to receiving numerous gifts in oversized boxes from Tiffany's, Lord & Taylor's and Nieman-Marcus, each received instead one box from Filene's Basement—and a small box at that. Fortunately, both family and friends grasped my situation and accepted their downsized presents with aplomb.

Pretty soon, though, my embarrassment over this loss of purchasing power turned into gratitude. For even now, with a somewhat more robust *personalia,* I am limited to small and inexpensive yuletide gifts. But this also means I am spared from spending hours and hours in crowded department stores during the weeks before Christmas and, as a result, have more time to enjoy my favorite time of year: Advent.

Perhaps since my nose is less buried in Christmas lists I am now better able to notice the burdens that others shoulder during December. A few weekends ago I visited Macy's for my annual abbreviated holiday shopping spree and was astonished not so much by the sheer number of shoppers (who were shopping, after all, in the self-described "World's Largest Store") but by the heavy freight with which everyone seemed to be ladened. Maybe it's just my imagination, but are Christmas gifts getting bigger and bigger? Some people were trundling around boxes that looked as if they contained small cars. I saw one poor woman carrying an infant in a Snugli, leading a toddler by the hand and toting in her other hand what looked like half the merchandise from the toy department.

Now, at this point, you might suspect that I am going to launch into a general diatribe against the commercialism of Christmas. That's what many people think about when confronted with the habits of the American buyer this time of year. And one would certainly be justified in commenting on this: the ridiculous pressure to consume, egged on by wall-to-wall advertising (tired of those Gap ads yet?), can crowd out any time to ponder the meaning of the season.

But more often than not, when I see people carting around those big, heavy bags, I think not about commercialism but something like: Boy, they must really love their children. Or, Boy, they must have a lot of friends and family that they care for. Not to say that buying is the best way of expressing love. By no means! as St. Paul would say. Rather, the effort and struggle that many people go through before Christmas is one way of showing that they care for their children, their parents, their friends, their neighbors. Sure, it gets insane at times and sure, some people get too focused on buying the most expensive gifts possible, and absolutely, we would all be better off if we lived much more simply; but at the heart of even the most crazed Christmas shopper lies the simple and holy impulse to give and to make someone happy. And that is surely something to celebrate.

The trick, of course, is remembering why we are doing all that late-night and weekend shopping, why we're spending hours online searching for the right color sweater, why we're sweating through our overcoats in those endless checkout lines, why we're struggling with those burdensome packages—why, in short, we are giving at all.

We give because of God's wonderful and everlasting gift to humanity: Jesus Christ. We offer our time, energy and love because of the time, energy and love offered by Mary and Joseph, two people whose lives were spent in generous service and sacrifice. And we struggle with those heavy packages because of the One who, in coming into our world, and in clothing himself with our humanity, willingly took on all of our burdens.

And surely those are things to celebrate even more.

—*America*, December 23, 2002

GALILEE

In this excerpt from Jesus: A Pilgrimage, *Martin offers a more academic take on Jesus and his followers, though one that emphasizes a familiar theme in Martin's work: the quest to rid oneself of entanglements and all else that prevents the process of finding holiness.*

We may have heard this story so many times the fishermen's responses seem foreordained. Of course they follow him, we think. That's what disciples *do*. But their decision was by no means an easy or obvious one. After all, they had commitments and responsibilities; they were settled. We know, for example, that Peter was married, because the Synoptics tell us about his mother-in-law. And for those who think that they were dirt-poor fishermen with nowhere to go (and so it's easy to pack up their crummy business) we should remember that fishing in Galilee was often profitable; the lake's fish were exported considerable distances. One commentary calls Capernaum an "important trade center." James and John are leaving behind a boat with "hired men," which indicates that Zebedee's business was at least successful. Likewise, Peter and Andrew were working together: a family business.

So there is the commitment to a job.

There is the obligation to family as well: Peter is married; James and John are leaving behind their father. (That Peter leaves his wife—unless he is widowed and caring for his mother-in-law—inserts an element of confusion into the story. What happens to her? The Gospels are silent.) And who is to say that Zebedee hadn't pinned his hopes on his sons taking over the family business? Duty to their father would have been paramount—not simply as a professional obligation but a reflection of the filial piety so prized in those days. In their book *Let the Little Children Come to Me*, a study of childhood and children in antiquity, the authors note that there was an expectation that sons would continue their father's work, and that such continuation was seen as a sign of true obedience.

Finally there are ties of habit and security: most likely their families had lived and fished on the shores of Galilee for generations. The historian Henri Daniel-Rops notes that not only had fishing on the Sea of Galilee existed since "beyond the memory of men," but that even the names of the towns along the shore highlighted the importance of the industry. Bethsaida means "the fishery," or "fishing town." And the Greek name for Magdala was Tarichaea, or "dried fish." Fishing was the *raison d'être* of these towns.

Galilean fishermen often worked together in groups—most likely family groups—pooling their resources not only physically, for the fishing voyages, which required a great deal of human labor, but also financially, to purchase the boats and equipment needed for their trade. There were two methods of fishing. The first was using a seine, or dragnet, weighted down and drawn behind a boat. Jesus would use this kind of net as an image of the kingdom in which the dragnet catches all sort of fish, which God will sort out. The second method was a smaller casting-net, of the type George and I saw, which could be deployed from the shore or from a boat, flung out by hand into the sea. Notice that there is no mention of a boat in Simon and Andrew's case; James and John are in their father's boat.

This may indicate that the second pair was slightly more well-off: larger dragnets were the more profitable way of fishing. But that does not mean that they were wealthy. Reed suggests that the father of James and John "probably owned a modest house, a boat, and some nets, and occasionally hired a few day laborers who were worse off. But in general fishermen were a motley crew." The ruins of the houses on the shores of the Sea of Galilee attest to the fact that the fishing industry was no "financial bonanza."

Overall, Peter and Andrew, James and John were accustomed to this way of life, and they were accustomed to this way of life *together*. Luke says that James and John were business partners with Peter. The four, then, knew one another well. Perhaps that's why Jesus called them together—intuiting that it would be easier for them to come with their brothers and friends.

And while it is true that Jesus doesn't call them as a mob, he does call people to work together with him as a *group*, an early indication of the communal element of his ministry. Jesus could have worked alone, or he could have selected a single person— say, Peter or Andrew or Mary Magdalene—as his assistant, but instead he calls many people to labor with him. Inviting people to work together is a constitutive part of Jesus's ministry, and it reflects his keen understanding of human nature—and perhaps his own need for a group of friends around him. Later we will see that when Christ rises from the dead he will appear to the disciples individually, but more often to a group. John R. Dona-hue, S.J. calls his activity "radically social."

Still, even with their common call, it must have been hard for the fishermen to leave behind their ways of life.

In that way, the Galilean fishermen were like many of us. It's difficult to let go—even harder to let go based on a few words from a stranger. Each of these men was held down by a variety of very real commitments. The nets they were holding are a mar-velous image of the intricate ties that bound them to their old lives—their entanglements.

—*Jesus: A Pilgrimage*, 135–38

3

The Care of Souls:
Solidarity with the Suffering
and the Wounded

One of the great spiritual insights of Thomas Merton's life is recounted in his book Conjectures of a Guilty Bystander, *during an unhappy period when he has found himself in a period of caustic judgmentalism of all those around him and a quick contempt for his fellow humans. He relates:*

> *In Louisville, at the corner of Fourth and Walnut, in the center of the shopping district, I was suddenly overwhelmed with the realization that I loved all those people, that they were mine and I theirs, that we could not be alien to one another even though we were total strangers. It was like waking from a dream of separateness, of spurious self-isolation in a special world, the world of renunciation and supposed holiness. . . This sense of liberation from an illusory difference was such a relief and such a joy to me that I almost laughed out loud . . . I have the immense joy of being man, a member of a race in which God Himself became incarnate.*

Merton's famous epiphany might be reduced to a less poetic axiom that would still capture the spiritual reality of the moment: it is pointless to seek the divine everywhere in life if the search does not lead to greater compassion for those who suffer. Perhaps the Buddhist has always recognized better than the Christian a stark reality of the Gospels: the evangelists comment on Jesus's exercise of divine power far less than they do on his compassion for the suffering and marginalized peoples he encountered.

So too in Ignatian spirituality, the realization of the many gifts God has given each of us should lead to a deeper compassion for the wounded and the suffering of the world as well as the desire to make a greater gift of oneself and one's life. This chapter brings together selections from a number of James Martin's writings on suffering as well as on the need to reach out to those inside and outside the church who suffer or find themselves alienated from the church and society. These include his spiritual reflections on his own physical and emotional sufferings, his clarion calls for justice for the marginalized of the church and American society (including gays and lesbians, immigrants, refugees, victims of sexual abuse, and victims of violence), and his in-depth reflections on horrific crimes like 9/11 or the genocidal wars taking place in Africa.

THE UNDERSTANDING CHRIST

How does Jesus's suffering change us? Help us? What does it mean to have an understanding Christ? Let me suggest a few things.

First, it helps us to feel less alone. There are few things as isolating as suffering. Everyone's suffering is largely incommunicable. The particular problems that you face in your family, for example, are so complex, so shot through with complicated family histories and relationships, as to be almost unexplainable to people. Struggles in the workplace are also complex, hard to explain. The physical problems you deal with are by their very nature private, since no one else can climb into your body and experience your pain. Overall, the struggles you face about almost any part of your life are so private, so personal and so unique, that even when you do explain them you may feel that you've given someone the wrong impression.

But there is one person who understands you fully: the Risen Christ.

Jesus understands your human life because he *lived* a human life. And so you are not alone in your suffering. The Risen Christ—alive and present to us in the Holy Spirit—is with you in your suffering. He is with you in his *divinity*—that is, he knows all things and therefore understands your suffering fully. And he is with you in his *humanity*—he went through all of these things. If you've ever felt alone in your struggles, you no longer have to. You can know that Jesus understands you in every way. And when you pray to Jesus you are praying to someone who understands you. This may help you to feel less alone.

Second, knowing that Jesus understands you may help you feel not only less alone but more able to speak to Jesus more openly in prayer. Perhaps you've had this experience: you are facing a difficult problem and struggle to talk about it. It's hard to find the words; you're not certain that people will understand; and you're worried that people might think that you're just complaining. Suddenly you meet someone who is going through the same thing. Perhaps you've met someone who lost a parent, just as you have. Perhaps you've met a person who is looking for work, as you are. Perhaps you've even found a support group of people living with the same illness that you have. Suddenly you feel more at ease, and can open up. It's a relief to be able to let down your guard and speak candidly with that person or that group.

You can do the same with Jesus. Let your guard down. Open up. Be honest with him in prayer. It's a relief to be honest after feeling that you won't be understood, that you can't complain, you can't ask for help, that you can't even mention your struggles. No, Jesus wants to hear your struggles and he understands them.   —*Seven Last Words*, 119–22

This essay and the two that follow it address Martin's own physical infirmities and how these have given him several important spirituals insights. These include the way even suffering can

*show one the presence of God in everyday life as well as the
importance of praying and developing healthy spiritual practices
when one is physically healthy, in preparation for the times one
is not.*

FINDING GOD IN THE OPERATING ROOM

The Story of Gethsemane is one that I've always found enor-
mously appealing, and it has been the source of much prayer
throughout my life. But while I think that I've always understood the frustration and confusion that Jesus felt in the Garden—the confusion of not knowing what to do, the frustration
that comes with seeing one's plans scuttled—I never fully understood his fear. Never, that is, until one day on the phone my
doctor mentioned that a small "spot" had made an unscheduled
appearance on my last CAT scan. "It may be a tumor," he said.
"But then again, maybe not."

I had been to see the doctor a few weeks earlier, after a spate
of migraine headaches. He seemed relatively unconcerned, as it
had been a stressful time in my otherwise sedate life (preparing
for comprehensive exams, sending out invitations for a graduation and diaconate ordination, contemplating a move to a new
city). Still, the doctor advised that some CAT scans be taken.
"Just to be sure," he said.

After a few days he called with the results. "Your brain looks
fine," he said reassuringly, "but there is a spot near your parotid
gland."

Excuse me? A what? On my what?

"It's probably nothing to be alarmed about," he said, at this
point trying to sound reassuring, "but you should probably see
a specialist." He began to explain—though by now I had pretty
much stopped listening—that the parotid gland was another
name for the salivary gland and that tumors can occasionally
develop near there.

I put the phone down gingerly, feeling stunned. Momentarily
I felt the urge to cry, but it passed after I realized what I needed

to do. Quickly I made an appointment with an otolaryngologist, a specialty I could barely pronounce, much less define.

"You have a tumor," said the otolaryngologist (ear, nose and throat specialist) a few weeks later as she snapped the CAT-scan film down from its lighted display case. Before I could respond, she pressed on with a torrent of clinical bad news that I was wholly unable to digest. "There's an 85 percent chance it's benign, 15 percent that it's malignant," she said. "The tumor is very near the facial nerve, so there's a chance of partial paralysis of the face. You'll almost certainly lose feeling in your left ear and at the site of the incision for a few months. It's a very difficult dissection." She paused to take a breath and wheeled her chair over to me. She placed a cold forefinger above my left ear. "The incision will start here and go to . . . here." She drew her finger slowly past my ear and down my jaw line. "Then back to here," she said, moving behind my ear. "And here." She drew her finger forward, along my neck. "You'll need a biopsy, too, ASAP."

It was about as much as I could take. I felt queasy. "Are you going to faint?" she asked blandly. I said I wouldn't, and didn't. But in the car, driving home from the hospital, I was seized with fear. And anger. And sadness. But mostly fear. What a lousy time for this to happen, I thought.

Then I actually laughed. When, exactly, would be a *good* time for this to happen?

The Body of Christ

Almost from the moment I learned about my tumor, I began thinking about Jesus on the cross. ("Well, I would *hope* so!" said a Jesuit friend.) And for me the most poignant realization concerned the profound intimacy of bodily suffering.

Our bodies, it can be fairly said, are the most intimate parts of our existence. So thinking about surgery, "invasive" surgery as they say, was daunting. The idea of someone laying open the left side of my face, manipulating my facial nerves and muscles, fishing around for a tumor and sewing it all up again made me wince with fear and nausea.

Yet Jesus in his passion welcomed a similar invasion—a piercing of his body—or at least he *accepted* it as part of God's plan. Normally, we attempt to avoid pain or try to alleviate it. This is good and healthy. Yet it is this very human desire that makes Jesus' actions all the more meaningful and astonishing. The day before my surgery, while attending Mass, as I wondered what it would be like to have my neck sliced open with a scalpel, I thought about Jesus. And I heard anew the words "This is my body, which will be given up for you."

In the past I had imagined the words of consecration as representing Jesus' total offering of his self—his entire life—and of course it was. But it was also Jesus' offering of his own physical body—the most intimate, personal part of himself, the part that we normally wish to shield from any pain—to a painful crucifixion. What I would have given anything to avoid, he took on willingly, and in doing so gave everything.

"What Is It That You Want?"

St. Ignatius Loyola counsels us to pray to understand our deepest desires. His own experiences had taught him that God is revealed most often in our wants, our hopes, our longings. But sometimes (strange as it sounds) it is hard to know what you really want. Should I take this job or that one? Go this way in life or not? I seem to want both things, but what do I *really* desire?

Surgery, I discovered, has a wonderfully clarifying effect on all of that. When I was being wheeled into the operating room, staring up dumbly at a rapidly moving row of fluorescent lights on the ceiling, I thought of how I would feel if the tumor turned out to be cancerous and my life ended sooner rather than later. And suddenly I thought of how much I wanted to be a priest. I wanted to be able to celebrate Mass; I wanted to baptize my sister's child soon to be born; I wanted to be a good priest. And

I understood this with a clarity and strength that I had never felt before. It was a great grace after years of wondering precisely how *much* I wanted to be a priest.

What I would have given anything to avoid, Jesus took on willingly, and in doing so gave everything.

Now I knew. It was clear, or rather, it was *made* clear to me.

When I woke up after the surgery in the recovery room—dazed, a mask of cold, cloudy oxygen over my mouth—I heard the nurse calling a name: "Father Martin! Father Martin!"

I smiled and went back to sleep.

"I Will Bind up Your Wounds"

I awoke later only dimly aware of the outside world but acutely aware of my own body, my "meatness" as the Catholic writer Andre Dubus has termed it. At the time, though dopey from the anesthesia (and soon to be drugged with morphine), I felt an IV tube snaking out of my arm and a long drainage tube coming out of the back of my neck. Whichever way I moved, something pulled painfully at my body. I felt like nothing so much as an insect trapped in a spider web. Added to this was a throbbing pain in my jaw and a constricting tangle of bandages swaddling my neck. I felt, in a word, helpless, caught in a web of discomfort and fatigue.

An hour later a Jesuit friend came to visit. As I lay there unable to move, he spooned ice and Jell-O into my mouth—all I could eat at the time, but good and cool nonetheless. Later in the week, after five days without bathing, I asked if he could help me shower. (Believe me, I needed one.) Eating and bathing: both simple things I had taken for granted that I could do for myself and by myself. True, it was an experience of humility to feel oneself so totally powerless and dependent on others, but it was also a signal grace to feel myself cared for by friends and, in my case, by brother Jesuits.

The experience of unexpected graces like this came rushing in frequently throughout my little ordeal, and frequently enough I again realized the link between suffering and grace.

But is this the reason for suffering and pain? Does God make us suffer to show us his grace? Is this the *why* of suffering? I don't think so. But it certainly is the *that* of suffering, if we are open to it.

Prayer during Pain

"Make sure that you pray when you're well, because when you're real sick you probably won't." That's what Cardinal Joseph Bernardin wrote in his magnificent work *The Gift of Peace*. Now I greatly admire Cardinal Bernardin (for one thing, I know his intercession helped me through some rough spots during my recovery), but I wonder about this striking observation of his about the spiritual life.

He's right, of course: When you are in pain it is difficult to pray. A few days after I returned from the hospital I noticed that my face had begun to swell and swell and swell, until the pain became overwhelming. (Fear kicked in, too: Can stitches come apart?)

The kind Jesuit doctor with whom I was staying advised patience, suggesting that we wait to see if there was any improvement in the morning.

At dawn, when the pain killers wore off, I was awakened by pain that I can only describe as stunning; it felt as if a nail were being driven into my jaw. I staggered from the bed and instinctively dropped to my knees, trying to pray for relief and some patience. But no verbal prayer came, just tears. In the midst of such pain, though, came another feeling. It was not so much a "why me?" (for I had long ago passed from "why *me*? to "why not me?") but a crushing disappointment that there could be such intense physical pain in a world of God's making.

I also remembered Cardinal Bernardin's comment and decided that it might need to be amended. Yes, it is difficult to express yourself in prayer when you are in pain, but perhaps this is only true if we think of prayer as purely verbal. When you are in physical pain, if you are conscious of your need for God, your whole body yearns, begs, explodes for God. And so

I think you *are* praying—but with your whole being. In fact, during the two weeks I was recuperating, I stopped saying the *examen,* the nightly prayer reviewing one's day that St. Ignatius recommended.

Since becoming a Jesuit 10 years ago, I had never once missed praying the *examen* at night. But for two weeks during recovery the need to pray at night simply evaporated. My whole day, spent asking God for healing, for help, for grace, for patience, became a sort of silent prayer.

Being Watched

During the next few weeks, I grew accustomed to having people stare at me. In the past, I used to think that when people stared, or gave me a second glance, or when their eyes lingered a second longer on my face, it was because (maybe!) I was good looking. But as I walked through the streets of Oak Park, Ill., where I was recuperating, my face misshapen and marked by the stitches that coursed down its side, hair unwashed and greasy, I knew that the covert stares and surprised glances of the people I passed came because I was, well, ugly.

One day I walked with a friend into the Ernest Hemingway Museum and strode up to the information desk. The young woman at the desk, pony tailed, in her 20's, began describing the current exhibits at the museum. She cheerfully pointed out a new display to her left. I turned my head, following her outstretched hand, and displayed the left side of my face to her. She stopped in mid-sentence and began stammering. I realized she was looking at my scar, and I flushed red.

I turned to look at her and grinned sheepishly, trying to put her at ease. "Oh, I'm sorry," she sputtered. "I got a little distracted."

All of this made me think of what it was like to be someone who, for whatever reason, appears "different"—whether overweight or wheelchair-bound or too tall or too short or with a physical trait that marks one as extraordinary. For me, it was unsettling. The very thing I wanted most to hide was exactly what everyone was staring at.

After I got over the embarrassment of being stared at, I began
to wonder if the experience, besides being yet another exercise in
humility, might have some other value. For one thing, it magnified my feelings of compassion for those who appear "different."

"My Covenant in Your Flesh"

Surgery, I think, is a little death. You hand your body over to
others, if only for a little while, and in some sense it ceases to be
under your control. You do this in complete trust, not knowing
what it will be like on "the other side."

Indeed, for days after my surgery I kept finding telltale signs
of my lack of control over my person. A portion of my stomach
was painted orange. (Who had done *that?*) One morning, a full
week after surgery, as I sat in a chair reading, I spied a metal-
lic band, about an inch wide, taped to my ankle. A small body
thermometer, apparently attached while I was snoozing in the
O.R. "Wow, it's like you were abducted by aliens!" said a friend.
"Very 'X-Files.'" After an operation, life is different somehow.
You may appear different, carrying an indelible mark, a permanent scar, on your body. You may be healed of something that
was troubling you. A friend who recently had heart surgery told
me that soon he will be better than he was before—i.e., different. Perhaps this is why another friend told me he thought of
his surgery as not only a "little death," but also a "little life." "In
a strange way it reminds me of baptism," he remarked. You're
a new person after surgery, he noted, and a new life, unlike the
one you've been living previously, begins. And, like the original
intent of, say, circumcision, you now carry on your body the
mark of your complete dependence on God.

What Awaits Us

Particularly sobering after my operation was the realization that
this—lying in an uncomfortable hospital bed, losing control of
my body, feeling helpless and sick—is something that probably
awaits me in the future, as it awaits most of us.

The tumor turned out to be benign, and so I hope it's not for another 40 or 50 years that I will face my final hospital visit. And, who knows, what takes me to God may not involve a visit to the hospital. (Bricks have been falling lately with alarming regularity from Manhattan skyscrapers.) Nevertheless, it's the way most of us will end our lives.

All of this is very instructive. Our lives are framed by experiences of helplessness and pain—that is, birth and death. And this framing helps to put the years in between into sharper perspective. For if we can realize our radical dependence on God at the beginning and the end, then the life in between becomes more realistic, and ultimately we are made more aware of our constant need for God, in both sickness and health.

—*America*, September 26, 1998

PLOUGHING THE SOUL

Most essays on the spirituality of suffering are written at the end of a difficult time, offering wise insights learned from the past: "Now that I can look back on my suffering, here's what I've come to understand." The subtext, of course, is: "Thank God that's over!" This is not, however, one of those essays. Instead, I write as I am still making my way through a tough phase in life and still trying to make sense of it.

An explanation: I'm not dying. I've no serious illness. I have plenty of food and a roof over my head. And thank God for all of that. But a few months ago I was diagnosed with "repetitive strain injury," or "cumulative trauma disorder," depending on which doctor I talked to. It's a painful condition in the hands and wrists that follows repetitive motion; in my case, typing. "This is nature's way of telling you to slow down," said doctor number one. That sounded fine, I thought, and hoped that it might subside after a few days of rest.

But that's not what has happened. Instead, some 10 months later, I'm still in pain and only a little closer to recovery. It has been frustrating.

Simple tasks are no longer simple: drying dishes, opening jars, doing up buttons, opening doors. I imagine that people with arthritis suffer from the same things. It's maddening to explain constantly what's wrong—especially when it isn't readily apparent that anything is amiss.

One day, opening a door for myself in a restaurant, I realized that there was someone following me. The polite thing to do would have been to hold the door open for her. Instead, I could barely open the door for myself, and hoped that she would be able to squeeze in behind me. But the door slammed in her face. "That was so rude!" she yelled. (This was, after all, New York.) I was tongue-tied. I could hardly pipe up with: "But you see, I have repetitive strain injury, which is to say a painful inflammation of the tendons and joints in the hands and wrists." As she swept passed me I was left instead with a flushed, embarrassed face.

And as with any infirmity—large or small—I've been relying on friends for all sorts of unexpected favors. Packing to go away for the summer meant asking patient friends to carry boxes up and down the stairs for me, while I repeated "Thanks" a thousand times. As a student, I couldn't write or type, so I had to ask to borrow colleagues' notes, or to take examinations orally. And in one of God's more inscrutable jokes, I had, just a few weeks earlier, signed a book contract.

Ironically, as the pain started, I was just beginning a theology course called "Suffering and Salvation." ("You should get extra credit," said a classmate.) One lesson was about how very alone sufferers can feel, a theme that often crops up in Scripture. It's difficult to communicate exactly what's going on with your body and inside your head. And one sometimes feels, during the worst moments, that God is far away. Read some of the Psalms of lament—"How long, O Lord? Will you forget me forever?" (Ps.13:1)—and this becomes obvious.

But I discovered that much of what we were studying, while making sense intellectually, was overwhelmingly difficult to put into practice in my own life. One scholar we studied in the course was Dorothee Soelle, whose magisterial book *Suffering* sets forth a comprehensive theological understanding of the phenomenon. One chapter proposed three stages of suffering: first, one is helped to recognise one's limitations; secondly, one opens oneself up to God; and thirdly, God helps to transform the sufferer. All of that seemed theologically sensible and intellectually appealing. So why was it so difficult to put into practice? Here I was, understanding the theology, but still frustrated and angry, and sometimes despairing.

The answer, I think, is that any kind of rare, transforming insight depends less on knowledge and more on God's grace. Not that the two aren't often related. But, sometimes, they're not.

And so, in quite unexpected places, I've seen some glimmers of God—that is, when I'm not too centered on myself. In Kathleen Norris's wonderful new book, *The Cloister Walk*, she recounts a parable told by St. John Chrysostom. I read her book at night, quickly before my hands became numb, struggling to hold the pages open. St. John asks us to imagine a man observing a farmer at work. The farmer first places a supply of seed in a silo to prevent it from getting wet. A few days later, he sees the farmer sowing the seed on damp ground. "But it's getting wet!" thinks the onlooker.

Clearly, the impatient observer has no idea what's going on. If only he could wait, he might see healthy plants sprouting in a few weeks. How much more, says St. John, should we "await the final outcome of events, remembering who it is who ploughs the earth of our souls."

That brief parable was the truest thing I've read over the past few months. God ploughs up our souls, frequently. It's painful—as the rocks and clods tumble over one another—and confusing—as all sorts of new dirt is exposed. It makes one want to shout to God, like the impatient observer, "You don't know what you're doing!"

Will anything fruitful sprout from my situation? I've not a clue. But I hope that if God is starting to plough, he must have something in mind. And so I wait.   —*The Tablet*, March 1, 1997

REFLECTIONS ON CHRONIC ILLNESS
AND PAIN, AMONG OTHER THINGS

A broad topic, I know—but one with which I've recently become familiar.

A "chronic" illness, I have discovered, is defined as any that takes longer than six months to heal or subside. About three years ago, I developed a malady called "repetitive strain injury," a painful tendinitis of the hands and wrists. I am in pain for much, if not all of the day. As a result, I've been given, as a (relatively) young adult, the opportunity to experience something that theologians, mystics and saints have long pointed to as one of the best ways to grow closer to God, that is, through suffering and pain. So what—as my third-grade teacher used to ask at the end of class—have we learned?

Doctor, Heal My Self

First, some unbidden commentary on the medical profession. Over the last few months I've seen (by conservative estimate) twenty different doctors: rheumotologists, internists, neurologists, orthopedists, general practitioners, not to mention physical and occupational therapists, massage therapists and even an acupuncturist.

Anyway, after a completely involuntary and unscientific study of the medical profession, here's my conclusion: There are good doctors and bad doctors. A good doctor is one who listens, a bad doctor is one who doesn't. And I've come to see that a doctor's skill at listening is intimately related to how well a doctor deals with pain and uncertainty, the twin companions of chronic illness.

Here's a story, and a personal one at that, to illustrate the point. The first neurologist I visited instructed me to have an EMG test done "immediately" (a word that always strikes me as worrisome when it issues from the lips of doctors). As it turned out, an EMG, or electromagnetic graph test, consists of having electric shocks passed through your nerves, in order to test their functionality. "It's just a little uncomfortable," said the neurologist. I always wonder whether doctors know something like this from personal experience, so I asked. "No, I've never had one," she replied confidently, "But I *know* it's not painful."

A few days later I found myself lying on a vinyl-coated hospital table as another neurologist taped small metal disks to my wrist, elbows and shoulders for what was initially billed as a one-hour procedure. I would be given electric shocks, which would pass from metal pad to metal pad, through my arm. ("Wow," said a Jesuit friend when I described the procedure, "Who's your neurologist, Dr. Mengele?") I might add that this was of course precisely the area where I was most sensitive. "Ready?" said the neurologist smiling.

"You'll feel a slight tap as I turn on the electricity," he said cheerfully. And then suddenly—crack!—a strong, painful electric shock, akin to one you get if you stick your finger in an electrical outlet, coursed through my arm and convulsed my wrist, which leapt a foot off the table.

Immediately I felt a wave of frustration and confusion sweep over me. I was aware that my neurologist needed the results of the test, yet I knew that I couldn't endure this for an hour. I felt months of pent-up frustration coalesce as I lay on the cold table. Before I knew it—and much to my surprise—tears fill my eyes and spilled onto the examining table.

"Here's comes another one," said the neurologist, and I heard another crack. Turning to look at me, he saw my by-now wet eyes, and abruptly turned away from me. Furtively, I dried my eyes with the sleeve of my hospital robe. "This is," I finally admitted, "more unpleasant than I thought it would be."

He said nothing and continued fiddling with his EMG machine, still unwilling to look at me. It was astonishing that he felt so uncomfortable with a person in pain that he couldn't even *look* at me. "Here's another one," he said again with his back turned. Pressing another button, he sent another shock through the metal pads.

Finally I asked him to wait. "Oh," he said over his shoulder. "Do you want to stop?"

"What I want," I said evenly, "is a Kleenex."

After a brief and impersonal conversation, in which he admitted that he probably had gathered enough data for my physician, I told him I wanted to stop. "Whatever," he said blandly. When I left the room he was still staring at his machine. Now, *here*, I thought, is a doctor who needs a course in pastoral care.

So one of the first lessons I learned was a practical one: find a good doctor, that is, one that listens, and one that seems genuinely interested in your well-being. It's not as easy as it sounds, but it's worth the effort for one's own physical, mental and spiritual health.

Send My Roots Rain

Poor Gerard Manley Hopkins. For some reason, I always think of the English Jesuit when I'm tempted to despair. There's an excellent biography of the poet called *Gerard Manley Hopkins: A Very Private Life* in which author Robert Bernard Martin details Hopkins' difficult career as a Jesuit, stuck in a school he didn't like, grading endless Greek exams. His familiar poetry, of course, is full of his flirtations with despair. "How Long will failure all I endeavour end?" he wrote in one of his cheerier moods.

Sad to say, reading Hopkins only makes me more blue. And a great battle with any sort of chronic illness is the temptation to despair. One's mood tends, quite naturally, to fluctuate with one's physical well-being. (Think of how happy you are during a bout of the flu and you'll know what I mean.) Living every day with a chronic illness can occasionally lead one to the brink of despair, something that the saints, Ignatius among them, caution us to avoid.

Thomas Merton wrote in *New Seeds of Contemplation* that, at its heart, despair is a form of pride. "Despair is the absolute extreme of self-love . . . Despair is the ultimate development of a pride so great and so stiff-necked that it selects the absolute misery of damnation rather than accept happiness from the hands of God and thereby acknowledge that He is above us. . . ."

In other words, despair says that things can't change. That is perhaps why Ignatius saw it as the product of the "enemy of human nature." Despair also says that I will never learn how to live with my difficulties, that God will not be able to use them to his own ends. Merton, I think, was right.

One of the Noble Truths

Buddhism has it right, too, or at least part of it. Suffering is part of life. Yet that cold fact points up perhaps the most wrenching of spiritual questions, against which all others—with the possible exception of the existence of God—pale. That is, why is there suffering? And its corollary for those in pain or suffering: "How long, O Lord?" in the words of Psalm 13.

Last year, I gave a homily at a Novena of Grace in Boston. The Jesuit scholastic who ran the novena offered the homilists their choice in topics. We were able to choose between things like the liturgy, the sacraments, the Eucharist, community, and so on. One look at the list and I knew immediately what I wanted to preach about: my topic would be "Jesus as Healing Life." I knew in advance that the listeners would probably include a fair number of elderly Catholics, people who doubtless had experienced a good deal of suffering. It would be a good opportunity to pull together some of the things I had come to understand over the past few years.

I'll spare you the details of the homily. My goal, though, was not to shy away from the question of suffering, which many homilists tend to gloss over in a most cavalier fashion. How many times have you heard someone say, "Jesus suffers with us?" You want to shout back, "What does *that* mean?" In any event, I offered some of the traditional theological and scriptural understandings of suffering. But the line that drew the largest response was a story that my mother had told me a few months before.

My mother used to regularly visit my ninety-year-old grandmother in a nursing home. At the home lived a very old nun, who was living with constant pain, as a result of her many illnesses. One day, as the nun recounted it to my mother, the sister was visited by her (younger) religious superior. The elderly nun confessed how much pain she faced in her daily life. "Well," said the superior to her elderly charge, "just think of Jesus on the cross."

"Jesus," said this holy old sister pointedly, "was only on the cross for three hours."

Like I said, the crowd during the novena liked this story more than anything else I said. The expression "burst into laughter" would be accurate. "Boy, that nun was *right!*" said one gray-haired man after the Mass.

Here's another brief story. Recently, after having written a story in these pages about faith healing, I received a phone call from a man who I had never met. He described his progressively worsening illness and, most tellingly, told me that his parish priest had instructed him *not* to pray for healing. Just accept it, he was told. It's your lot. My caller friend wanted to know if that was true. Could he pray for healing?

"Could and should," I said. Isn't that what people did in Jesus' time? Isn't that what people do at Mass? "Lord I am not worthy to receive you, but only say the word and I shall be healed? After all, the woman with the hemorrhage in Luke's gospel (8:43–48), to take but one example, doesn't simply sit there and wait for healing, she seeks it out. As do a host of others: the centurion ("say but the word"), the father of the demoniac. They *ask* for help.

Then why, the caller wondered aloud, would his priest tell him not to pray for healing? The only reason I could offer was that either the priest had never suffered or he was very foolish.

The point is that whatever your "answer" to suffering is—it's a test, it's a way to bring us closer to God through trials, it's a way of identifying with Jesus on the cross—be exceedingly careful not to impose it on people who are suffering. Better to let them tell you.

Blessed Be the Name of the Lord

With chronic pain one is overly aware of one's physical well-being. Is it better today? Worse? Should I see a doctor? Change my treatment? (After seeing many doctors there's also a tendency to become an expert and second guess the physicians, which only adds to the uncertainty.) And there's that nagging, distracting and sometimes completely consuming pain that reminds you of your situation. As a result, it's easy to become overly focused on yourself. As a result of that, it's also easy to miss the many pleasures of life—the wind on your face, a phone call from a friend, spending time with your family, the quiet of snow, the smell of strawberries in the summer. These joys are still around, occurring right in the middle of your illness, which is a good thing to remember, and to be thankful for. "The Lord gives and the Lord takes away, blessed be the name of the Lord," as Job said, who knew a thing or two about suffering. And sometimes the Lord is giving and taking away at the same time.

The Sacred Heart

Feeling compassion for others can dramatically increase when you're in pain. I've found myself much more solicitous of the elderly, the infirm, the disabled, and homeless men and women on the street. For this I am thankful. Suffering, I think, makes one more Christian. It's a strange thing really, but painful experiences can open up your heart more than you would ever expect. I would imagine that it was the same with Jesus, "a man of suffering well acquainted with infirmity," as Isaiah foretold (53:3). More to the point, St. Paul writes that because Jesus suffered, he wonderfully understands our suffering (Heb. 2:18).

I work every week with inmates in a jail in Boston. In the womens' unit, I normally run a sort of Bible study-cum-communion service. Each week we sit at a particular table in the middle of the recreation area, that is, the large space between the women's cells. Most weeks, there is a group of women awaiting me, but last week at that table sat a solitary figure: a young African-American woman, weeping.

I sat down at the table, and since there was nothing else I could do, I sat with her while she cried. I had no idea what she was crying about (though being in jail seemed enough reason). After a few minutes, she dried her tears with the sleeve of her yellow prison jumpsuit and explained her situation: She had been in jail for twenty days (her first time) and was due to give birth in just two weeks. Then she leaned back in her chair, away from the table, and patted her large belly. Her arrest had come when she was visiting a friend's house, where drugs were being used. To make things worse, her friend was with her in her unit; she motioned vaguely over her shoulder in the direction of some other women.

She talked for a long time about her problems. Then she paused and said, quite unexpectedly, "I like to read the Bible." I asked her which parts she liked best.

"The psalms," she said. "They make me feel like God is listening."

We talked about Scripture, and especially the psalms, and how they helped people feel better, for years. The psalms were written by people who knew suffering, I said. And I thought of my own experience over the past few years with them, how Psalm 13 ("How long, O Lord?") helped me to express my frustration and how Psalm 62 ("Only in God do I find refuge") enabled me to find a measure of comfort.

As we talked, I suddenly realized that I would probably not have been able to connect with her on this level—as two people who have experienced suffering, though in utterly different ways—had I not faced some trials myself.

So, in the end, I've realized that with pain and suffering can come compassion, and an ability connect more deeply with others who suffer. It is, I suspect, what helped Jesus to be compassionate: the suffering that came from his loneliness, his distance from his family, the contempt from religious officials of the time, the misunderstanding and rejection of his closest friends. The passion and death of Jesus, then, helps the Risen Christ to understand with a profound intimacy those who suffer, which is to say, everyone.   —*America*, March 21, 1998

Written at the height of sexual abuse allegations in the Catholic Church, this essay and the one that follows it explores two

*questions many lay Catholics asked themselves (or were asked)
during the scandal: how did this happen? And why do I stay?
Martin's answers to the latter question are simple: fidelity and
hope.*

WHY STAY IN A CHURCH
SO CLEARLY FLAWED?

Five years ago this summer I knelt on a cold marble floor in a
church in Boston, before a Jesuit archbishop. Placing his hands
on my head, he prayed silently. By tradition, when I stood up I
was a priest.

The ordination Mass is one of the most elaborate liturgical ceremonies in the Roman Catholic Church, with rituals
stretching back to the earliest days of Christianity. At various
points in the liturgy one hears echoes from the worlds of both
late antiquity and the Middle Ages. Near the beginning of the
ceremony, those to be ordained, the *ordinandi*, kneel before the
bishop and place their hands between his, recalling the pledges
of fealty offered by vassals to their overlords. After declaring
their obedience, the men lie prostrate on the bare floor, facing
the altar, hands tucked under their foreheads, in a gesture of
humility before God and the church. Following the episcopal
"laying on of hands" the *ordinandi*, clad in white albs tied with
cinctures (a traditional symbol of chastity), are vested with the
symbols of the priesthood: the long stole (a sign of authority in
ancient Rome) and the chasuble (the poncho-like garment of
Greco–Roman times). Finally, they are anointed on the palms
of their outstretched hands with the chrism, or holy oil, as the
bishop pronounces a ritual formula: "May Jesus preserve you to
sanctify the Christian people and to offer sacrifice to God."

In light of the sexual abuse crisis in the Catholic church,
the above paragraph carries overtones that are both unwanted
and unavoidable. Today the "obedience" of priests and bishops
to the church suggests a desire to protect an institution at all
costs. "Humility" before the church may connote a willingness

to overlook crimes committed against children. Any "authority" that priests enjoy, at least in this country, has been severely eroded. The notion that a cleric would be needed to "sanctify" others may seem an arrogant one, effectively elevating the priest from the plan of the average layperson. Indeed, that ordination is limited to men is a continuing source of pain for many Catholic women (and men) and underscores the insular nature of the hierarchy, a target of withering criticism during the last two years. The term "laying on of hands" after the sexual abuse of so many minors is especially fraught. And chastity may be the last thing associated with the contemporary Catholic priesthood.

But this collision of the new and the old, the contrast between beautiful ideals and sometimes ugly realities, as well as the negotiation of clerical life during a period of crisis are only a few of the hurdles that face the Catholic priest today.

Though the life of a priest is almost unimaginably rich, many people I meet are interested not in joys of celebrating Mass, the deeply moving experience of hearing confessions, the challenges of balancing the active and contemplative lives, or the struggles of representing a church in a secular world, but something else: the sexual life of a priest. Such interest only intensified in the wake of the clerical abuse crisis, which led many Americans to conclude that priests were (pick one): sexually active, utterly un-aware of their sexuality, pedophiles, or, wholly incapable of keeping their promise of celibacy.

Even strangers and the most casual of acquaintances have felt free to ask me questions about the following topics: my sexual history (before and after my ordination), my sexual orientation (and that of my brother Jesuits), and even whether I think masturbation violates the vow of chastity. It is as if the mere appearance of a Roman collar sets people free from the normal conventions of contemporary conversation.

One challenge, therefore, is not to take personally even the most offensive comments, and to bear in mind that many such questions come from a lack of knowledge about the priesthood. After all, there are fewer and fewer priests around. A recent

Georgetown University study reports that the number of Catholic priests in the United States declined from roughly 59,000 in 1975 to 47,000 last year. The number of active priests (the total figure includes retired clerics) is pegged at only 22,000. While the Catholic population in this country has grown rapidly (from 49 million in 1975 to 63 million in 2003) the number of priests has declined dramatically. So it is not surprising that misunderstandings would grow over time.

Underneath some of these pointed and personal questions seems to rest a natural curiosity about the meaning of sexuality, which the Catholic church has defined as a precious, indeed holy, gift not to be squandered. Whatever one may think about the church's attitude toward sex, this facet of Catholic moral theology always strikes me as healthier than almost any other message that one receives in a culture in which sex and sexuality are increasingly commodified.

Such questions about sexuality are neither surprising nor difficult to understand, especially these days. During the early months of the sexual abuse crisis, in 2002, as I learned more about the grotesque crimes of the former Boston priest John Geoghan, I found myself repulsed by the details of his actions and outraged that such a person would have been allowed to continue functioning as a priest. Still, I remained hopeful that such cases would prove rare.

But as more and more instances of abuse were unearthed, and evidence uncovered that some bishops had moved abusive clerics from one parish to another, I found myself, like most priests, confronting a host of warring emotions. Certainly I knew that many bishops had in the past relied heavily on the expertise of mental-health professionals, who had sometimes given even serial abusers clean bills of health. Nonetheless, the consistent reshuffling of abusive priests time and again flew in the face of basic common sense. Eventually, I found myself angry (at the ineptitude of many bishops), embarrassed (as the term "pedophile priest" slowly entered the lexicon), sorrowful (over the awful plight of the victims), confused (at the bewildering variety of reasons offered for the scandal) and despairing (as the litany of cases seemed without end).

As the crisis wore on, every priest seemed to admit to one tipping point—the piece of news that finally moved him, if even temporarily, to a state of demoralization, depression, or despair. Perhaps it was reading the repellent details of a predatory priest's crimes in one's diocese; perhaps it was meeting face-to-face with a victim of abuse living in one's parish; perhaps it was knowing a colleague abruptly removed from active ministry as a result of a decades-old crimes. For me it came as I read the nearly unbelievable story of Paul Shanley, the serial abuser and former member of Nambla, the organization that celebrated "man-boy love," and who was later called "a priest in good standing" with "no problem that would be a concern in your diocese" in a letter from Cardinal Bernard Law's office to the bishop of San Bernardino, California. For a while I wondered how I could publicly represent a church that countenanced or at least tolerated criminal behavior. And for the first time in my short career as a priest, I was embarrassed to wear the collar.

The fallout from the crisis in the lives of active priests—that is, the vast majority, who have led healthy lives of service—is immense. Beyond the disappointment in the institutional church and sorrow for the victims of abuse, there are less well-known consequences for priests: tightened budgets resulting from justifiably large legal payouts means less money for educational and social-service programs in parishes; working with lay-run organizations like Voice of the Faithful, as well as developing and implementing sexual misconduct policies, rightly demand more time and attention; dealing with bishops whose schedules are now packed with meetings with lawyers and psychologists means that other pastoral issues must take a back seat.

There are other, more personal, results. Many priests will now, as a rule, never get close to a child, no matter how benign the circumstances. After a recent Sunday Mass, a young girl standing beside her mother spontaneously hugged me, and I was surprised to find myself wanting to push her away. I wondered:

Would this hug be later misinterpreted? Priests and members of religious orders teaching in Catholic schools say that their work has been affected dramatically. One friend who works in a Catholic high school for poor boys is frequently approached by students seeking counseling about their complicated family lives. In the past, the students could count on privacy. Now they must air their problems in a classroom with an open door, and so are less willing to discuss their struggles, for fear of other boys overhearing. While these concerns are a small price to pay for the crimes committed by priests, they nonetheless have an effect on many hardworking priests who struggle to carry out their day-to-day ministries.

Why do I stay in a church so clearly flawed? Why do I stay a priest? These are fair questions, and they reminds me of Father Andrew Greeley's trenchant comment that the question today is not why so many Catholics leave the church, but why they stay.

First reason: I freely made a vow to God, and I intend to keep my word.

Second reason: I love being a priest. I feel it is where I am meant to be. I love celebrating Mass, presiding at baptisms and weddings, preaching homilies, hearing confessions. I love talking with strangers on the bus or subway about faith and doubt. The Trappist monk Thomas Merton expressed this gracefully when he wrote, in 1949, that the priesthood "is the one great secret for which I had been born."

Third reason: Like anyone who reads church history, I am not surprised by the presence of scandal and even grave sin in the church. As any organization, the church has long had its share of fools and villains, some of whom held high offices. After all, Saint Peter, by tradition the first pope, sinned famously—denying Jesus three times before the crucifixion. Centuries later, Renaissance popes like Alexander VI (of the rapacious Borgia family) and Paul III were widely known to have granted ecclesiastical offices to both their illegitimate children and grandchildren.

Even the greatest of Christian saints recognized this. During the fourteenth century, when two and sometimes three men claimed the papacy for themselves, Catherine of Siena excoriated them. "You are flowers that shed no perfume," she wrote to a group of Roman cardinals, "but a stench that makes the whole world reek."

While historical precedent does not excuse the contemporary sins of abusive priests or the bishops who reassigned them, it stands as a reminder, especially to Catholics accustomed to thinking otherwise, that the institutional church is made up of sinful human beings, and is therefore constantly in need of change and reform: *Ecclesia semper reformanda*. The theological model of the church as a "pilgrim people," always on a journey, was underlined by the Second Vatican Council in its 1963 "Dogmatic Constitution on the Church," a key document: "The Church . . . at once holy and always in need of purification, follows constantly the path of penance and renewal."

But it is insufficient simply to admit sinfulness. As any priest worth his salt will tell you in the confessional, a penitent also needs to show a "firm purpose of amendment" and a desire to undergo a form of penance. There is also the long-standing requirement to participate in the larger reform of the community. During the Donatist controversy in the fourth century, when a group of Christians wanted to admit only the "holy" into the church, Saint Augustine disagreed, arguing that the Christian community should welcome as well those who have sinned and repented. Yet as Peter Brown notes in his biography *Augustine of Hippo*, the saint understood that this was only part of the solution. Early Christians striving for holiness must, of necessity, co-exist with other sinners in the church, but they should also "be prepared, actively, to rebuke and correct them."

I see some signs that after a very public "rebuke," penance and reconciliation are finally beginning in the Catholic church in the U.S. Last July, the new archbishop of Boston, Sean Patrick O'Malley, a Capuchin Franciscan, declared on the day of his appointment his desire to work for reconciliation, no matter what the cost. "People's lives are more important than money," he said simply. O'Malley's subsequent swift resolution of legal settlements, his willingness to sell the archbishop's palatial residence in Brighton, and his personal outreach to victims of clerical abuse show that it is possible to work for reconciliation with compassion, intelligence, and, yes, speed.

At the beginning of the ordination Mass, the bishop offers a short homily to the *ordinandi*. Though the rubrics of the ceremony provide a standard homily, the bishop has the option of foregoing this in favor of a more personal message. But I'm always a bit disappointed when he chooses to do so, since the traditional text includes this exhortation:

"Let the example of your life attract the followers of Christ, so that by words and actions you may build up the house which is God's church." All in all, that's a good goal for priests during this period of crisis, and I look forward to helping rebuild a church sorely in need of repair.　　　　　*—Portland*, Fall 2004

HOW COULD IT HAPPEN?

The terrible revelations of sexual abuse in Ireland and Germany have confirmed the reality that the abuse of children by clergy is not a phenomenon confined to the United States. Nor, as Kieran Conroy, the bishop of Arundel and Brighton in the U.K., stated recently, is the crisis a media creation. "It is real," he said. "It is a reality." Outrage among the Irish and German public is the predominant, natural and justified response. But buried beneath the shock and anger, especially for Catholics, however, is a searing question: How could this happen?

There is an important resource that may begin to answer this question: the detailed analysis of the roots of clerical abuse in this country, which was conducted by The National Review Board, the group of lay people who researched and reported to the U.S. Conference of Catholic Bishops in 2003. Some questioned the independence of the board, but I think that their situational analysis, carried out by committed and highly qualified lay Catholics, is accurate.

Looking at what the National Review Board viewed as the root causes of the crisis in this country may shed light on what happened in Ireland and Germany and elsewhere. On the whole, the board's analysis is about the most accurate and insightful that we have about the American situation. Of course, these are presented by the board as reasons, not excuses. There are no excuses for these crimes.

The board asked two main questions. First, why did so many priests abuse minors in the U.S.? Second, how could the U.S. bishops have dealt with the issue so poorly, or not at all?

Regarding the first question, as I far as I understand, roughly 4% of U.S. priests from 1950 to 2000 were accused of abuse. This is slightly higher than that in other professions, including those who deal with children, like schoolteachers. (Most abuse, most studies show, takes place within families.) But any number is too high and leads to the question of how, especially in a religious organization committed to helping others and living out what Christians call Gospel values, this could happen.

The board answers how so many priests could have been abusive by looking at two causes. (Their responses are italic. My own comments follow their points.)

1.   *Improper screening for candidates in the past.*

From many conversations with men who entered minor seminaries or religious orders in the 1940s and 1950s, I know that the entrance requirements were less rigorous than today. One priest explained to me that to enter his religious order one needed merely to submit a recommendation from another priest and meet with the local provincial. If the provincial gave his approval, the candidate was accepted.

Compare this to what I faced when I entered the Jesuit Order in 1988: a battery of psychological tests (which culminated in a lengthy psychological evaluation to the Jesuits), six face-to-face interviews, an eight-day retreat, as well as having to submit a comprehensive autobiography, recommendations from six friends and co-workers, a physician's examination, and so on.

Such procedures today—and especially those put in place after 2002—help to begin to weed out those with any serious psychological problems, such as pedophilia. Tragically, they were not in place many decades ago, in this country or abroad.

2. *Poor formation or training for candidates.*

Once again, it should be noted how different priestly formation and training are today as compared with even 30 or 40 years ago. At least in the U.S., it is difficult for a man to reach ordination without substantial exposure to issues on sexuality, intimacy and chastity, as well as questions of sexual abuse and professional boundaries. In the past, however, a great many priests at the time of their ordination failed to receive adequate training or counseling in any of these issues, setting the stage for problems in the future.

The board's second question was: Why did the church leaders respond to the problem so poorly for so many years? Here is where the board's analysis is especially astute.

1. *Some bishops and other leaders did not understand the broad nature of the problem, but treated it sporadically.*

Like many other people, even well-educated men and women, particularly if we are talking about the 1960s, 1970s and even 1980s, most of the American bishops simply did not grasp the terrible prevalence in our society of such things as pedophilia, incest and spousal abuse. (Megan's Law, for example, was passed as late as 1996, a testimony to this fundamental lack of understanding of these things in American society.) The bishops were among those still in the dark about this dark side of human behavior, and simply were at a loss to appreciate the magnitude of the problem. The same was most likely true in Europe as well.

2. *Many bishops put needs of institutional concerns above the concerns of the people. Historically, there is a deep antipathy to "scandal" in the Catholic Church.*

In the church, where the community is seen as the "Body of Christ," that is, a visible representation of Christ's presence, and where Tradition is seen as one way that the Holy Spirit leads the Christian community over time, an attack on the church is often interpreted as tantamount to an attack on the faith itself. Similarly, the notion that the faithful needed to be "protected" from scandal (lest it lessen their love and respect for the church) made bishops less likely to admit even obvious problems with abusive priests. The horrible irony was that in protecting the faithful from "scandal" by concealing evidence of abusive priests, as well as shuffling them between parishes, some of the American bishops created the greatest scandal in the history of their church in this country. The Irish and German churches are also now seeing the fallout from "avoiding scandal."

3. *The threat of litigation caused many to adopt an adversarial stance.*

Protecting the church is, particularly for a bishop, much more than simply protecting the "institution." The financial losses that might be incurred from lawsuits were also (accurately) seen as losses that would damage the great many social services provided by the church: parishes, schools, hospitals, shelters. Some American bishops felt the need to protect this network of social-service agencies and so followed the advice of those lawyers who suggested adopting the most aggressive attitudes towards lawsuits. Sadly, those bishops failed to realize that those institutions, noble as they are, were not the only things that they should have been protecting.

4. *Some bishops failed to comprehend the magnitude of the harm suffered by victims.*

Needless to say, when some U.S. bishops failed to even meet with victims, a shockingly callous act, it was easy to ignore their suffering.

5. *Many bishops relied too heavily on psychiatrists, psychologists and lawyers when making decisions.*

Even today, and even more so in the 1960s and 1970s, when many cases were first brought to light, many bishops turned to mental-health professionals who themselves held conflicting opinions about the treatability of pedophilia. Is it curable? Is it genetic? Can a man be placed in active ministry after treatment? What is the best type of treatment? Would being placed in active ministry help the man in his "cure"?

Bishops, hardly experts in these matters, often relied on flawed advice. Or they chose experts who told them what they most wanted to hear: that the man could be cured and returned to ministry. Still, it needs to be underlined that this does not excuse the bishop who moved the man who repeatedly abused and was just as repeatedly reassigned. One need not be a psychologist to see the stupidity of such decisions. And of course more recent decisions, say in the 1990s, are even more indefensible, given society's (and the psychiatric profession's) growing knowledge about pedophilia.

6. *Many bishops avoided confronting abusive priests.*

The simple inability to confront and deal with difficult situations, whether out of apathy, ignorance or fear of conflict, seems to have played a major role in the crisis. This is something that cuts across cultural lines, and may have even been worse in European countries.

7. *Many bishops placed interests of priests above those of victims.*

The image of the bishop as the "spiritual father," who protects and guides his priests has deep roots in the Catholic Church. Tragically, often overshadowed was the bishop's larger and more important role as "pastor" or "shepherd" of all of the people in his diocese. Even worse, the welfare those who were most vulnerable—young children—was often ignored.

8. *Canon law made removal from ministry onerous.*

The process of "laicization," that is, returning the priest to the "lay state," and stripping him of his rights as a priest (the ability to celebrate Mass, wear a collar, call himself "Father") is a cumbersome ecclesiastical process, designed to preserve the rights of the priests. Entering into it may have seemed overwhelming for some bishops. Indeed, Archbishop Rembert Weakland of Milwaukee, as reported this week by *The New York Times*, was forced to appeal directly to the Vatican to remove a notoriously abusive priest from ministry.

Those were the board's findings. I would like to add four more reasons that I note from my own observations over the years.

1. Some American bishops, mostly elderly men, were themselves uncomfortable, for a variety of reasons—some personal, some cultural, some familial, some related to their formation—discussing any matters of sexuality, particularly homosexuality, as well as the more frightening topics of pedophilia and ephebophilia, and the terrifying prospect of child sexual abuse. Again, this may be even more pronounced in Ireland and Germany among bishops and clergy.

2. Some bishops here were hampered by the inability to discuss the possibility that the scandal would lead to dramatic change in the church. If one fears a discussion of difficult church issues (celibacy, clerical culture, episcopal authority) one will naturally be more afraid of an issue that might provoke open up such discussions.

3. Some bishops were unable to accept personal responsibility or their own sinful (sometimes criminal) actions. From the beginning of the crisis, many of the bishops seemed to confront the crisis in the manner of a C.E.O., rather than as a Christian pastor. Some seemed to have forgotten that an essential part of the traditional "sacrament of reconciliation" (that is, "confession") in the church is penitence: the need to make amends for one's sins. It is not simply enough to confess, to admit sinfulness, and to beg for forgiveness from God and the person you have offended. One needs also a "firm purpose of amendment" and the willingness to engage in some form of penance. But public penance, like the resignation of Bishop John Magee in Ireland last week—is too rare.

And of course, like anyone else, clergy are subject to the law of the land, and, if found guilty of crimes, should be treated like anyone else.

Around the time that the scandals were breaking in the U.S., a Catholic sister I know said that the Christian response was at odds with what she called the "corporate response." Quoting from the parable of the Prodigal Son in the Gospel of Luke, she described what a Christian response from an offending bishop would have sounded like: "I have sinned against God and you, and I no longer deserve to be called your bishop. I will resign and spend the rest of my life praying for victims." Beyond any criminal penalties to be paid, such an action might have been understood by Catholics. Tragically, some bishops, the "teachers" par excellence in the community often ignored the treasures of their own Christian heritage.

4.   When cases of abuse were raised prior to 2002, some bishops viewed the media as adversaries. Prior to the crisis, Cardinal Bernard Law said that he "called down" the power of God against *The Boston Globe*. Despite some lingering anti-Catholicism in the American media's coverage of the crisis (for example, their facile conflation of celibacy and pedophilia, the overlooking of abuse in other professions, and their stereotyping of all priests as abusers and all bishops as conspirators), the church needs to be grateful for the role of the media for revealing what the church itself was unwilling to confront. The "Charter for the Protection of Children and Young People," adopted by the U.S. bishops in their meeting in Dallas in 2002, would not have happened without *The Boston Globe*.

Those are but a few reasons for the causes of the sexual abuse of children by clergy in the United States, as a board of committed Catholic laypersons saw them. This may begin to explain how and why these sinful actions and awful crimes happened. And how and why these terrible crimes and grave sins happened in Ireland and Germany, and elsewhere.

—*Huffington Post*, May 25, 2011

This long selection from This Our Exile *and the short essay that follows address a central question every believer must face: how do we explain suffering that seems pointless?*

JOHN MUTABURUNGA AND HIS COWS

For sighing comes more readily to me than food, and my groans well forth like water.   —Job 3:25

John Mutaburunga was a middle-aged man who came from a family of cattle herders in Rwanda. Whenever he visited our office he wore a threadbare blue corduroy jacket and an old fedora covered with the red dirt that covered everything else in Nairobi. John asked us to help him buy a few cows. He told us that a friend had offered him free ground for grazing outside of the city. It seemed incredible, but since cows were cheap and grazing land in Nairobi proper was unavailable, we gave him the capital to purchase four cows, the necessary feed, and some tools.

I heard nothing from John for some months. One day, he appeared in my office, looking wan. His cows were doing poorly. "They are very thirsty," he said. Two had already died. Could I please come and see them?

The next afternoon, I drove out to meet John in Ngong, a town a few kilometers outside of Nairobi, populated primarily by Maasai herders, who strode deliberately through the dusty streets wearing their red plaid *shukas* and carrying long herding sticks over their shoulders. John waved at me from in front of a small bank.

He climbed into my jeep, and we drove over the green Ngong Hills to the other side of the plateau, where the landscape became progressively drier and dustier. Though Nairobi was almost always cool and breezy, once you ventured outside of Nairobi it became, as a friend liked to say, "Africa hot"—the very heat you imagine that Africa would offer. As we descended from the mountains the landscape opened up into the plain, with dry grasses, low bushes, and thorn trees. Impala slept in the distance, and vultures wheeled overhead in the clear sky. Hopeful Maasai women stood by the side of the road selling fresh honey in soda bottles. The dirt road was deeply rutted, and eventually enormous rocks made the road impassable, even for the sturdy jeep.

We got out of the jeep and examined the landscape. Far off in the distance was a cluster of tiny white shacks. "I live just there," said John, gesturing vaguely. Though it was late afternoon, I was astounded at the heat and asked him how he could expect to raise cattle here. He told me that this was the only land he could find. It was free and his Maasai friends allowed him to graze his cattle there. Every day he led his donkey into town and carried back two jerrycans of water. It had taken us an hour by jeep to ride to this point, and we had yet to reach his house. How long did it take him to walk back and forth with his donkey?

"Three hours, Brother. But if I had a truck I would be making the trip much faster."

It was unbelievable to think that he expected to raise cattle here. There was no water and no grass. As biting flies buzzed around us, we tried to come up with solutions to his problem: Could he take his cows elsewhere? No, he would have to pay to graze anywhere else. Perhaps he could sell the cows' milk to make a little money. No, he explained patiently, if the cows don't drink water, they don't give milk. What did his neighbors do with their cattle?

"They are Maasai. They migrate with their cows. But my family does not know how to live like that, Brother."

So we stood silently under the blazing sun and surveyed the bleak landscape. John Mutaburunga had no money to pay for a bus ticket to Rwanda, and at this point, who would choose to return? His remaining relatives, all Tutsis, were most likely dead. His wife had recently died of AIDS, leaving him with three children. He had no money. John had one talent: he knew how to raise cows. So, of course, he had asked us for cows. And John had only one place to graze, the arid land offered by his generous Maasai friends. But by following the only things that were certain in his life and working diligently, he had met with disaster. It was the plight of most of the refugees in Nairobi.

John was, I saw clearly, doomed to fail. A wave of profound and inarticulate sadness swept over me as I realized that there was little I could do for him. John wept when I told him that it would be impossible for us to buy him a truck; we simply didn't have enough money. Perhaps the best thing would be for John to sell his remaining cows before they died. "But, Brother, what will I do then?"

I didn't know, I said.

And I still don't.   —*This Our Exile*, 180–84

GOOD FRIDAY ON BOYLSTON STREET

Those of us who love Boston, those who were born there, those who live there, and especially those who were in Back Bay yesterday, are still taking in the appalling scenes from yesterday's massacre. Not only on the most enjoyable day of the year in Boston, but also in the absolute heart of the town, Copley Square, on the most pleasant streets imaginable, on a beautiful New England day. Seeing blood in a familiar locale on such a hopeful day was almost impossible for the mind and heart to understand.

Seeing Boston damaged was like seeing a relative hurt. To be sure, I am a proud New England Province Jesuit, having done my novitiate and theology training in the city. My first spiritual director used to say that he was a Bostonian "by birth and by choice," and I know many friends who would echo that sentiment, so deep is their love for Boston. Seeing injury come to the city was shocking, difficult to comprehend in such a familiar setting—the Jesuit community in Back Bay, on Newbury Street, is only a block away from site of the bombings. It was the same here in New York on Sept. 11, 2001. Familiar surroundings, laden with happy memories, suddenly became places of immense sadness.

When Jesus was crucified, his friends and family—the Gospels describe not only his mother but also his aunt at the crucifixion—must have had similarly overwhelming emotions. Seeing Jesus beaten, bloodied and finally nailed to the cross must have seemed unbelievable. How can this be? Just the week before, on Palm Sunday, Jesus was moving through the great city in triumph, as people clapped and cheered him on. I imagine that some of those who lost loved ones, and saw loved ones injured, felt something of the same yesterday in Boston. Joy and celebration quickly gave way to shock and sadness. Perhaps they had just clapped their hands for a friend, or waved on a husband or a wife, or cheered on a neighbor or a work colleague, who had been training for months, as they saw them run across the finish line in triumph. As in Jesus's time, friends and family members entered the great city prepared for joy, not agony.

But agony is what they received. Jesus received agony as well: beatings, torture and bloody wounds gotten from the hands of the Roman soldiers. In the original Greek the Gospels do not stint in describing his pain on the cross. When he is on the cross he "screams out" and tells God he feels abandoned, shouting so loudly that people who had previously taunted him take pity on him. Before he dies he screams out one more time. We are not told what he said. One Bible commentary said that it was simply the cry of someone in terrible pain. Those watching felt an unfathomable sadness and horror and helplessness.

In this Easter season, Boston is now back in Good Friday. And one insight of that terrible day is that we do not have a God who does not understand suffering. Everyone on that first Good Friday in Jerusalem knew suffering: Jesus's disciples, who had expected a joyful victory but received a miserable failure; and his family and friends who had followed him to the great city in happiness, but were met with sadness. Like the people in Boston, who had prepared for joy, they must have been at a loss to take in all the misery. Here was the person we loved, the one we knew well, for whom we had such hopes, cut down. In this familiar setting that is such a part of our lives—Jerusalem, Boston—violence, maiming and death. It doesn't make sense. Finally, Jesus himself—God on the Cross—was miserably treated. A victim of senseless violence as sure as those on Boylston Street were.

Why bring this up? Because Jesus is not someone who does not understand pain. Jesus is with us in our suffering, not only because he loves us but because he suffered.

But suffering is never the last word. There is always the possibility of new life. How will this happen? It may be difficult to see now, as it was impossible for the disciples on Good Friday to see, but the God who has suffered is ready to help us, and always holding out the promise of something new, something that will help us move beyond the blood and tears.

That was true in Jerusalem 2,000 years ago and it is true in Boston today.   —*Huffington Post*, April 16, 2013

These two essays deal with a defining moment of tragedy for the city of New York (and the nation), as well as a powerful moment of encounter with physical suffering and the resulting emotional trauma that follows, both for the ones suffering and for those ministering to them.

THE LAYING DOWN OF LIFE

Two days after the terrorist attack on the World Trade Center, I made my way to one of the emergency trauma centers in Manhattan. It had been hastily set up in a cavernous sports facility called Chelsea Piers, on the Hudson River. I had been there earlier, on the evening of Sept. 11, still stunned from the day's events like many New Yorkers, and, also like many New Yorkers, wanting desperately to do something. But on that surreal and awful night, I simply waited with dozens of doctors, nurses, police officers, firefighters and volunteers for what officials expected would be hundreds of survivors. I ran into three young Franciscan friars, who were planning to spend the night there. They were full of energy and devotion. But though we wanted to help, after a few hours the stunning reality dawned: there would not be many survivors to attend to.

When I return to Chelsea Piers two days later to offer assistance, I discover that I have already been preceded by scores of members of the clergy. "Another priest," says one harried,

sweating volunteer as I enter. "Go upstairs and ask for Ellen."
Ellen tells me that she already has plenty of priests, ministers and
rabbis. I wander downstairs, trying to think about where I might
be able to help most. The day before I had spent at a center set
up by a local Catholic hospital, where family members painfully
searched dog-eared sheets of paper that listed the names of survivors. But at that hospital too there was a surfeit of help: there
are so many mental-health care professionals in Manhattan.

Outside, surrounded by ambulances, U.S. Army vehicles,
police cars, fire engines and dump trucks, I ask a police sergeant
a question upon which I had reflected not at all. But it seems the
right thing to ask: "Do you think they might be able to use a
priest downtown?"

He knows where I mean. And I am terrified he will say yes.

"Of course," he says; "yes." Almost instantly a police car
materializes to bring me to the site of the former World Trade
Center. One of my spiritual directors used to say that sometimes
if God wants you to do something, he removes all roadblocks,
and I feel this intensely as we sail downtown. I ask, he answers,
we go.

My own fear increases with every southerly block. With me in
the back seat is a well-dressed psychiatrist. "Have you dealt with
trauma victims?" he asks, as we speed through the streets. "No,
I say; please give me some advice." He does.

The sights of the first few minutes of the drive are familiar,
comforting: the river on the right, the Manhattan skyline on
the left. We make a left-hand turn, and there are fewer and
fewer people walking on the street. When we stop briefly at
an intersection, crowds of people surround the car, cheering
and clapping, waving flags. My window is open, and a hand
is thrust in, offering muffins, donuts, bottled water. We turn
again, and presently there are many parked cars covered with
fine soot. Our car passes the line that cordons off the press
from the rescue area; I see cameras, reporters, news vans. And
then we make another turn: here are cars crushed by falling
debris, papers floating in the breeze, and more and more pale

grey ash. We continue on and I catch sight of a burned, twisted building. The psychiatrist gets out of the car, wishes me well and sprints away.

The car turns once again, and I see the sight familiar from repeated viewings on television: the horrible remains of the Trade Center, issuing forth a brown, acrid smoke that chokes one and brings tears to the eyes. It is repellent. I feel the urge at once to vomit and to weep.

A U.S. Army soldier walks over and greets me, providing me with a sort of friendly escort. Ashamed that I cannot tear my gaze from the site of the embrowned buildings only a few yards away, I make an effort to ask after the soldier's welfare. But, instead, he ministers to me. "That's O.K., Father," he says. "Everybody stares when they see it. It's hard to see, isn't it?" He hands me a face mask, which I notice everyone is wearing, to protect against the smoke and dust.

"Okay, Father," he says and points. "Just over there, that's where everyone is; it's the morgue." The temporary morgue is a formerly tony office building that, though I know the area well, I am now totally unable to recognize.

The streets surrounding the morgue are covered by two inches of soot. More paper blows around; I notice an office memo with its edges charred brown. Twisted girders covered with grime must be stepped over. All I can think of is a banality. But, though banal, it is true: this is like hell—full of immense sadness and terror and pathos.

And yet, here is grace. There are hundreds of rescue workers: firefighters and police officers and army personnel and construction workers and truck drivers and counselors and doctors and nurses. Almost all are in motion. They are purposeful, efficient, hard-working.

Some of the firefighters and police officers sit by a staging area near the doorway of the temporary morgue, resting. Though most are New Yorkers, a surprising number are not, having traveled great distances (from Massachusetts, says one; from Florida, says another) to help. We talk about what they have seen, how they feel, what they think. In the midst of this hell, they are inspiring to speak with, and say simple things, made profound to me by their situation: "Just doing my job, Father." "One day at a time." "Doing the best I can, Father." I cannot resist the urge to tell them what great work they are doing.

Suddenly I realize that I am standing beside grace. Here are men and women, some of whom tell me I lost a buddy in there, who are going about their business—a business that includes the possibility of dying. Greater love has no person, said Jesus, than the one who lays down his life for another. And this is what that looks like. Here it is.

As I think this, four men carry a small orange bag past us holding the remains of a victim of the attack. I am afraid of what I might see, so I do not look.

Next to the building, three African-American N.Y.P.D. officers sit on salvaged office chairs in front of cardboard boxes that are stacked perhaps six feet high. We talk about their work here. All are New Yorkers, who say how disorienting it is to consider downtown without the World Trade Center. We talk about friends we know who were at or near the Trade Center at the time.

One of my friends, I tell them, who worked at a nearby building, emerged from his subway station at 9:00 a.m. on Tuesday, as crowds of people raced by. "What happened?" he asks someone. "A plane hit the World Trade Center!" He goes to his office anyway; he thinks it must have been a small plane that hit. No need to worry.

Once at his desk, he looks out the window and sees the appalling sight of the Trade Center wreathed in smoke. When he tells me the story, he pauses, and says what many New Yorkers say: "I couldn't believe it. I couldn't understand it." Now he rushes to the stairwells with co-workers, and begins racing down 18 floors. Once outside, a police officer shouts at him. "Run! Run! Run!" As he runs, dazed, someone cries out, "It's collapsing!" He tells me he thinks to himself: don't be surprised if you die.

The police officers nod. They know many similar stories, and, of course, far worse ones. "It is hard to take it all in," one says. They talk more about their experiences and say they are worried that it will get worse once the recovery of the bodies begins. "Here are the bags," says one, gesturing behind him, and it is suddenly clear what is in that tall pile of boxes.

When I feel that I have talked with as many people as I can (at least those who are not busy with their work), I leave. One police sergeant tells me the way out: "Walk up this path," he says. As I do, streams of fire companies pass me, and almost everyone greets me. "Hello, Father." They touch the brim of their helmets. They shake my hand as I leave and they move in toward the wreckage.

Leaving is stranger than coming. All I have to do is walk north. The rubble eventually recedes, so there is nothing to step over; the soot becomes less distinct and the pavements are cleaner; the smoke clears and I remove my mask; there are more and more pedestrians. And then I am back in New York on a sunny fall day: people in Greenwich Village sit in outdoor cafes; women in tank tops jog by; taxis race past. I remember reading about soldiers in World War I who would fight in the trenches in France during the day and then, granted a day's leave, would be in the theaters of London in the evening. Is this what it is like for the rescue workers?

A subway entrance presents itself. A policeman sees me and walks over. I suddenly realize I must look strange: in clerics, sweating, covered in grey soot, a face mask dangling from my neck. "What subway do you want?" I am astonished to find out that I am so disoriented that I cannot tell him, but can only say that I want to go uptown. I feel foolish—a New Yorker takes pride in knowing where he's going. "Were you down there?" he asks. I nod and he brings me downstairs, past the ticket counter, and motions for the subway attendant to open up the gate, to allow me in for a free ride, a last gesture of kindness and solidarity in a city overwhelmed by grief but united in overwhelming charity.   —*America*, October 1, 2001

LOOKING BACK ON SEPTEMBER 11

At the World Trade Center in October 2001, after working there for several weeks alongside fellow Jesuits and other volunteers, I wondered what would become not only of the physical site but of the people we had met. One ironworker, who spent long days at Ground Zero cutting apart the steel beams of the destroyed buildings, said that when he went home at night, he could hardly bear to see his wife and child, for they reminded him of the people he had pulled out of the pile. A firefighter told me that when he first arrived at the site, he had run one way, and his friend another. He lived, while his friend died. A police chaplain said that he felt as if he were the one being ministered to at the site.

What would happen to these people? What sort of meaning would they find in their experiences? Five years after the terrorist attacks on the World Trade Center, family members of victims, rescue workers and chaplains are still coming to grips with the legacy of that day. Over the past weeks I have spoken with a few, who reflected on where they have been and where they are today.

"Sheer Luck or the Grace of God"

Last month a journalist told me that when you ask someone about Sept. 11, 2001, they seem almost compelled to recount the entire story of where they were that day as if a partial telling would be an insult to those events. So it was not surprising that Joe Lauria, a 15-year veteran of the New York City Fire Department, would speak at length about the day.

On Sept. 11 Joe's fire company in Queens was immediately dispatched to the World Trade Center. But they were held up from entering Manhattan out of fear that the traffic tunnels under the East River would be bombed. When he reached the site, Joe was horrified to see people leaping to their deaths from the towers. They were like mannequins falling through the air, he said. We said prayers that they would face as little suffering as possible. Joe watched as the upper floors of the North Tower leaned slowly, then split in two and collapsed, creating a deluge of debris and choking smoke.

"I stood motionless, not believing it, frozen in time," said Joe. "Then all of a sudden we were trying to outrace this huge storm cloud." He spent the entire day and the following weeks working at the site, almost around the clock. The time he spent excavating and searching for survivors and, later, remains, Joe describes as "horrific."

The delay in getting into Manhattan probably saved his life. "If my company had been there 20 minutes earlier, we would have been in the lobby of those towers. There were 343 firefighters who perished, and I would have been one of them."

Today Joe, a Catholic, often thinks about how close he came to dying; he also wonders how God could allow so many of his friends to die. He was angry at the terrorists but not at God. And though he has no easy answers, his faith has not been shaken: "More because it was a man-made event, as opposed to Hurricane Katrina or the tsunami."

Did Joe feel that God had spared him? "It was either sheer luck or the grace of God," he said. "Why were we held up? Who knows? That's a question I'll have to ask the Big Guy when I get to heaven."

The 38-year-old firefighter husband of Carol (who asked that her real name not be used) was not as fortunate as Joe was. Carol's grief has been complicated by the very public nature of the event that took her husband, the father of their two children. She spoke passionately about her emotional struggles from her home in Long Island. "Every year at 9/11, you try to please both sides—those who want public grief and those who want it private," she told me recently.

"But I don't need the world to help me remember. I will never forget him going off to work that day, or the phone call or the worst thing of all: telling my children."

Carol and her husband, both Episcopalians, were not especially religious. After the tragedy, she found it difficult to attend services: hearing certain hymns raised emotions too painful to bear. But eventually, Carol's children, now 10 and 13, wanted to return to church to prepare for first Communion and confirmation. Today, she says, "I'm trying to become more spiritual, because I realize more that there are so many things over which I have little control."

When Carol was 24, her mother died. She now sees that event as a kind of spiritual preparation that helped her to bear her husband's death. There was also a striking coincidence, or providential moment, that connected her mother to the events of Sept. 11. "They found my husband's body on the day of my mother's birthday," she explained. "It was as if she were bringing him home to me."

Like Joe, Carol does not blame God. "I'm a realist," she says. She realizes that a firefighter's job means that he might not come home at night. Men and women in her husband's profession are often called upon to save people at risk to their own safety and even lives. "So I don't place blame on God. It could have been any circumstance that led to his death."

Lately, church has become consoling for Carol. It offers a private time for her to think about her mother, her husband and when they will all be reunited. But she is honest about the complexity of her emotions. "Sometimes I yell at him for leaving me," she said.

"Naturally, God Is There"

The passage of time has not reduced the immediacy of the most painful question: Why? It was the question the rescue workers asked most frequently of my brother Jesuits while we were ministering at Ground Zero. Why would God permit this to happen? In essence, they were asking the same question that has preoccupied saints, theologians, philosophers and other Christians for centuries (the problem of evil or theodicy): How could a good God allow evil?

For the Rev. David Baratelli, a Port Authority chaplain who also serves at St. John's Byzantine Catholic Church in Bayonne, N.J., the day's grief was matched by the goodness he witnessed around him. One day, after Father Baratelli finished celebrating Mass at a nearby chapel, a police lieutenant told him that some of the workers had not been able to receive Communion that day. So Father Baratelli grabbed a large ciborium and walked into the pile of rubble. "All of these cops and firefighters saw me coming," he recalled with emotion. "And they took off their helmets and with the greatest devotion received the Eucharist."

Father Baratelli said he was "captured" by the thought that God would have his way, that God's way is one of goodness, and that God would triumph by the virtue of the good. "I have to believe that Christ was present in that Eucharist and that he was helping those people."

For others, the grief remains raw. Anthony and Maryann, who live in northern New Jersey, were told on Sept. 11 that their son, Anthony Jr., a police officer with the Port Authority, "never came out" of the towers. His father said, "Naturally I was mad. He was a good boy, and they never recovered the body. You pray that they might discover him so that we could just bury him."

The devout Catholic couple found solace from the local parish priests, who rushed to their house to pray with them after the tragedy, and from Catholic Charities. "They were terrific. I can't say enough about them," said Anthony. Once a week the two visit a local shrine to St. Joseph in Stirling, N.J., to pray for their son, who was 47 at his death. "I feel the closeness of my son there, and naturally God is there," said Anthony.

He is not angry with God. "I say my prayers for my son and I'm happy I can pray for him. But what can you say? There's nothing you can say." His comment reminded me of the observation from some commentators on the Holocaust, that the best response to overwhelming tragedy is often silence.

The fifth-year anniversary is doubly poignant for Steve, 36, who lost his wife, an employee of a firm with offices at One World Trade Center. The two were married exactly one month earlier, on Aug. 11, 2001. In Washington, D.C., on a business trip that day, Steve heard the news of the attack from a taxicab radio, went into a nearby restaurant and saw the second plane slam into the South Tower. After the tragedy, he stayed with friends for a month.

Steve (not his real name) is an active parishioner of St. Ignatius Loyola Church in New York City, which he had attended with his wife before her death. Like Anthony and Maryann, he did not feel abandoned by God. And like Joe Lauria, he understood the event as a "man-made" tragedy. But at the same time Steve does not think this event was part of God's plan. "I don't believe things happen for a reason," he said.

"It's Only Fair to Give Back"

Mass provides more comfort for Steve now. He admits that this might have as much to do with the fact that attending Mass was something he and his wife used to enjoy doing together. But he has changed, Steve said. He is trying to become a "better person," trying to be closer to his wife's family, trying not to be as judgmental and trying to be more open with people. The tragedy has lent his life more perspective, he believes.

"It's understanding what matters and what doesn't," he said. In the weeks and months after Sept. 11, Steve became politically active, traveling to Capitol Hill with family members of victims. Today he laments that the country seems to have lost the feeling of unity that existed immediately after 9/11.

"It makes you wish for what we were back then with all the bipartisanship and everyone not stuck up on petty differences. I'm amazed that we're still dealing with things like same-sex marriage and the flag-burning amendment, when there are more important issues."

When I asked how long he felt that spirit of unity existed in the country, he was blunt: "About six months."

When Joe, the New York City firefighter, also lamented the loss of the common spirit that existed at Ground Zero, I felt as if I knew something of what he meant. During the few weeks I worked there, I remember walking north from the site one day and hearing people applaud. After I looked around and saw no firefighters or police officers, I asked a Jesuit who was walking

with me, "Who are they clapping for?" He said, "I think for us."
There was a strong sense of support from the city, the country
and even the world. As I finished an interview with a French
journalist, the man threw his arms around me and said, "*Nous
sommes tous américains*" (We are all Americans).

The spirit within the site was even more palpable. During
the weeks I spent there, I found a tremendous spirit of unity
and concord, which for me betokened the presence of the Holy
Spirit. People from all over the country—firefighters, nurses, Red
Cross workers, National Guard volunteers—united in a common cause made for a strangely comforting environment.

Joe felt that Sept. 11 forced people in New York to move
out of "their own little worlds" and "pitch in." One reason, he
believed, was that for New Yorkers it happened close to home
without the buffer of television. "It allowed them to see it first-
hand, and forced them to look within themselves."

Father Baratelli told me the story of an employee of the Port
Authority who fled from the burning towers, disoriented and
bloody, and ran into some total strangers who said, "Let us help
you." They brought her to a nearby physician who cared for
her, and even brought her back home. "In the darkness of this
moment, the goodness of God came forth," he said.

But Joe Lauria felt that this spirit has ebbed considerably.
In the days following Sept. 11, the New York Fire Department
had logged a marked decrease in the number of false alarms,
but today it's back to where it was five years ago. "As that day
becomes more distant and as the site is cleared up, things dis-
appear and people go back to their own routine. Most of the
firemen felt that there was this tremendous feeling at the site, but
they also found out that it was to be short-term."

Anthony, the New Jersey father who lost his son, was not
surprised that people have changed. "What's the use of kidding
ourselves?" He wears a wristband with his son's name on it, and
though people ask about it and sincerely express their sorrow, it
usually ends there. "That's about as far as it goes."

Carol, the woman who lost her husband, saw a change, but she also sees a lasting effect today. After her husband's death, a candlelight vigil was held on her front lawn. That night over 200 of her neighbors came out to support Carol and her children. Since then Carol has made many more friends in the neighborhood and feels that if she ever needed anything, she would receive it. This has also helped her feel more generous to others. "So many gave to me," she says. "It's only fair to give back. I will never forget that." After Hurricane Katrina she donated a washer and a dryer to a school in New Orleans.

"No Easy Answer"

Last month I visited a Jesuit friend who works in a high school in Jersey City, N.J., just across the river from the site of the World Trade Center. When I emerged from the subway, I found myself standing next to a colossal bronze monument to the Katyn Massacre, which dominates a popular plaza. One reason for the site's popularity is its commanding view of Lower Manhattan. Five years ago, I had heard stories of people watching the collapse of the towers from here. But it seems almost impossible to imagine: it's too close.

That evening I took a train that passed through a stop named "World Trade Center." Still, I was shocked that it ran directly through the site itself. On the way over I had been reading a book and so missed the sight. The windows gave a full view of the monstrous hole and the retaining walls: the massive space that is, in essence, a mass grave. Passing through Ground Zero on a subway car seemed shocking, an offense. Some passengers paused to stare, but others continued with their business. I thought of the final lines from a favorite poem by Robert Frost, called *Out, Out*, in which a boy dies after a terrible accident with a buzz saw. The narrator ends by describing the onlookers: "And they, since they/ Were not the one dead, turned to their affairs."

But that is overly harsh. Most likely, those commuters had passed through the site many times and were first shocked, but then settled into a more placid reaction. That workaday response, then, was both surprising and not surprising. As Anthony said, "What's the use of kidding ourselves?"

My discussions with these people indicate that things are still too raw. Like the World Trade Center site, it is still an open wound, yet to heal over. They grapple with finding meaning, and probably will for some time. As Joe, the firefighter, said toward the end of our conversation, "Did it shake my faith? No. You could ask why God didn't stop those guys from doing what they did, but I guess I just don't ask that question."

"Because I know that there's no easy answer," he said. "And who's to say which answer is the correct one?"

—*America*, September 11, 2006

OBAMA AND CIVIL RIGHTS

In his regular columns for America, *Martin regularly comments on contemporary political and social issues, including this essay after the 2008 election of Barack Obama to the presidency of the United States.*

Seeing the throngs of men, women and children in Chicago's Grant Park cheering the nation's first African-American president-elect; hearing civil rights lions like Jesse Jackson, John Lewis, Roger Wilkins and Andrew Young grope for words when describing their feelings about the election; listening to black schoolchildren on television express in simple phrases what Barack Obama's achievement meant to them; watching replays of the Rev. Dr. Martin Luther King Jr. declaim "I have a dream" on the steps of the Lincoln Memorial; and downloading videos of jubilant crowds in the Nairobi slums chanting a Kenyan surname over and over—all this made me think of a passage from the New Testament: the Magnificat.

Fifty-six million voters did not vote for Senator Obama; some reports claim that almost 50 of the 267 active U.S. Catholic bishops stated that it was a grave sin (some called it cooperation in murder) to cast a vote for the Illinois senator; many priests warned parishioners against making such a choice; and millions of Catholics, even if they did not agree with their pastors, did not vote for Obama because their overall political views were more closely aligned with those of Sen. John McCain.

But were there many Christians, even Obama opponents, who watched their African-American brothers and sisters weeping tears of jubilation and pride, whose hearts were unmoved by the transformation among a people who had suffered for so long? Many must have heard echoes of Mary's words in the Gospel of Luke: "He has . . . lifted up the lowly; he has filled the hungry with good things. . . ." In Mary's song of praise, God visits an oppressed people and restores their fortunes "according to the promises he made to our ancestors."

The civil rights movement sprang from African-American churches that believed God would rescue the poor, that the Spirit would lead them and that Jesus loved them. Dr. King used familiar biblical imagery—in particular, the exodus of the Hebrew people out of Egyptian slavery—to call a community to hope in the face of fear. "One day every valley shall be exalted, every hill and mountain shall be made low, the rough places will be made plain, and the crooked places will be made straight, and the glory of the Lord shall be revealed, and all flesh shall see it together," he said in 1963, paraphrasing Isaiah. This is prophetic language. It looks ahead to the "one day" when God's justice will set things right.

But who would have thought that the upending of the status quo would happen so quickly? Robert F. Kennedy, for one. In 1968 Senator Kennedy said, "Things are moving so fast that a Negro could be president in 40 years." It must have seemed outlandish at the time. Five years earlier, Dr. King had been arrested in Birmingham. And just a year earlier, riots in Newark and Detroit had stripped the country of hope. But the prophet sees that some day "one day" will be today.

John LaFarge, S.J., adverted to this hope in one of his most popular books. Father LaFarge, a longtime editor of *America*, was deeply involved in interracial issues in the 1930s, when Robert Kennedy was still a boy. In *The Race Question and the Negro*, published in 1943, he examined the perils of racism and confidently concluded that even someone infected by prejudice will "by the logic of his own principles and by the light of his own experience . . . come to this road at long last."

That is why the scenes in Grant Park were so moving. The "one day" had come "at long last."

Despite the passionate rhetoric used to describe Mr. Obama, he is neither a messiah nor the anti-Christ. But his election is a sign that believers downplay only if they wish to downplay God's activity in the world. It is a sign that the "lowly" can be lifted up—to previously unimaginable heights. That the "hungry" can be filled with the nourishing food of jubilation, pride and hope. That the valleys shall be exalted. That the mountaintop is a real place.

Not every Christian rejoiced in the election results. But every Christian who knows the Gospels, even those who disagree with Barack Obama's politics, can be gladdened to see this particular sign of progress. "We rejoice with the rest of our nation," wrote Archbishop Donald T. Wuerl of Washington, D.C., "at the significance of this time."

For this sign our souls should magnify the Lord.

—*America*, November 24, 2008

SIMPLY LOVING

Perhaps no topic has drawn the ire of James Martin's critics over the years than his stubborn defense of the rights and dignity of gays and lesbians in the church. Here he returns to a familiar theme: before you condemn those on the margins of the church, ask yourself if you have listened to them and their experiences.

Everybody knows that same-sex marriage and homosexual acts are contrary to Catholic moral teaching. Yet that same teaching also says that gay and lesbian people must be treated with "respect, sensitivity and compassion." As more states pass laws legalizing same-sex marriage, more gay and lesbian Catholics are entering into these unions. This leaves some Catholics feeling caught between two values: church teaching against same-sex marriage and church teaching in favor of compassion. In Seattle a few months back, for example, many high school students protested the ouster of the vice principal, who was removed for marrying another man.

Most people who oppose same-sex marriage say they do not hate gay people, only that the traditional understanding of marriage is important and perpetually valid. Other opponents of same-sex marriage invoke the oft-repeated mantra, "Hate the sin, love the sinner." If that is so, then why do so many gay people say they feel hatred from members of the church?

Let me suggest a reason beyond the fact that many gays and lesbians disagree with church teaching on homosexual acts: only rarely do opponents of same-sex marriage say something positive about gays and lesbians without appending a warning against sin. The language surrounding gay and lesbian Catholics is framed primarily, sometimes exclusively, in terms of sin. For example, "We love our gay brothers and sisters—but they must not engage in sexual activity." Is any other group of Catholics addressed in this fashion? Imagine someone beginning a parish talk on married life by saying, "We love married Catholics—but adultery is a mortal sin." With no other group does the church so reflexively link the group's identity to sin.

The language of "hate the sin, love the sinner" is difficult for many gay people to believe when the tepid expression of love is accompanied by strident condemnation. And the notion that love calls first for admonishing the loved person seems to be applied only in the case of gays and lesbians. To take another example, it would be like telling a child, "You're a sinful child, but I love you anyway." This can end up sounding more like, "Hate the sinner."

Look how Jesus loved people who were hated in his day. Take the story of Zacchaeus, the diminutive man who climbs a

sycamore tree to catch a glimpse of Jesus as he passes through
Jericho (Lk 19:1–10). As chief tax collector, and thus head of all
the tax collectors in the region, Zacchaeus would have also been
seen by the Jews as the chief sinner in the area. When Jesus spies
him perched in the branches, he calls out, "Zacchaeus, hurry and
come down, for I must stay at your house today." Zacchaeus
then promises to repay anyone he has defrauded. "Salvation has
come to this house," says Jesus.

Notice that Jesus shows love for Zacchaeus even before the
man has promised to do anything. That is, Jesus loves him first,
by offering to dine with him, a powerful sign of welcome in
that time. Jesus does not say, "Zacchaeus, you're a sinful person because you're gouging people with taxes collected for the
oppressive occupying power, but even though you're a public
sinner, I love you anyway." He simply loves him—first.

The story of Zacchaeus illustrates an important difference
between the ministry of John the Baptist and of Jesus. For John
the Baptist, conversion came first, then communion. First you
repent of your sins; then you are welcomed into the community.
For Jesus, the opposite was more often the case; first, Jesus welcomed the person, and conversion followed. It's not loving the
sinner; it's simply loving.

What might it mean for the church to love gays and lesbians
more deeply? First, it would mean listening to their experiences—
all their experiences, what their lives are like as a whole. Second,
it would mean valuing their contributions to the church. Where
would our church be without gays and lesbians—as music ministers, pastoral ministers, teachers, clergy and religious, hospital
chaplains and directors of religious education? Infinitely poorer.
Finally, it would mean publicly acknowledging their individual
contributions: that is, saying that a particular gay Catholic has
made a difference in our parish, our school, our diocese. This
would help remind people that they are an important part of the
body of Christ. Love means listening and respecting, but before
that it means admitting that the person exists.

—America, June 2, 2014

WHERE WERE YOU, GOD?
A PRAYER FOR NEWTOWN

The Sandy Hook Elementary School shooting took place on December 14, 2012, in Newtown, CT. At the time it was the deadliest school shooting in U.S. history. A single assailant shot 20 kindergarten-aged children as well as six adults before committing suicide himself. Martin asks a question straight out of the Book of Job: God, I believed in you; how did you let this happen?

Where were you, God?
We are crushed with grief, God.
    We cannot bear to think of so many people killed.
    We cannot bear to think of children being killed.
    It is unthinkable to us, the worst tragedy.
Children.
Where were you, God?
    How could you let this happen?
    Why is your world like this?
    We are sad and angry and confused.
But God, we know that you know what it means to have
    a child die.
    For your Son died a violent death.
And we know that your Son understands grief.
    For he wept bitterly when his friend Lazarus died.
    And he was moved with compassion when he saw
    suffering.
    His heart broke like our hearts do.
    He cried like we do today.
We know too that your Son raised Lazarus from the dead.
    And that you raised your own murdered Son from the
    grave,
    As a sign of the eternal life you have planned for us.
    The life into which you now place the victims, whom

you loved.
And love.
We know that you understand our terrible anguish.
You accept our bitterness and our confusion too.
And we know that your Son is beside us, weeping with
us.
We know that you are still with us God, in the darkness.
In our compassion for the families and friends of the
victims.
In the love that moves us to care for one another.
In the anger that drives us to put an end to violence,
As your Son tried to do in his time with us.
Most of all, eternal rest grant unto them, O Lord,
And let perpetual light shine upon them.

—*Huffington Post*, December 15, 2012

4

More by Deeds than by Words: Models of Holiness

$$\frac{\text{א} \quad \text{m}}{\text{δ} \quad \text{G}}$$

"The only real sadness, the only real failure, the only great tragedy in life, is not to become a saint." These lines by Leon Bloy, quoted by spiritual authors time and again since he first penned them more than a century ago, are simultaneously a challenge to the self-satisfied Christian and a consolation to the perplexed seeker. On the one hand, Bloy's aphorism seems to suggest that the implicit message of bourgeois Christianity, that God wants us only to be the good enough Christian, is a terrible fiction and that true faith (and God) demands far more than a complacent or easy journey. On the other hand, the reality of who the saints truly were, once that reality is fully understood, casts Bloy's line in a new light: everyone, from the most pious and pure to the most doubtful and dark, is called to the same vocation—and many who succeed are the ones who seemed least likely at one point or another in their journey. One could easily rephrase Bloy's quote in the simple words of Lumen Gentium *(which Martin often references in his writings): the call to holiness is a universal one.*

This chapter offers selections from Martin's voluminous writings on such people, whose lives have provided him perhaps his favorite topics in his writings: the personal quest for holiness in life and the communion of saints who are ever present to help us each in that quest, whether through intercession or example. These include some of his most famous reflections on his own lifelong conversations with the saints, including figures such as Teresa of Calcutta, St. Ignatius, St. Bernadette Soubirous, and the Holy Family. They also return to a constant theme for Martin: the holiness that each of us can find within us if we keep the faith, if we remember that holiness is a lifetime process, and if we do the slow, hard work of eliminating all that keeps us from our relationship with the Holy One.

LIVING WITH THE SAINTS

You might have heard the story of the Jesuit and Franciscan who are driving to the L.A. Congress. Well, they're driving to Anaheim and they get into this big argument over liberation theology, they swerve off the road and hit a telephone pole, and go straight to heaven.

The Jesuit and Franciscan suddenly find themselves standing in front of the gates of heaven, which are hidden behind some clouds. They're both excited, thinking, "Hey, I can't wait to see what heaven is like!"

In a few minutes, the clouds part, and the gates of heaven open, and trumpets sound and hundreds of angels start flying around and start singing. Then a long red carpet rolls out, all the way up to the Jesuit. And out come all these Jesuit saints—Aloysius Gonzaga, Francis Xavier and Ignatius Loyola himself. They all hug the Jesuit, who is just overjoyed. And then . . . out comes Mary, and St. Ignatius introduces her and she hugs the Jesuit, too. Then there is this a trumpet blast and out comes . . . Jesus, who embraces the Jesuit says, "Welcome to heaven." They all hug each other, and everybody starts singing St. Louis Jesuit songs, and then they all go inside to heaven, laughing and singing.

Then the carpet rolls back up and the angels go away and the gates close and the clouds come back. And the Franciscan is left standing there in front of the gates by himself. Well, he's pretty excited, wondering what his welcome is going to be like. He waits some more. And some more. After about a half-hour he starts to get ticked off.

Finally, after an hour, a little side door opens up and St. Bonaventure says, "Hey!" And the Franciscan says, "Who, me?" And St. Bonaventure says, "Yeah, you." And the Franciscan goes up to the door and St. Bonaventure says, "Oh yeah, hi, m . . . so . . . welcome to heaven."

And the Franciscan says, "That's it?" And St. Bonaventure says, "Is what it?" And the Franciscan says, "Come on! That's the welcome I get? I mean, the Jesuit gets the trumpets and the angels and the red carpet and the saints and Mary and Jesus, and all I get is this lousy welcome?"

And St. Bonaventure says, "Oh yeah . . . well you have to understand something. We get Franciscans up here every day. We haven't had a Jesuit in heaven for three hundred years!"

Now, I'm not a saint either, but after spending ten years working on a book on the saints that just came out, I know a little bit about them . . .

We often think that the saints had the benefit of constantly feeling that they were in God's presence. Therefore, we imagine that things were easier for them, at least spiritually. So we think, well, Thérèse of Lisieux may have suffered physically, but she always had the comfort of prayer. But sometimes it was harder for the saints than it is for us.

Take Mother Teresa. You probably know that she left Albania as a teenager to join the Sisters of Loreto in Ireland. You probably also know that she was sent by the Sisters to work at a girls school in India. After working there for several years, Mother Teresa was sent away for an extended vacation in Darjeeling. On the train ride to Darjeeling she had what she would later name a "call within a call." And when Mother Teresa's papers were read after her death it was discovered that she had enjoyed a very rare grace: what spiritual writers call a "locution," actually hearing the voice of Jesus, asking her to leave behind her work and care for the poorest of the poor.

But there was something else discovered in her papers, too, something much more surprising. When her private papers and letters were finally opened it was learned that shortly after this train ride, Mother Teresa experienced an intense spiritual darkness that some say lasted for many decades, some say for the rest of her life. This is a little known facet of her life.

Here is what Mother Teresa said in a letter to her spiritual director. "In my soul," she wrote, "I feel a terrible pain of loss, of God not wanting me, of God not being God, of God not existing." That's Mother Teresa saying that she struggled with feelings that God did not exist. Eventually, she began to see that this sense of abandonment as a way of God drawing her even closer to the figure of the abandoned Christ and to the abandoned poor.

So there you go. Many of us think that the saints might have hard lives—what with all the working with the poor and founding religious orders—but had it easy when it came to faith and prayer. And that kind of thinking sometimes acts as an excuse. We say, "Well, the saints had this sort of mystical union, so following the Gospel was easier for them. So let's leave the radical Christianity to them."

But as Thérèse and Teresa show us, this is not always the case. Sometimes they had it harder than we do. This makes their examples more inspiring and helps us to feel much closer to them. It helps to know this when we are struggling with our faith that even the saints struggled.

Reading the story of Thérèse of Lisieux in the novitiate led me to track down other lives of the saints—some of them well known, some more obscure.

St. Aloysius Gonzaga, for example, is someone else who is usually depicted as a sort of delicate flower, but who, in reality, was pretty tough. Coming from a noble family in Renaissance Italy, he told his father that he would be turning down his inheritance, renouncing his title and entering the Jesuits. This prompted his father, the Duke of Mantua, to fly into a rage and threaten to have Aloysius whipped. When that didn't work he sent Aloysius on a trip to meet the crowned heads of Europe, to show Aloysius what he would be giving up. Finally, worn out after an 18-month battle of wills, his father gave up, and sent the Jesuit superior general a letter saying, "I merely say that I am giving you the most precious thing that I possess." After a few years as a Jesuit, Aloysius died, at age 21, after caring for plague victims in Rome. Today he is often invoked not just as the patron of youth but as the patron of people with AIDS.

During the novitiate, then, I read the lives of dozens of other saints, as well as some other near-saints, like Angelo Roncalli also known as Pope John XXIII. I was introduced to him during a retreat in Gloucester, Massachusetts. Instead of praying, which I should have been doing, I was poking around the retreat house library and came upon an old paperback book called *The Wit and Wisdom of John XXIII*.

Until this point, about all I knew about John XXIII was that he had convened the Second Vatican Council. I had no idea he was so funny, though I had heard the story of the journalist who asked John XXIII, very innocently this question: "Your Holiness, how many people work in the Vatican?"

And John answered, "About half of them."

But the best story was the one that placed John XXIII in a hospital in Rome, called the Hospital of the Holy Spirit, a place run by an order of sisters. One day, the pope stopped by for a surprise visit, and the sister in charge rushed up to greet him and say, "Your Holiness, I am the Superior of the Holy Spirit!" And John said, "Oh you're very lucky. I'm only the Vicar of Christ!"

One thing that John XXIII shows us is how wrongheaded is the idea of the grumpy and depressed saint. And he shows us the value of humor in the spiritual life. As the French novelist Leon Bloy once said, "Joy is the surest sign of the Holy Spirit." And he shows us, like Therese, the value of humility: that is a constant thread through his life. He never saw himself as above other people and consistently referred to his simple background. When he was pope a little boy named Bruno wrote to him about a dilemma. "Dear Pope," he wrote. "I am undecided. I want to be a policeman or a pope. What do you think?"

John wrote back. "My dear little Bruno, if you want my opinion learn how to be a policeman, because that cannot be improvised. As regards being pope, you will see later. Anybody can be the pope: the proof is that I have become one. If you should ever be in Rome, come to see me. I would be glad to talk this over with you."

After reading the stories of the saints I found myself growing more attracted to these men and women, and feeling a real friendship with them. I began to see them as models of holiness relevant to my own life and to appreciate the marvelous particularity of their lives. Therese was very different from John XXIII who was not at all like Thomas Merton. Each saint was holy in his or her own unique way, and revealed God's way of celebrating individuality.

This gave me enormous encouragement. It dawned on me that none of us are meant to be exactly like Thérèse of Lisieux or Aloysius Gonzaga or Pope John XXIII. We're meant to be ourselves, just like they were themselves. As Thomas Merton wrote, "For me to be a saint means to be myself." That's the theme of this book I just finished, *My Life with the Saints*.

Each saint lived his or her call to sanctity in different ways, and we are called to imitate them in their diversity. There is no need for anyone to do precisely what Mother Teresa or St. Francis of Assisi did. They've already done it! Instead, we are called to lead holy lives in our own way.

In his beautiful book *Journal of a Soul*, the autobiographical work that runs from his young adulthood to his death, Pope John XXIII himself meditated on this idea in 1907. Reflecting on the lives of the saints, Angelo Roncalli wrote this: "I am not meant to be a dry, bloodless reproduction of a model, no matter how perfect." Rather, John realized that he was called to find sanctity in his own life, according to his own capacities and circumstances. "If Saint Aloysius had been as I am," he concluded, "he would have been holy in a different way."

Every saint has been "holy in a different way."

Just think of the variety of holy men and women throughout Christian history. And I don't mean simply when they lived, where they were from, what languages they spoke, and what they looked like. I mean something more basic: who they were and how they were.

Just think for a minute about Thérèse of Lisieux and Dorothy Day. Dorothy Day was born in 1897 and, as a young adult, attended the University of Illinois. After graduation she moved to New York City to begin a career as a journalist. While there she fell in with an influential circle of friends in Greenwich Village that included Emma Goldman, John Dos Passos and Eugene O'Neill. At one point, while she was working as an orderly in a hospital, she fell in love with a man, got pregnant and had an abortion, an episode omitted in her autobiography *The Long Loneliness*.

Gradually, Dorothy became more concerned about the plight of the poor and marginalized and what religion had to say about this. Around the same time she fell in love with a man named Forster, who became her common-law husband. When their child Tamar was born, Dorothy discovered herself in the midst of a religious conversion, and found her way to the Catholic church. It was, she felt, the church of the poor and the church that most appealed to her intellect. Her conversion ended her relationship with Forster, since he was not at all interested in organized religion. Actually, he was an anarchist, so wasn't interested in organized anything.

In 1932 Dorothy met Peter Maurin, a self-described French peasant, who held out a utopian vision of the world to Dorothy based on the Gospels. He was a great visionary, and a great talker. Dorothy Day said that Peter Maurin who "could talk you deaf, dumb and blind." From their conversations came the Catholic Worker movement, which focused on service and companionship with the poor and nonviolent opposition to war and injustice. As an aside, though they both cared for the poor, Dorothy Day looked at things a little different from Mother Teresa, who specifically avoided confronting the systems that gave rise to poverty, choosing to devote all of her time to be with poor individuals.

Dorothy Day led an active and activist life. And a joyful one, too. When I was researching my book I spoke with Robert

Ellsberg, the publisher of Orbis Books, who had lived with Dorothy at the Catholic Worker house in New York while a young man. He told me that far from the usual portrayal of her as a humorless person, the real Dorothy was a joyful woman who loved a good story, took an interest in people and laughed a lot. A human person who loved to read, and he surprised me by telling me this—even liked to watch TV. She liked *Masterpiece Theater*.

Now, as I said, let's think about Therese of Lisieux and Dorothy Day. Thérèse realized that God had called her to spend life cloistered behind the walls of a Carmelite convent, while Dorothy Day understood that her invitation was to spend a life very much on the "outside," working among the poor and marginalized in the big cities. Both understood their calls. But both also appreciated styles of sanctity that varied from their own. Thérèse admired the Catholic missionaries working in Vietnam. And Dorothy Day admired Thérèse enough to write a short book on her. The two were holy in different ways. They were Christian in different ways.

Perhaps the very earliest example of the variety of ways to be Christian is the call of the first disciples. One Scripture scholar, William Barclay, once offered some insights on why Jesus of Nazareth might have chosen fishermen among his first disciples. If you think about it, fishermen have traits that correspond to what a good Christian needs.

Fishermen, or fisherwomen, are patient, just like a Christian needs to be patient waiting for the message to take hold. They are brave in the face of storms, just like a pastoral associate in a parish who needs to be brave in the face of trials in the church. They know how to fit the bait to the fish, just like the good catechist who needs to know what approach fit the catechumen. They know how to stay out of sight, just like a good preacher who knows to make the homily about Jesus and not about himself. The traits that make a good fisherman make a good Christian, and a good Catholic.

But that explains the reasons for choosing only a few of the disciples, those four who were fishermen. What about everyone else? Why would Jesus call, say, a tax collector and a religious zealot, and, among his wider circle of disciples, a prostitute?

One reason may have been that Jesus saw each disciple's ability to contribute something unique to the community. The unity of the church, both then and now, encompasses a tremendous diversity. Man and woman. Young and old. Married, vowed, single, ordained. Gay and straight. As another saint, St. Paul says, "There are a variety of gifts, but the same Spirit . . . To each is given a manifestation of the Spirit for the common good. . . ."

Each of us manifests an individual holiness that builds up the reign of God in ways that others may not be. You know that famous saying of Mother Teresa's that everyone quotes? "Let's do something beautiful for God?" Well, that's just part of it. The complete saying is much more beautiful, and addresses this wonderful diversity in the Christian community. "You can do something I cannot do. I can do something you cannot do. Together let us do something beautiful for God." This holy diversity is an outgrowth of the role of simple human desire, whose place in the spiritual life is underlined by St. Ignatius Loyola in his *Spiritual Exercises*. Put simply, the different desires of the saints led them to serve God in different ways. Their desires affected not only what they did, but who they became. In these natural inclinations are ways that God accomplishes his work in various places and in a variety of modes.

When I was studying theology, our Jesuit community had a small poster in our living room that said:

> Bernard loved the valleys,
> Benedict the hills,
> Francis the small towns
> and Ignatius the great cities.

Each of those four men found his home in a place suited to his own likes and preferences, and was in that way moved to accomplish his own particular task. Ignatius, for example, with all of his big plans, would probably have felt frustrated living in a small town. And Francis of Assisi would certainly have gone crazy trying to run a large religious order from an office in Rome!

God awakens our vocations primarily through desire. A man and a woman, for example, come together in love out of desire and discover their vocations as a married couple. Out of desire, a husband and wife create a child and discover their vocations as parents in this way. In the desire for companionship, friends come together. Desire works the same way in the lives of the saints, drawing them to do certain types of works, giving rise to special vocations. And ultimately, one's deepest desires lead to God and the fulfillment of God's desires for the world, because one's deepest desires are God's desires planted within you.

The primary difficulty in grasping the universal call to holiness is that many people feel that they have to be something else, or someone else in order to be holy. A generous young mother who spends most of her waking moments caring for her children, for example, may say to herself, sadly, "I'll never be like Mother Teresa." A hardworking pastoral associate in a parish in an affluent neighborhood might say, "I'll never be like Dorothy Day." And a priest who finds himself swamped with administrative details in his parish might say, "I'll never be like Francis of Assisi."

But you're not meant to be Mother Teresa or Dorothy Day or Francis of Assisi—you're meant to be yourself. That's not to say you can't learn, and learn a lot from their lives, but you're not meant to be them.

Sanctity consists, as Thomas Merton said, in discovering your "true self," the person you are before God, and striving to become that person.

In other words, a young mother, for example, is not meant to be Mother Teresa. She is not meant to enter the Loreto sisters, and then found a religious order and work in Calcutta. She is meant to be a woman who loves her children, loves her husband, loves her friends and neighbors and, if she's working outside the home, her coworkers. She is meant to experience God in her life and in the lives of the people with whom she lives and works. Sometimes this means doing big things with love, like raising children. And sometimes it means doing smaller things with love. That's the "Little Way" that Thérèse wrote about. Part of this process may mean that this young woman has to let go of the desire to be someone else. Because, in reality, she might be lousy at the type of work that Mother Teresa used to do. To underline this point, Mother Teresa might have been lousy at the work that this working mother is doing! And to underline it even further, could you imagine Thomas Merton, that famous complainer, raising children? Oh man. He'd probably be complaining that those early-morning feedings were making him too sleepy to write the next day.

Most of the problems arise when we begin to believe that we have to be someone *else* to be holy. We use someone else's map to heaven when God has already planted in our soul all the directions we need. When admirers used to visit Calcutta to see Mother Teresa, she would tell many of them, "Find your own Calcutta." In other words, bloom where you are planted. Discover sanctity in your own life.

The saints show us that being holy means being ourselves. That's a powerful message to carry to the ends of the earth. And a powerful message to carry to a parish or a school or a retreat house. So, by way of conclusion, how might you increase an understanding and appreciation of the saints in your own spiritual life and in the lives of the people with whom you minister?

First, for your own personal life. Let me give you three easy ways.

1. *Read.* There are few things more enjoyable than reading a good biography of a saint or soon-to-be-saint. And when faced with a choice between a scholarly treatment over the more fictionalized versions, I'd start with the scholarly one. Because it's almost impossible to improve on their real lives. For example, as wonderful a movie as is *The Song of Bernadette*, the real life of Bernadette Soubirous, the visionary of Lourdes, is even more inspiring. Did you know, for example, that after the apparitions,

Bernadette always turned down offers of gifts, even though she was desperately poor? And did you know that she could be blunt when confronted with people who wanted to use her? When a photographer told her to pretend that she was looking at the Blessed Mother, she said, "But she's not here!"

In scholarly biographies you always find the kinds of things that are left out of some the pious stories—specifically, places where the saint struggled and felt discouraged. There you'll learn about Mother Teresa's dark night and Thomas Merton's struggles with pride. And in those scholarly biographies you'll also learn about how those human struggles helped to draw them closer to God.

2. *Pray.* After reading a saint's life it's natural to meditate on his or her life and ask for some intercession. And I have a theory that is unprovable: I think that we start praying to a saint because that saint is already praying for us. But that shouldn't become the only reason for devotion to the saints. In other words, the saints shouldn't be reduced to people whose only function is to intercede for us, to get us things. That's like being friends with someone only if he did you favors: that would be a pretty unhealthy friendship. Still, everyone needs help from time to time.

By the way, I guess you all know the prayer to St. Anthony. Can we say it together? "St. Anthony, St. Anthony. . . ." But do you know the saint you pray to find a parking space? That's Mother Cabrini. My theory is that since she lived in New York, she's the go-to person for parking spaces. Anyway, the prayer goes: "Mother Cabrini, Mother Cabrini . . ."

So the saints are our patrons and our companions. We ask for intercession and we feel encouraged by their example. But the saints are also there for our enjoyment. If you take Therese of Lisieux's image of the garden, the flowers aren't there to do something for us, but to be enjoyed, like you enjoy a good friend's company. And meditating on the lives of the saints is one way to enjoy their company.

3. *Evangelize.* It's fun to introduce other people to the saints: that's one reason I wrote this new book. After all, it's natural to want your friends to know one another. So why not share the life of your favorite saint with friends, if they're open to it? Sharing these stories helps your friends in their Christian lives. By introducing them to a saint you are offering them encouragement and help. And it may also help you feel closer to your friends, with whom you can now share your affection for that saint. For me, there is something special about talking about Thomas Merton and Therese with fellow admirers—a sense of participating in their spirituality that is exciting and encouraging. It's like being fans of the same sports team.

Next, how can you incorporate the saints into the life of your ministry? Here are three basic ways to incorporate the saints into your work in parishes and high schools and colleges and hospitals and chanceries and retreat centers.

1. *Teach.* The biggest obstacle to devotion to the saints is a lack of understanding of how amazing their lives were, and how interesting they are. Some Catholics still see them frozen in stained glass, or as perfect, unattainable models far removed from any relevance. Or too boring. You know, that's the last word that people would have used to describe, for instance, Francis of Assisi—"crazy" would have been the more likely one!

So the best way to overcome those obstacles in your parish or school or retreat center is to teach the real stories of the saints, and suggest resources and books to help people meet the real person. And here's a secret: sometimes movies are just as good. The best way to get to know Thomas More may be through *A Man for All Seasons* and the best way to get to know Archbishop Oscar Romero may be with the film *Romero*. Sometimes a DVD is a great way to evangelize.

2. *Worship.* Another easy way to introduce people is through liturgical celebrations. The most natural way, the way already provided for by the church's tradition, is to tell their stories on their feast days, even if briefly. And since all the saints patterned

their lives on Christ, there is always a way to link their stories to the Gospel reading. Feast days are when people are most open to hearing those stories. And, if you're really stuck for a homily, the lives of the saints are always good resources for material.

3. *Innovate.* Be creative. If you're a pastor or pastoral associate, do you plan to celebrate the feast day of your parish's patron saint? Maybe that might help educate new parishioners and help them feel more attached to the parish. If you're a religious ed teacher or a D.R.E., have you ever sponsored an essay contest about the patron saint of your school? Maybe that would help your students better understand the concept of the universal call to holiness, and help them feel more comfortable about who they are. If you're a campus minister, could you ever point your students to the saints as role models? Maybe they would discover that even the most traditional saints were powerful models of social justice. If you're a spiritual director, are you only giving people material from the Gospels for prayer? Maybe you could supplement this with material from the lives of the saints. Innovate. Be creative. And pray to the saints for new ideas. They'll help you: they're pretty creative.

Those are just a few ways to introduce others to the lives of the saints.

Over the course of my life, and quite by surprise, then, I have gone from someone suspicious of devotion to the saints to someone who counts it as one of the great joys of my life. And these days I wonder which companions I will meet next.

—*LAREC*, 2006

WHERE HOLINESS MAKES ITS HOME

This selection from A Jesuit Off-Broadway *emphasizes Martin's theme that oftentimes the saint is simply the person who has realized what God has meant him or her to be.*

One morning in late January, we were moved to a rehearsal space in a building across the street from Martinson Hall while the set for Judas was being constructed. There we began talking about the inherent humanity of the disciples. Many Christians who are interested in the saints tend to overlook their natural failings. Elizabeth Rodriquez told me, "I just never thought of the saints as human when I was growing up. They were, you know, saintly. And there was this huge distance between them and us, between what they did and what we did."

More often than not, sanctity is confused with perfection, which means that the saints are often seen as either inhuman or superhuman. Thus the revelation of any flaws is viewed as a threat to their "image." When Pope John Paul II died, a few weeks after the play's opening, criticisms of his papacy or admissions of his personal failings were seen by many Catholics as off-limits-embarrassing blots on his saintly record. But no saint was perfect. Holiness makes its home among human imperfections.

Some of the saints could even be unpleasant, particularly in their single-minded pursuit of their vision. Stories of their quirky behavior are sometimes related by their most devoted admirers as marks of their underlying humanity. When Mother Teresa once visited the United States, she immediately instructed the American sisters in her religious order to get rid of their washing machines. The sisters should be living more simply, she declared, and should wash the clothes and bedsheets of the sick by hand, as her sisters in India did.

The lives of a few well-known saints feature episodes of outright nastiness. Saint Jerome, a brilliant polymath who translated the Bible into Latin, was a noted theologian, writer, and spiritual director. He was also surprisingly uncharitable when confronted with opposition. In the early fifth century he wrote a snide public letter to a theologian named Rufinus, addressing him "my most simple-minded friend." For good measure, he said that his opponent walked "like a tortoise." Jerome continued with his invective even after Rufinus's death, when a gentler appraisal of the man would have been expected.

Likewise, Saint Cyril of Alexandria, archbishop of the Egyptian city from 412 to 444, is described by *Butler's Lives of the*

Saints as "brave but sometimes over vehement, indeed violent." During a church council in Ephesus in 431, Cyril led a group of his followers who deposed and sent into exile a bishop who had disagreed with some of Cyril's theological writings. Reconciliation and forgiveness were apparently not his strong suits. Edward A. Ryan, a Jesuit professor and church historian, said wryly, "We don't know anything about the last ten years of Cyril's life. Those must have been the years in which he became a saint." Another misconception is that the saints are carbon copies of one another: all of them blandly pious men and women locked in constant prayer. But even the most cursory glance at their biographies reveals an extraordinary diversity in their personalities, their likes and dislikes, and the courses their lives took. They worked, prayed, and loved differently. They thought differently, too—and even quarreled. Perhaps the earliest example of this is the fierce debate that took place around AD 51 between Saint Paul and Saints Peter, James, and John over whether the Christian message should be extended to non-Jews. Paul won out, and the gospel was taken to the "Gentiles," with Peter and his friends no doubt nursing disappointment for a time.

A striking example of the variety among saintly men and women is the counterpoint between Dorothy Day and Mother Teresa, near contemporaries. Dorothy Day, the American-born cofounder of the Catholic Worker movement, spent much of her life caring for the poor in the United States, not simply by opening up a network of homeless shelters, but also by advocating publicly and often loudly for systemic political change. She was frequently jailed for her nonviolent protests. Hers was what the writer Robert Ellsberg has called a "political kind of holiness." Mother Teresa, on the other hand, famously cared for the poor but also pointedly refrained from commenting on the political factors underlying the causes of poverty, except in the most general of terms. The two women had different ways of responding to the demands of Christianity.

A more contemporary understanding of sanctity is that it means not perfection, which is unattainable, but being true to the person you are meant to be, the person created by God. Believers are called to follow as best they can their individual paths to personal holiness. This is part of what the Second Vatican Council termed the "universal call to holiness." The goal of every Christian is to grow in love and charity, but this common goal is lived out in different ways.

The lives of the saints show us, as Karl Rahner wrote, what it means to be holy in this particular way. Mother Teresa was not meant to be Dorothy Day. And Saint Peter was not meant to be Saint Paul. "If St. Aloysius had been as I am," wrote Pope John XXIII in an entry in his journals in 1903, "he would have become holy in a different way." Or, as Thomas Merton put it: "For me to be a saint means to be myself." But being oneself, or even being a saint, does not mean being perfect.

This concept—the essential humanity of the saints—was absolutely central to Stephen's presentation of the story of Jesus and his disciples, and I didn't think it was possible to stress it too much. After all, it's difficult to listen to Saint Thomas, as played by Adrian Martinez, a stocky man with frizzy black hair, stand before you holding a beer and admit that Judas was "a bit of a jerk off" if you haven't accepted the fundamental humanity of the apostles.

So the cast began talking about the disparate crew of apostles that Jesus gathered around himself. Matthew worked as a tax collector; as an employee of Rome, he would have been despised by the Jews in Palestine. Peter, Andrew, James, and John were simple fishermen from the backwater of Galilee. The idea that a supposed prophet chose to continue to hang out with friends from Galilee was shocking for sophisticated people of the time. ("Can anything good come out of Nazareth?" asks Nathanael in the New Testament.)

I recalled an insight from a Jesuit priest many years ago. Think about Peter, this Jesuit had said. The Galilean fisherman was at once good and deeply flawed. A man who repeatedly didn't "get it." A man who doubted the miracles he saw, questioned the mission, refused to allow for the possibility that Jesus would ever have to suffer, and denied his best friend three times. Of the original twelve apostles, Peter perhaps best exemplified what Avery Cardinal Dulles, the dean of American Catholic theologians, called the "obtuseness of the disciples." Yet this was the person whom, according to the Gospels, Jesus chose to lead his church—perhaps because Peter was the one who understood his own human flaws well enough to recognize his need for divine assistance.

It was clear, I suggested to the cast one day, why Jesus selected Peter. Peter was a strong man, full of passion and energy and zeal for spreading the message of Jesus. He was strong enough to lead the church. But he was also weak, because he understood the need for both confidence in God and humility before God. Peter was weak enough to lead the church.

For a few seconds, there was silence around the table. Finally, Phil sat up and said, "What?" I was happy that the insight seemed to strike the cast as forcefully as it had struck me all those years ago in the Jesuit novitiate.

Talking with cast members after the play had ended its run, I learned of the effects that our talks about the humanity of the saints had made. "I realized," said Adrian Martinez, "that these were real people dealing with real events and that real sacrifices were made in their lives. Thinking about it like that makes all those Bible stories seem more visceral and more relevant to the present day." For Jeffrey DeMunn, it was something of a revelation. "The saints and apostles had always been semimythical to me. But during the table readings, I thought, Wait a minute! They were real human beings. That was revolutionary and just opened up the whole play."

If I had been in theology studies, I would have said that the cast and I were engaging in exegesis, the careful breaking open of the text. When I described how seriously the director and the cast took their work, an elderly priest said to me, "We should all take the New Testament so seriously."   —A Jesuit Off-Broadway, 109–13

PATRONS AND COMPANIONS

This essay was adapted from an address given at the Catholic Theology Society of America meeting in San José, CA, in June 2011.

Over the past few years, I have spent a good deal of time speaking to groups both large and small about the saints. After listening to the comments and questions of people in parishes, colleges and universities, retreat houses and conferences, as well as reading scores of letters, I have noticed two extremes in contemporary Catholic devotion to the saints, both of them perilous.

The two main ways of understanding the saints in the Catholic tradition are to see them as patrons and as companions. These two models are elucidated in most scholarly studies of the saints, among them *Friends of God and Prophets* by Elizabeth Johnson, C.S.J. They also find voice in the Preface of the Mass for Holy Men and Women, used on the feast days of the saints: "They inspire us by their heroic lives and help us by their constant prayers."

The main challenge in fostering devotion to the saints lies in steering between the extremes surrounding those two models. On the one hand, there is in some quarters an exaggerated emphasis on the patron: the canonized saint in heaven who intercedes for us. In this understanding, the focus is on the one who prays for us in company with the risen Christ, the Blessed Mother and the communion of saints, after having led an earthly life beyond any critique; the patron never entertained an unorthodox thought, never suffered doubt for even a moment, never experienced conflict with the institutional church. Seen thus, saints are supposed to be acceptable in every way to people of every devotional type. Catholics who overemphasize this model are sometimes shocked to hear about the flaws of the saints, the areas where they did not follow the status quo and those times when they found themselves in conflict with church leaders.

On the other side are those who overemphasize the companion model: the earthy, sinful, struggling man or woman who shows us, through sometimes flawed actions, how holiness always makes its home in humanity. In this conception, the saint is someone who, once dead, serves no other role than that of model—as if their lives ended once they died. People in this camp often recoil from the parts of saints' lives that include apparitions, visions or anything that remotely smacks of the supernatural. They are often aghast at talk of intercession, pilgrimages, novenas for the saint's help and, of course, miracles.

A healthier (and more accurate) model is to see the saint as both patron and companion: the manifestly human being whose earthly life shows that being a saint means being who you are, but who now enjoys life in heaven and intercedes for us.

By way of illustration, let me share two stories from the two dangerous extremes.

Human Lives

A few years ago I wrote a brief article for the op-ed page of *The New York Times* that described the incredible life of Mother Theodore Guérin, the newest American saint. Mother Guérin was born in 1798 in France, entered religious life and eventually journeyed to Indiana. There this remarkably determined woman founded the Sisters of Providence of St. Mary-of-the-Woods and started a college and several schools in the region. One might think that such zeal would have won her favor from the local bishop.

It did not. The idea of a strong, independent woman deciding where and when to open schools apparently offended the bishop of Vincennes, Ind., a man whose name sounds like that of a villain in a Victorian-era potboiler: Celestine de la Hailandière. In 1844, when Mother Guérin was away from her convent raising money, the bishop, in a bid to eject her from the very order she founded, ordered her congregation to elect a new superior. Obediently, the sisters convened a meeting. There they re-elected Mother Guérin—unanimously. Infuriated, Bishop de la Hailandière informed the future saint that she was forbidden to set foot in her own convent, since he, the bishop, considered himself its sole proprietor.

Three years later, Bishop de la Hailandière demanded Mother Guérin's resignation. When the exceedingly patient foundress refused, the bishop told her congregation that she was no longer its superior, that she was ordered to leave Indiana and that she was forbidden from communicating with her sisters. Her sisters replied that they were not willing to obey a dictator. At one point, the bishop locked Mother Guérin in his house until her sisters pleaded for her release. The situation worsened until, a few weeks later, Bishop de la Hailandière was replaced by the Vatican.

My op-ed noted that for a time the future saint, through no fault of her own, found herself in conflict with the church hierarchy. Within just a few days, I received a letter from a bishop with whom I am friendly. My article, he said, was damaging to the faithful. Was I saying that the only way to be a saint was to oppose the hierarchy? By no means, I replied. Rather, Mother Guérin's struggles with her bishop were part of her spiritual journey, her very human life on earth.

Coincidentally, I had just returned from a pilgrimage to Lourdes, where I had spent time cheerfully chatting with this friendly bishop. I am surprised that this would come from someone who visits Lourdes, he said in his letter. In response, I pointed out that St. Bernadette Soubirous, the visionary of Lourdes, had herself been booted out of the town's rectory by the local pastor, after she first reported her visions of Mary. Here was another instance of a future saint being, for a time, rejected by the church. (The story of Mary MacKillop, the new Australian saint who was for a time excommunicated, is another of many such examples.) Understanding the saints as bland figures whose lives were free of any conflict indicates an exaggeration of the patron model, where any "controversial" aspects of a saint's life are seen as irrelevant, now that they are in heaven.

Some Catholics who gravitate toward this extreme are discouraged to hear that the saints sometimes sinned even after their conversions; that they did not follow the "expected" things that saints are supposed to do; or that they were, in a word, human. Once, during a parish talk, I quoted St. Thérèse of Lisieux on the rosary, as an example of how different were the saints. They were not cookie-cutter models of one another, nor were their spiritualities. "The recitation of the Rosary," said the Little Flower, "is as difficult for me as wearing an instrument of penance." The crowd—believe it or not—gasped audibly.

"Why did you say that?" said a Catholic sister afterward. "Because it's true," I said. "Well, you shouldn't say such things," she said.

One extreme to be avoided, then, is an excessive emphasis on a homogenized, noncontroversial blandness. For the one who prays for us in heaven also lived a human life.

Saints Alive

The other extreme is an overemphasis on the companion model, which stresses the saints' humanity. More explicitly, it is an approach that shies away from what happens after the saint's earthly death. A few years ago after another trip to Lourdes, I told a Catholic theologian about my visit there and about the pilgrims with whom I went.

"That's dangerous," he said.

"What is?" I asked.

"The notion that the saints pray for us, that miracles happen—like magic."

But that is what we mean by "patron," I responded, quoting the prayers of the Mass: "They help us with their constant prayers." After all, I said, the law of prayer is the law of belief (*Lex orandi, lex credendi*). Besides, the records of miraculous cures are available in Lourdes for all to see, authenticated by physicians, many of them nonbelievers. And that is just for St. Bernadette. Read the canonization papers for any modern saint and you will be gobsmacked by the cures: immediate, irreversible, inexplicable. From the look on my friend's face, however, you might have thought I was telling him that I believed in the Great Pumpkin.

But if God can create the universe and raise his Son from the dead, then miracles—miracles today, that is—seem easy in comparison. Regarding the question of why some prayers are answered and others are not: I have no idea. Why, if millions visit Lourdes annually, have only 67 miracles been authenticated? I have no clue. But that is no cop-out; it is on the same theological plane as the problem of evil: Why do some people suffer? I don't know, but I do not need to understand God fully to believe in God fully or to love God fully. But those miracles, whether or not we understand why they happen, do happen.

When the doubtful or suspicious ask about intercession I often ask them this: If we ask for the prayers of friends on earth, why not from friends in heaven—unless we do not believe that they are with God, or that God somehow destroys their unique selves after their death, which I cannot believe. If our fellow sinful believers on earth pray for us, why wouldn't the saints? Regarding intercession, it is also important to look at the *sensus fidelium*. Millions of Catholics pray to the saints for their help; they can recount personal stories of being helped in ways that go beyond credulousness, gullibility or stupidity. So I pray to the saints regularly. But I do not get overly upset when my prayers are not answered.

The dangerous thing is not so much "believing in miracles" or even "believing in intercession." The dangerous thing is limiting God. In essence, it is saying, "God cannot possibly work like this."

Both/And

When it comes to devotion to the saints one must hold in tension their dual roles as patron and companion. An overemphasis on one destroys the saint's humanity, renders their earthly lives almost meaningless and negates their roles as models, examples and companions as Christian disciples. An overemphasis on the other makes their new lives in heaven meaningless, renders the tradition of intercession irrelevant and negates their current place in the communion of saints.

There is an obvious parallel to Christology. In classical Christian theology, Jesus Christ is understood as "fully human and fully divine." An overemphasis on the divinity of Christ (for example, saying that Jesus could not suffer because he was God) is as unhelpful as is overemphasis on Jesus' humanity (for example, denying his ability to perform miracles). Both need to be kept squarely before us as Christians, to be held in tension for us to begin to understand Jesus Christ. The same tension needs to be held when looking at the saints, balancing hagiography "from above" and "from below."

So in my own work and life I am trying to restore a little balance. And I'm happy to do so with the help of the saints, my patrons and companions.   —*America*, November 7, 2011

After many centuries in which saintliness was all too often conflated with virginity, the church since Vatican II has struggled to hold up a model for holiness that makes sense for married couples and parents; here and in the two following essays on the Holy Family, Martin offers some useful if complicated models for married holiness, and also emphasizes the sanctity to be found in embracing the sacrifices both large and small we can make for our families.

HIS WIFE IS A SAINT . . .
SO IS HER HUSBAND

After their wedding in Alençon, France, on July 13, 1858, Louis Martin and Zélie Guérin refrained from sex for 10 months. The impetus for that arrangement, known as a "Josephite marriage" (after the celibate relationship between St. Joseph and his wife, Mary), came from Louis, who had earlier hoped to enter a monastery. Eventually, a frustrated Zélie escorted her husband to a local priest, who assured them that raising children was a sacred activity.

They took his advice: Before her death in 1877, Zélie bore nine children—five of whom joined religious orders.

We would know little about Louis or Zélie were it not for their youngest daughter, Thérèse, who entered a Carmelite monastery in Lisieux and became one of the church's most popular saints. St. Thérèse of Lisieux, the "Little Flower," was canonized in 1925.

This Sunday in the basilica of Lisieux, Louis and Zélie will be beatified, the Catholic church's final step before canonization, positioning them to join the rarefied company of saints who were married. That brief list includes Saints Peter, Monica, Thomas More and the American-born Elizabeth Ann Seton. The roster of saints married to one another is even shorter: Isadore and Maria, 10th-century Spanish farmers, are among the few.

The Lisieux ceremony follows the Vatican's approval, in July, of the required miracle—the healing of a man with a malformation of the lung. But the beatification raises questions about the models of life being presented to Catholics. What can a man and woman who planned to live celibately say to married couples today?

The two traditional roles of the saints are the patron (who intercedes on behalf of those on earth) and the companion (who provides believers with an example of Christian life). And the paucity of lay saints—more specifically, married ones—in the roster is somewhat embarrassing.

Two reasons underlie this anomaly: the outmoded belief, almost as old as the church, that the celibate life was "better" than married life, and the fact that the church's canonization process is an arduous one, requiring someone to gather paperwork, interview contemporaries if that is still possible and present the case to the Congregation for the Causes of Saints.

Certainly there have been as many saintly wives and husbands as there have been holy priests and nuns. But religious orders and dioceses know how to navigate the canonization procedures on behalf of bishops, priests, brothers and sisters. By contrast, how many families have the resources to embark on the decades-long process on behalf of even the holiest mother or father? As a result, married Catholics have few exemplars other than Mary and Joseph, whose situation was hardly replicable.

Since the Second Vatican Council, which emphasized the "universal call to holiness," Rome has stepped up its efforts to canonize more lay and married people. The Vatican hopes to expand the "calendar of saints" beyond those who sport miters, collars and veils in order to provide Catholics with lives that they can emulate, not simply admire. But do Louis and Zélie fit the bill?

No one doubts that the Martins led the traditional life of "heroic sanctity" required for sainthood. Though obviously biased, St. Thérèse wrote: "The Good God gave me a father and mother more worthy of heaven than of earth." They were devoted to one another, to their children and to their faith. During their first year of marriage, the couple took into their home a young boy whose mother had died. And whenever Louis and Zélie were apart, they exchanged the tenderest of letters. "Your husband and true friend who loves you forever," Louis wrote.

One lesson that believers might take from the new "blesseds" is that sanctity comes in many styles. If it were up to their youthful selves, neither would have married: Zélie wanted to be a nun as much as Louis hoped to be a monk. After setting aside their celibacy, they provided a warm home for their children, five of whom fulfilled their parents' thwarted hopes for life in a religious order. The wife died early; the grieving husband struggled with mental illness, including hallucinations in which he saw "frightful things," according to his daughter Céline.

Throughout their complicated lives Blessed Louis and Zélie Martin tried to love as best they could, something that is still relevant—and not just to married couples. And whose life, and which saint's life, is "typical" anyway? Holiness, as the lives of the saints remind us, always makes its home in humanity.

—*WSJ*, October 17, 2008

JESUS, MARY AND JOSEPH!

"Jesus, Mary and Joseph!" my dad used to say, and not entirely in a devotional way. That was one of the most frequent expressions out of his mouth when he was annoyed—in particular when he was driving and someone cut him off. Or when he banged his finger with a hammer, trying to fix something. Or when he was frustrated with me. That was one of his most frequent expressions. The other frequent expressions are not best not shared in a religious setting.

That's my topic this morning—not my father's salty language—but those three persons, so familiar to us, yet still so mysterious. What can the distinctive lives, experiences and spiritualities of the members of the Holy Family teach us? How can their extraordinary lives help us in our ordinary ones?

Let's start with Jesus. Now, obviously, Jesus Christ, the Second Person of the Trinity, the Son of God, is a big topic. But that too often we think only of his divine life, forgetting that he was also human. We remember his miracles and forget his struggles. You know the story of Jesus coming back to earth for the Second Coming, and deciding that there were all sorts of things that he wanted to do that he never got around to. So he thinks, "Well, now's the time to do them." And the first thing he decides is that he wants to golf. So he asks around to find out who is the greatest golfer, and everyone tells him Tiger Woods.

So he meets up with Tiger Woods for his first lesson. And Tiger says, "Okay, well, we're going to tee up your first ball." And he shows him how to hold the club and address the ball, and keep his head down. So Jesus is watching and then he steps up to the tee, and takes out a driver and puts his head down and swings. And the ball goes way over into the rough, into the tall grass.

Then from out of nowhere a little deer comes up to the ball, and gently nudges it with its little deer nose onto the fairway. Then a chipmunk climbs down from the tree, picks up the ball with its little hands and runs down the fairway to the green.

So Tiger Woods is watching all this, and then a flock of doves comes down from the skies and with their wings flutter so hard that the ball moves towards the cup, just inches away. Then the sky clouds over and a big lightning bolt zaps the ball, which jumps into the air and goes into the cup. And Tiger Woods looks at Jesus and says, "Look are you going to play golf or are you going to screw around?"

That's the way a lot of us can think about Jesus, as this sort of magical person. Fully divine but not really fully human. But that's a heresy of course. Today we tend to downplay his humanity.

So today let's focus on one particular aspect of his human life, and how it might help us in our own lives. Specifically, how Jesus came to understand what he was meant to do and who he was meant to be. How can his understanding of vocation help us with our own vocation? How does his path towards self-knowledge and his relationship to his Father, help us understand our own self-knowledge and our relationship to God? Let's look at how the Jesus that we find in the Gospels helps us to find our path.

Much of the answer to that question turns on what theologians call his "self-knowledge." I am no theologian or academic or scholar. So I won't be proposing any new theology. Besides, the tradition says it best: fully human and fully divine. But that doesn't settle the question of how Jesus thought of himself and his vocation.

And anything we say about his inner life is speculative. During my theology studies, one student asked our New Testament professor about Jesus's self-knowledge. When did Jesus know he was divine? When he prayed, how did he relate to God the Father? How did he come to know what his vocation was? What did he think about the miracles he performed? Overall, what was his inner life like?

My professor listened carefully and said, "We have no idea."

While it's true that we know little about the inner life of Jesus, there are some things that we can know. First of all, as a first-century Galilean Jew, he wouldn't have used the same language that we use to describe himself. As the theologian Elizabeth Johnson says in her book *Consider Jesus*, "Jesus did not wake up in the morning saying, *I am the Son of God with a truly human nature and a truly divine nature that comes together in one hypostasis.* I do not know what he said in the morning, but we can virtually certain that it was not that!"

So how did Jesus understand his true self and his vocation?

Well let's do a sort of imaginative exercise to explore the human way in which Jesus of Nazareth might have grown into understanding his vocation. St. Ignatius Loyola, the founder of the Society of Jesus, encouraged us to place ourselves imaginatively in Scripture, which is what I'm about to do. And as I spin out this story, see if you see any resonances or intersections or parallels to your own life, your own quest for self-discovery and your own vocations. Along the way I'll pose some questions to prompt you in those reflections.

If we're talking how Jesus came to understand his vocation, we might begin in his adolescence, when many people first start thinking about who they are and who they want to be. For a boy in first-century Palestine, this might have started as early as age 13, which in later Jewish life became the traditional time of coming of age marked by the *bar mitzvah*.

Unfortunately, the Gospel writers say nothing about the life of Jesus between the time he is discovered teaching in the Temple, at age 12, and the beginning of his public ministry, around age 30. The Gospel of Luke says: "And Jesus increased in wisdom and in years, and in divine and human favor." And that's it! There is an eighteen-year gap in our knowledge about the life of Jesus. Yet this period, often called the "hidden life," was undoubtedly crucial in the growing self-awareness and maturation of Jesus.

What might this time have been like for Jesus?

As Mary and Joseph meditated on the unusual birth and early childhood of their son, they most likely came to understand that he was destined for a unique vocation. Perhaps some of their own reflections were passed on to Jesus. At the same time, their son probably spent much of his time preparing for what he may have thought would be his lifelong occupation: a carpenter, or what we might also call a craftsman or construction worker. You know the Gospels refer to Jesus more frequently as "the carpenter" rather than "the rabbi."

Have you ever thought about Jesus's working life? The same virtues that Jesus acquired as a carpenter (patience, hard work, honesty and so on) would serve him well in his later ministry. As he matured, in conversations with Mary and Joseph, and in his daily work in Nazareth, God may have been preparing Jesus for his eventual work, much as God can use our own backgrounds and talents for the good. So the first question that comes from Jesus's life: how in your life's background, has God prepared you for the work you're doing today?

Jesus's young adulthood may have been when he first started to wonder if he was meant for some special purpose. Perhaps this came from his own prayer, or from the way he felt when he read certain Scripture passages—especially the prophetic writings, like the Book of Isaiah. Perhaps when he saw people in Nazareth who were sick, he felt his heart moved with pity. Perhaps when he saw the religious leaders laying heavy burdens on the people, he sensed the injustice in life and how far this was from what God wanted.

Perhaps he started to believe that his life should be about alleviating suffering. Perhaps he felt within him a desire that became progressively clearer and clearer: to preach the word of God and to lessen the suffering of those around him. Perhaps, as he looked at Nazareth and the surrounding Jewish towns, he wondered whether he didn't have some great part to play in the liberation of his people. Perhaps he began to desire to liberate his people. Now a second question: in your life, what desires are moving you towards your full vocation?

Overall, I like to think of Jesus as a pensive young man, who thought hard about the person God intended him to be.

But, even when he reached the age of 30, Jesus may still have been a bit unclear about things. After all, many of us are still unclear about things at that age, and Jesus had a lot to be unclear about!

Because at the very beginning of his public ministry, Jesus seems unsure about what he's supposed to do. You could make a case that when Jesus went to the Jordan River to be baptized, it was because he was attracted, like so many people, to the message of John the Baptist. That is, he may have gone to see what John's message was all about and whether it would help him understand what he was meant to do.

Indeed, his baptism seems confusing even for some of the Gospel writers. The Gospel of Mark says that Jesus had a "baptism repentance." Why did he need that? If anything, shouldn't the Son of God be doing the baptizing himself?

Whatever the reasons that drew Jesus to the banks of the Jordan River, something happened at his baptism that was so astounding (the Gospels describe it as the heavens opening and a voice being heard) that it convinces Jesus that he has a unique mission. And so he is driven into the desert to continue his process of prayer and discernment.

Clearly Jesus was sorely tested in the desert. Whether you believe "Satan" appeared in some physical way to do the testing personally or whether Jesus experienced these tests, or temptations, within himself is to my mind beside the point. And this episode was most likely passed along to the disciples by Jesus himself, and so needs to be taken seriously.

The testing in the desert may be the easiest part of Jesus's life to understand. Jesus, now thinking intently about his mission, was subject the same temptations that all of us are: for power, for security, for easy answers. But he rejects these temptations and returns to Galilee to begin his ministry.

These few weeks in the life of Jesus, as he turns away from power, security and easy answers, are critical for any reflection in the search for his vocation and his true self. You could see it as a fundamental rejection of the temptation to become the "false self." For underlying all the impulses that Jesus experienced in the desert was a temptation to do things in a way that would contradict who he was called to be. The temptations said to him: "Don't become what you were called to be. Be someone who is more in line with your selfish desires and wants, with what society demands, with what will give you superficial success and pleasure. Be someone who fits in, who never poses a threat to the status quo. Be someone who craves only respect. Be your false self."

But Jesus may have also faced temptations that were more subtle than that. For example, Jesus may have been tempted to assume worldly power as a means to help people. After all, why not be the powerful and influential person if that power and influence can aid others? But gradually, Jesus realizes that God is calling him to a different kind of power.

In facing down these temptations in the desert, in turning away from a self-centered life and a life of worldly power, Jesus rejects his false self and embraces his true self. So a third question for you: what places in your life are you called to reject your false self?

Even after his stay in the desert, Jesus still seems reluctant to embrace his mission. For his first miracle seems a distinctly reluctant one. There he is at the Wedding Feast at Cana when the wine runs out. When his mother points this out to him, in effect, suggesting that he *do* something, Jesus says, "Woman, what concern is that to you and to me?"

In other words, What does this have to do with me? I'm not the person you want! I'm not yet the person I am called to be!

Here is Jesus still grappling with his mission, with his vocation, with his true self.

In response, his mother gives him the freedom to do what he wants. "Do whatever he tells you," she says to the hosts. Why is that? Well, Mary may have understood his mission earlier than Jesus did. Perhaps because she had a longer time to think about it. So the fourth question: Who points you to your vocation? Who are your Marys?

Somehow Jesus now understands what is required of him. Confidently now, he tells the steward to fill large earthen jars with water and serve the guests. But it is not water that comes out of the jars, it is wine.

Did you ever wonder if Jesus himself wasn't surprised by his first miracle? In his journey towards self-knowledge, if there were ever a time when he might have been surprised, it is in Cana. I'm sure in your own lives, you are surprised by the results of your ministry, or your service, or your love. You say just a few words to someone that unlock emotions and feelings that have long been hidden away. You casually mention a Gospel passage that turns out to be precisely the right one for someone to experience healing or hope. After a chance remark, someone during a homily or a class or a counseling session, someone approaches says through tears that this was just what she needed to hear.

The fruits of one's ministry and one's life are often astonishing, and the hand of God can be seen as clear as day—even when the results are simple ones. How much more surprising what happened at Cana might have been for Jesus!

At the same time, Cana seems to have strengthened Jesus's understanding of his mission and emboldened him to trust even more in God, to trust even more in his own judgment and discernment, and to trust in his ability to do miraculous things in the name of God. It may have helped Jesus to see the value of his true self, and understand the mission that his Father had sent him for: to be the revealer and revelation of God.

This is also the case in our own lives. The more we live out of our true selves, the more we become the person that God intended, the more we see the spectacular effects of a well-lived vocation. The father who fully embraces his vocation as a father becomes a better father, and his children find love. The mother becomes a better mother. The doctor becomes a better doctor. The friend becomes a better friend. And the Christian becomes a better Christian. So a fifth question: where do you see the signs of God's confirmation of your own vocation?

As the Gospel stories continue, it is easy to see Jesus growing in confidence in his mission and in his identity. His miracles are a measure of his confidence in himself, and in his mission, which flows from his relationship with his Father. In other passages, this assurance virtually leaps off the page. Like in a story that is told in Matthew, Mark and Luke: "If you choose," says a leper, "you can heal me."

"I do choose! Be made clean!"

Throughout his ministry, Jesus continues to grow in his awareness of his mission and his true self.

Towards the end of his earthly ministry, Jesus is clearly able to see what needs to be done. He has now fully embraced his identity and his ministry.

But there is one last test: his time in the Garden of Gethsemane immediately before the Passion. Near the end of his life, he struggles with a complete embrace of his mission. "If this cup may pass me by," he says, hoping that perhaps that suffering is not what God intends.

But somehow he realizes, through prayer and reflection, that his impending suffering, whatever it would be, is what God is asking of him at this moment in his life. He realizes that it is part of the reality of his life. And it is here, it seems to me, that in accepting the cup of suffering, Jesus fully accepts his identity. Part of his life and vocation includes suffering, as do all of our lives and vocations. In the Garden, Jesus accepts this essential human truth.

Jesus is then completely free. He is not disturbed when he is arrested in the Garden, having just been betrayed by one of his closest friends. In response to Peter's striking one of the high priest's guards, Jesus calmly heals the man and points the disciples to a peaceful acceptance of his path. In the face of Pilate's questioning, he refuses to allow himself even the chance to defend himself. He is, in fact, largely silent during the Passion. And as he moves towards death, carrying his cross, he is firm in his acceptance of his true self, a vocation that includes suffering and death.

His crucifixion becomes a deeply human act, not only because dying is perhaps the most human thing he does, but because it is an outgrowth of his great "yes" to the totality of his true self. So a sixth question: Where are you called to surrender to the future that God has in store for you?

But that's not the end of the story: there is Easter!

Did you ever wonder if Jesus knew for certain that he would be raised from the dead? Now, I may be completely wrong, but I think that while Jesus lived his life in perfect faith, and trusted that something wonderful would come from his acceptance of his mission and his obedience to his Father—as it always had in the past—he may not have known precisely what this would lead to.

There are indications of this in the Gospels. Even while he hung on the cross, though freely giving himself to his mission, he cried out in pain and confusion.

For me, this possible ignorance of his own future makes his acceptance of his humanity more meaningful. He trusted God so completely that he knew that by following his vocation, even in the midst of unimaginable suffering, he would bring new life to others. And perhaps even Jesus didn't know what this new life would be, until the morning of that first Easter, when his true self was finally revealed in all its splendor and glory. It's wonderful to think that even he was surprised at the new life given him by God. It was only then that in Elizabeth Johnson's beautiful phrase, "his ultimate identity burst upon him with all clarity."

The life of Jesus Christ is the central metaphor for the Christian life. And the way that Jesus came to understand who he was, what he was meant to do, and how he was meant to do it, can help all of us on our journeys. All of us are called to meditate deeply on our own true selves, to embrace the reality of our vocations and to let God transform our true selves into sources of new life for others. It's a long route, a lifetime journey, but we are not alone. And we can look to the humanity of Jesus for a roadmap to this journey.

Now, as I mentioned, the one who seemed to know his mission better than he did at the beginning was his mother. And I'd like to look at a part of the spirituality of this very human woman. And she was human. Completely human.

You know the story of Jesus and the woman caught in adultery? So he meets the poor woman who is about to be stoned, and the crowd says that the punishment for adultery is stoning. And Jesus stands in front of the crowd, draws himself up, and says, "Let you who is without sin cast the first stone!" And from way in the back of the crowd a little stone comes flying way up in the air and bonks the woman on the head. And Jesus looks up, and says, "Mother, I'm trying to make a point!"

So Mary is conceived without sin, but she's also a human being, with the normal worries and doubts and struggles.

And you know, this took me a while to figure out. When I entered the Jesuits, my primary image of Mary was as "the Blessed Mother" or the "Mother of God." The woman who prays for us; the woman who intercedes for us.

But in the novitiate, especially during the homilies at Mass, I met a different Mary. For rather than presenting Mary as a cool, distant presence, she was revealed as something different: a human being. In one homily we considered Mary as the "first disciple," the first one to carry to others the message of Jesus—as she does to her cousin, Elizabeth. In another the one who prays: Mary the contemplative, who "treasures things in her heart," as the Gospel of Luke has it. In another the resourceful young woman from a poor background, who bears a son at an early age, who flees with her family into another country, who raises her son in difficult circumstances, who lives with surprise, uncertainty and mystery in her life, and is able to do so because of her faith.

But it was—for some reason—the story of the Annunciation in the Gospel of Luke, the tale of the angel Gabriel's visit to Mary that led me into a real devotion to the mother of Jesus.

For a long time I wondered: What is it about the Annunciation that captivated me? More importantly, what is it that appeals to so many believers? Why is this passage from the Gospel of Luke the subject of more works of art—paintings, sculptures, mosaics, frescos—than almost any other passage in the New Testament, except the Nativity and the Crucifixion?

There are plenty of other incidents from the life of Jesus with greater theological importance—miracle stories, physical healings and sermons. There are passages from the New Testament with greater relevance for the life of the church—like the church, the feeding of the five thousand, for example. Why does the Annunciation have such a pull on Catholics?

Maybe because it depicts the dramatic entrance of the divine into our everyday world: God greets a young girl in her simple home in a small town. Maybe because the passage highlights he special role of women in the divine plan: Mary accomplishes something that certainly no man could do. Maybe because of Mary herself—someone whom many believers hope to emulate: humble, obedient, loving, trusting. Maybe all of these reasons.

But I think that the Annunciation is appealing for a different reason. For in that gospel story Mary wonderfully exemplifies the role of the believer. The Annunciation perfectly describes the growth of a personal relationship with God. And in doing so the story offers us a microcosm of the spiritual life. So let's look at that one story and see how it might help you in your spiritual lives. And I'll ask some questions to get you thinking about this: How is the Annunciation similar to our spiritual lives?

To begin with, the initiative lies entirely with God. God, through the angel Gabriel, begins the dialogue with Mary. ("Hail, full of grace.") So it is with us. God takes the initiative, begins the conversation. God speaks to us, and, as with Mary, in often unexpected ways.

We are surprised to find ourselves deeply moved while catching a glimpse of a spectacular sunset on an otherwise cold and cloudy day, by holding one's newborn child, by receiving Communion at Mass, by hearing a long-awaited word of forgiveness. And in these things, in our emotions in particular, we are surprised to experience God's presence.

But God makes the first step, as God did with Mary. So the first question from Mary's life: Where is God starting a conversation with you? When Mary first experiences the presence of

God, she is fearful or "perplexed," as some translations have it. How often this happens to us. When we begin to wonder if God might be communicating with us—through our emotions, our experiences, our relationships, our prayer—we are often confused, overwhelmed, even fearful. Often we feel unworthy before the evidence of God's love, since the presence of the divine often illuminates our own human limitations.

This sense of unworthiness was the experience of so many figures in the Old and New Testaments. Think about St. Peter in the Gospel of Luke. After Peter and his friends have been fishing all night without success Jesus orders them to throw out their nets again. When their nets are miraculously filled, Peter suddenly realizes who it is who stands before him. Standing before Jesus, Peter feels his unworthiness. And it is a painful experience. "Depart from me," he says. "For I am a sinful man."

This very human experience—fear—is common in the spiritual life. You realize God might be speaking to you, and you're terrified of the implications. This image repeats itself frequently in Scripture. It is the experience of the shepherds in their fields in the narrative from Luke. "The glory of the Lord shone around them," says the New Revised Standard Version, "and they were terrified." Much better at conveying this emotion is the old King James Version: "They were sore afraid."

In light of this fear, the angel of the Lord offers the message that God offers all who respond in this manner: "Do not be afraid." Jesus, in that same passage from Luke, says the same to Peter, "Do not be afraid, for now you will be fishers of people." God understands our fear. At the Annunciation God understands Mary's fear as well: in the presence of God, Mary is afraid.

So, says Gabriel, "Fear not." So the second question, where are you afraid of letting God into your life?

Then the angel offers Mary an explanation, with more detail, about what God is asking of her. "You have found favor with God," he says. "And now, you will conceive in your womb and bear a son . . ." Again, how similar to our lives. After the initial encounter and after we confront our fear of God, and after we have the chance to reflect on our experience with God, and it becomes clearer what God is asking us to do.

An experience, for example, of holding our newborn child is a vivid experience of God for parents. And again, while it may be initially frightening (You wonder, How will I ever care for this child?) it soon becomes clearer what God is asking us to do: Love.

Then Mary questions. How wonderful. What must have been a young, probably illiterate woman from a backwater town *pressed* the Angel of the Lord for an explanation. Pressed him! "How can this be," asked a practical Mary to God's messenger, "since I am a virgin?"

This is the part of the story that may be most familiar to us: Who hasn't questioned the will of God in their lives? Who, when confronted with the illness or death of a friend or relative hasn't questioned? Who, in the face of suffering or change hasn't questioned? Who hasn't said to God, "How can this be?"

Gabriel responds how God often responds to us. The angel reminds Mary to look around her. In other words, to consider the experience in her life and in others: "Know that your kinswoman Elizabeth is in her sixth month. She who was once thought to be barren is now with child. For nothing is impossible with God." Look around you. Look at what God can do, and has done.

Frequently in spiritual direction I meet people doubting that God is accompanying them during a difficult experience. Perhaps someone has lost a job. Or someone has grown ill or old. Or a relationship has ended. They begin to doubt the presence of God. But usually all it takes for them to regain their trust is a simple question: "Hasn't God been with you in the past?" Often they will think for a while and say, "Yes, now that you mention it, each time I thought I couldn't go on, I found that something or someone helped me to do so. I really felt God was right there with me."

It's like the story of the old abbot who used to speak frequently to his monks of finding God, searching for God and encountering God. One day one of his monks asked him if he had ever encountered God himself. The abbot, after some embarrassed silence, admitted that he had never had a vision or a direct experience of God. But, he said, there was nothing surprising about that—hadn't God said to Moses in the Book of Exodus, "You cannot see my face?" But God had also taught Moses that he could see his back as he passed by. "You will see me pass," said God to Moses. So looking back over his life, the abbot could see the "passage of God" in his life.

Peter-Hans Kolvenbach, the former Jesuit superior general, once wrote, "It is less a matter of searching for God than of allowing oneself to be found by him in all of life's situations, where he does not cease to pass and where he allows himself to be recognized once he has really passed."

What a wonderful insight. More often than not God is found by looking *back* over your life, or your week, or your day, and saying, "Yes, *there* was God."

Gabriel, in essence, says the same to Mary: Just look what God has already done. Look at Elizabeth. Nothing is impossible with God. So the third question from Mary: Where can you look in your life, backwards, to see signs of God's presence?

When Mary reflects on what she sees around her, on her own experience and on her knowledge of Elizabeth, she is able, even in light of what is being asked of her, to say yes. "Let it be done to me according to your will."

Mary does this in perfect freedom. As do we. God meets us in myriad ways, through nature, through prayer, especially through people. God invites us to join him, God invites us to follow her will, God invites us to create with him. But the decision is always up to us. Mary could have said no.

With her yes, Mary partners herself with the Almighty and is empowered to bring Christ into the world.

Just like us. With our own "yes" to God's voice in our lives we are also asked to nurture the word of God within us and bring Christ into the world—not exactly in the way that Mary was, but in our own situations and using our own talents and graces, we are called to bring Christ into the lives of others.

So the fourth question: what yeses of yours have brought new life into the world, and what nos of yours have prevented new life?

In describing the encounter between Gabriel and Mary, the Gospel of Luke perfectly describes the arc of the spiritual life: God initiates the conversation, we are initially hesitant and fearful; we seek to understand God's word in our life; God reminds us of our experience, and, free to choose, if we say yes to God, we bring new life into the world.

But that is not the whole story. A few months ago I was discussing my love of this passage with a woman religious. She said, "You're forgetting the most important part of the story! Then the angel left her!" she said. Isn't that always the way it is with us? After these encounters with God—whatever it is in our lives—we are left alone to carry out what we are asked to do. Frequently it seems very lonely! Who knows if Mary ever encountered God as deeply as she did before Jesus' birth?

That's the part of trusting that what God has told us is to be trusted. The part of faith.

So the last question from Mary: where are you called to be faithful to the word, even in the midst of silence?

Now let's turn to Mary's husband, Joseph. You know I always feel a little sorry for poor Joseph. On many Christmas cards these days you'll notice that Joseph is usually stuck in the back—old, balding, sometimes even leaving the scene. He doesn't get much respect, but he should! Not only did he help raise the Son of God, but his story has a lot to teach us. You know the story of the Latino Catholic pastoral associate who goes to church on a Sunday in the middle of March. After Mass, on the way out of church, she greets the pastor. And he says, "Will you be coming to the St. Patrick's Day celebration this week? And she shakes her head. "Well, you know that I don't have much of a devotion to St. Patrick," she said. And he says, Why not? And she says, "Well, nothing against St. Patrick, but I'm not Irish, as you know. I prefer saints that speak more to the Latino experience." And then she says, "But I *will* see you on the Feast of St. Joseph!"

And the priest says, "Well, technically, he's Jewish! How come you like him?" And she says, "Well, he's Latino by marriage." And the priest says, "What do you mean?" And she smiles and said, "Well, as I see it, he married Our Lady of Guadalupe, so he's one of us."

He is one of us. And his story speaks to our stories.

Now, like many saints whose lineage is traced back to the earliest days of the church, little is known about Saint Joseph, other than the few lines written about him in the gospels. He was of the line of King David, and was to be engaged to a young woman from Nazareth. Mary was found, quite unexpectedly, to be pregnant. But Joseph, "being a righteous man and unwilling to expose her to public disgrace," as the Gospel of Matthew says, planned to dissolve his betrothal quietly. And so, even before Jesus is born, Joseph's tender compassion and forgiving heart was on full display. That must have earned him the contempt of many in Nazareth.

So here is the first question from Joseph: Where are you called to be understanding even in the midst of a disbelieving or unforgiving community?

But God had other plans. As he did for another troubled Joseph—the patriarch of the book of Genesis—God used a dream to reveal his saving plans for the carpenter from Nazareth. In the dream, an angel let Joseph in on Mary's secret. That same angel, after the birth of Mary's son, advised him to take the child and his mother to Egypt, to flee the murderous Herod. Joseph listens.

A few more stories about the boy Jesus—he is lost on a journey and found teaching in the Temple—and we are into the hidden life.

This is Joseph's time. A time spent caring for his son—or to put it more precisely, his "foster son"—and teaching him the trade of carpentry or woodworking. In Joseph's workshop in Nazareth, Jesus would have learned about the raw materials for his craft: which wood was best suited for chairs and tables, which worked best for yokes, for ploughs. An experienced

Joseph would have taught his apprentice the right way to drive a nail with a hammer, the proper way to drill a clean and deep hole in a plank, the correct way to level a ledge or lintel.

As I had mentioned, Joseph would have passed on to Jesus the values required to become a good carpenter. You need patience (for waiting until the olive wood is dry and ready), judgement (for ensuring that your plumb line is straight), honesty (for charging people a fair price) and persistence (for sanding until the tabletop is smooth to the touch). Alongside his teacher, a young Jesus labored and built, contributing all the while to the common good of Nazareth and the surrounding towns. It's not hard to imagine that the skills Jesus learned from his teacher—patience, judgement, honesty and persistence—would serve him well in his later ministry? Joseph helped to fashion Jesus into what the theologian John Haughey, S.J., called "the instrument most needed for the salvation of the world."

The things that seem so insignificant, so hidden, so small—teaching an adolescent about carpentry—turn out to be quite important indeed. So the second question: Where in your life are you called to do small things with great love? And even if they seem unimportant can you trust that God will use them in ways that you might never understand?

As a father, Joseph would have been one of his son's primary teachers in his religious faith as well. Introducing him to the great men and women of the Scriptures, teaching him the Hebrew prayers, encouraging his boy to listen to the rabbis and religious leaders of the town. And talking to him about God. Children and adolescents are usually bursting with questions about God. It is probable that Joseph was the first one who Jesus went to with his questions. So Jesus's understanding of God the Father, his Father, may have been shaped not only by Joseph's own life, but by Joseph's answers to his questions. Joseph's faith was one of the foundations of Jesus's faith. Is it so hard to imagine that our understanding of God the Father was influenced by the kind of father that Joseph was?

But as soon as Jesus started his ministry, Joseph disappears, at least in the Gospel narratives. What happened to the guardian of Jesus? Tradition holds that by the time that Jesus began his began preaching, Joseph had already died. Joseph is not listed among the guests at the wedding feast at Cana, the beginning of the public ministry of Jesus. But did he die before his son had reached adulthood?

How they must have wished Joseph could have seen and heard about his son's work among the people of Israel. How they must have wished for the counsel of their father and husband during the confusing times Jesus's public ministry. And how Mary must have longed for his shoulder to support her during the Crucifixion.

Whenever the death of Joseph occurred, he is not mentioned beyond those few early passages in Scripture. After that, it is his life that now becomes hidden.

It is this hiddenness of Joseph's life that speaks to me. Appearing only briefly in the Gospels, given no words to speak at all, Joseph leads a life of quiet service to God, a life that remains almost totally unknown to us. It was, necessarily, a life of humility that you can see today.

But most especially in the lives of the poor. You know, during my Jesuit training I worked with the Jesuit Refugee Service in Nairobi Kenya for two years. My work there was to help East African refugees, who had settled in the slums of Nairobi, to open small businesses and support themselves.

And as part of my work, I frequently visited many of the refugees in their small homes, hovels really, in the slums of Nairobi. One day I visited a woman to whom we had given a small sewing machine to help with her business of mending her neighbor's clothes. She lived in a single dark room crammed with her few possessions: an old mattress on which slept her four children, a small hissing kerosene stove, a plastic pail of water, a cardboard box of clothes. Who is more hidden than the refugee, secreted away in her small hovel in a sprawling slum, huddled over her little sewing machine, trying to earn a living for her and her family? When the refugees used to visit me at our office in Nairobi, it sometimes seemed that, shorn of their connection to their country, bereft of friends, lacking money and facing the bleakest economic prospects, they were utterly submerged beneath a sea of poverty, hidden from the sight of the world.

The hidden life is shared by many people, even in the more affluent parts of the world. The middle-aged, unmarried woman who dutifully cares for her aged mother, but whose sacrifices and devotion remain largely hidden from her neighbors. The loving parents of the handicapped child who will care for him for his entire life, and whose worries and heartaches remain unknown to their friends. The black woman who knows racism and sexism, the gay man knows homophobia, both of whom lead quietly loving lives anyway. The single mother in the inner city working two jobs to provide an education for her children, and whose tiring night-shifts are still, after many years, a secret to her daytime co-workers. Countless hidden lives of love and service for others. The day-to-day pouring out of oneself for God.

This kind of hiddenness is attractive to me—and let me engage in some confession—because it is so far from the goals of my own selfish desires. In a culture that prizes the bold gesture, the public proclamation, the newsworthy article, I find myself often drawn to achieving things so that other people can see them. Doing a good work seems insufficient: others need to know that I have done this good work! In this way I find my appetite for fame in contradiction to what Jesus taught, "But when you give alms," he says in the Gospel of Matthew, "do not let your left hand know what your right one is doing, so that you alms may be done in secret; and your Father who sees in secret, will repay you."

I want humility but on my terms. I once told my spiritual director that I wanted to be so humble that people would recognize me for this. And we both laughed. I said "I want a humility that I can be proud of!"

So the third and final question about Joseph: Where is your most hidden holiness? Can you allow God to bless these hidden acts of charity that you do? Can you see your hiddenness as holy?

The burning desire for fame is a manifestation of pride, a pride that seeks not for the hiddenness of the desert or the humility of the unseen act, but the adulation and approval of others. Ultimately it is a destructive mindset, since one can never receive enough acclaim to satisfy the craving for attention or fame or notoriety. Inexorably, it to despair and so must be resisted. But while necessary, the path to humility is a difficult one to trod. In Henri Nouwen's phrase, one strives to seek the freedom to be "hidden from the world, but visible to God."

And I wonder if the more hidden the act, the more it is valued by God. I am always reminded of the story of a master sculptor in one of the great medieval cathedrals of France. The old man spent hours and hours carving the back of a statue of Mary, lovingly finishing the intricate curves and folds of her gown. But, someone asked the sculptor, what's the point? That statue will be placed in a dark niche against the wall, where certainly no one will ever see the back of it. God will see it, he answers.

The life of Joseph is the life of hidden holiness, the holiness most valued by God.

The lives of Jesus, Mary and Joseph may seem far removed from our own today. But if we look at them carefully we can see how their lives offer an invitation to grow in our own humanity and holiness. This morning we've looked at just a few windows into their lives. How Jesus helps us become who we are meant to be. How Mary helps us to understand our relationship with God. And how Joseph helps us to lead lives of hidden holiness.

So the next time you feel lost in your lives you may use the same words that my father did, my father who now lives with these three persons in heaven. And call on them for help, as "Jesus, Mary and Joseph!"   —LAREC, 2009

NEWBORN

Two young children have helped me see the nativity of the Lord in a new way. Their presence in my life has made the Christmas story an entirely new experience.

When I first started meditating on the nativity as a Jesuit novice, my meditations focused on the theological import of the event. Happily, I have a fairly vivid imagination, so it was easy to imagine the birth scene just as if I were there, as St. Ignatius Loyola suggests in his *Spiritual Exercises*. In my mind's eye, I could see the inky night, the crude shelter, the sleepy-eyed cows, the exhausted parents and the squalling baby. And it was easy to feel amazed by the Incarnation, when God chose to pitch his tent among us, as some translations of the Gospel of John have it (1:14).

But until the birth of my first nephew, I never appreciated how a newborn child can change everything. When he was born nine years ago, I was astonished by the way our family immediately changed its focus. Our hearts were now centered on a little child. What did he do yesterday? What is he doing today? What will he do tomorrow? How miraculous that God had created a brand-new person, someone we could never have imagined, who would change our lives. The same happened with my sister's second child, born two years ago, who is a gift in equal measure, but so different from the first.

Nor had I appreciated the accompanying worry, and sometimes fear, that goes with childrearing. (Still, I don't fully understand it, since I'm not a parent.) When I think about my nephews, I pray that nothing bad will happen to them, hope that they will be physically well and desire that they will be happy. But I know that at some point the world will be painful for them.

Most likely it was similar for Mary and Joseph as they pondered the future of their baby. While Luke's Gospel offers a brief sketch of how Mary discovered Gods plan for her (2:26–38), we have little idea of her innermost thoughts attending the birth of her son. As the New Testament scholar Joseph Fitzmyer, S.J., says about the annunciation, "What really happened? We shall never know." We have even less insight into Joseph's heart; Mary's husband is completely silent in Scripture.

We can assume that Mary and Joseph must have gathered from a variety of sources—the angelic messages, the dreams, the unique birth of their son, the strange utterances of Simeon and Anna—that their baby's life likely would be a strange one, filled with unusual joys and sorrows. And so they protected him as best they could, first sheltering him from the elements and later, in Egypt, from Herod's murderous wrath. But did they know, even then, that they would not be able to protect him forever?

All of us are called to emulate Mary and Joseph. We are invited to listen carefully to God, to respond with a trusting yes (often, like Mary, after some questioning) and, finally, to bring Christ into the world—not in his flesh, but in ours and in other ways important today.

And we are called to nurture our faith, which can be as precious and fragile as a newborn child. This does not mean that we jealously guard our faith from the world, but that we understand that our faith and our vocations need to be nourished, cared for and revered as gifts from God.

These are calls for every Christian, no matter who we are or where we came from. In the Christmas vigil Mass, the Gospel reading is taken from Matthew, who details the genealogy of Jesus family (1:18–25). That seemingly interminable list shows that the Messiah came from a long line of people who were not perfect. Within his family are a few unsavory characters. (You think your family is dysfunctional? Read Matthew.) Out of that holy but entirely human tree grew a new green shoot that would change everything.

How overwhelming the first Christmas must have been for Mary and Joseph. Few things can provoke such intense worry as a newborn child. Ask any parent. But few things promise such unreasonable hope, such unexpected change and such unbounded joy.

May your heart be newborn this Christmas.

—*America*, December 24, 2007

SAINTLY BAD BEHAVIOR

Many saints among us are not officially recognized by the Catholic Church; nevertheless, they remain role models of sanctity and witness to the faith. In this essay, Martin introduces people, canonized and not, who might have even behaved in ways that scandalize the rest of us, because of our political convictions, because of our conflation of holiness with blandness, or because our focus is on our own personal idols rather than on following God.

Recently, word came that the miracle required for Pope John Paul II's beatification may have happened: A French nun's Parkinson's disappeared after her religious community prayed to him to intercede. But amid the growing enthusiasm for the canonization of Pope John Paul II comes some dissent from a surprising place—within the Catholic Church. Not that the dissenters are airing their grievances publicly. Grumbling about someone's canonization is a little like complaining about a co-worker's promotion: It makes you look like a spoilsport.

The naysayers, mainly on the left, see John Paul not as one of the great religious figures of the age, but as a person with whom they often disagreed, particularly on issues of the ordination of women, the Vatican's response to the sexual-abuse crisis, and treatment of gays and lesbians. The most common arguments against his canonization can be boiled down to two: First, I disagreed with him. Second, he wasn't perfect.

Both objections fundamentally misunderstand who the saints are, and were. Many people envision the saints as perfect human beings whose flaws, if any, miraculously evaporated once they decided to become, well, saintly. Popular iconography does little to correct this misconception. Those pristine marble statues, romantic stained-glass images, and kitschy holy cards make it easy to forget that the saints were human beings who sinned not only before their conversions, but afterward, too.

Early sinning in the lives of the saints has always been a staple of hagiography, the study of saints. Biographers played up the

preconversion badness to make clearer postconversion goodness. Even pious biographies of St. Augustine mention his dissolute early years, his living with a concubine and fathering a
child out of wedlock. ("Lord, give me chastity," he prayed, "but
not yet.") According to *Butler's Lives of the Saints*, the standard reference manual, the party-hearty young Francis of Assisi
spent his father's money "lavishly, even ostentatiously." And St.
Ignatius of Loyola, the founder of the Jesuits, may be the only
saint with a notarized police record, for nighttime brawling with
intent to inflict serious harm.

But even after their decisions to amend their lives, the saints
remained stubbornly imperfect. In other words: human. And the
history of sinful saints begins right at the start of Christianity. St.
Peter, traditionally described as the "first pope," denied knowing
Jesus three times before the Crucifixion. As the priest in the film
Moonstruck says, "That's a pretty big sin."

Four centuries later, St. Jerome, the brilliant polymath who
translated the Bible into Latin, was a famously nasty Christian.
When confronted with criticism, he was reliably uncharitable.
In the early fifth century, the future saint wrote a snide public letter to a prominent theologian named Rufinus, addressing
him as "my most simple-minded friend" and commenting that
he "walked like a tortoise." Jerome kept up the invective even
after Rufinus' death, when a gentler appraisal might have been
expected.

Likewise, St. Cyril of Alexandria, archbishop of the city from
412 to 444, is described by *Butler's Lives* as "brave but sometimes over vehement, even violent." Reconciliation was apparently not his strong suit. During a church council in Ephesus in
431, Cyril led a group of unruly followers to depose and exile
another bishop who had disagreed with Cyril's theological writings. The late Edward A. Ryan, a Jesuit church historian and
seminary professor, said wryly, "We don't know anything about
the last years of Cyril's life. Those must have been the years in
which he was made a saint."

Contemporary avatars of holiness also had their foibles. Trappist monk Thomas Merton, one of the great spiritual masters of the 20th century, could be vain, impatient, and short-tempered. Late in life, he also broke his monastic vows by sleeping with a young nurse he met during a hospital stay, sneaking off the monastery grounds to meet with her. (Afterward, Merton repented over misleading the woman and recommitted himself to a life of chastity.) And Mother Teresa could be occasionally tart with any of her sisters whom she suspected of malingering. "You live with the name of the poor but enjoy a lazy life," she wrote to one convent.

All these men and women were holy, striving to devote their lives to God. They were also human. And they knew it, too. Of all people, the saints were the most cognizant of their flawed humanity, which served as a reminder of their reliance on God.

Unfortunately, well-meaning hagiography often tries to dial down the saints' human side to make their lives seem more virtuous. So, the modern-day conception of Francis of Assisi ends up depicting him as a kind of well-meaning peacenik, rather than the complicated man who was something of a hothead. (Francis once clambered atop the roof of a house his brothers built and began tearing it apart—he felt it was not in keeping with their life of poverty.)

While I disagreed with some of Pope John Paul's positions, and while the late pope wasn't always a fan of the Jesuits, I believe he was a saint. The man born Karol Wojtyla was devoted to God, devoted to advancing the Gospel, and devoted to the poor. And, just like his critics, he was aware of his faults. (He went to confession weekly.) Those who oppose the idea of St. John Paul might remember that perfection is not a requirement for holiness. And sanctity does not mean divinity.

Supporters of John Paul, on the other hand, should remember that his inevitable canonization does not mean he was flawless, and that it isn't heretical to criticize a saint. As another saint, Frenchman Francis de Sales, wrote in the 17th century, "There is no harm done to the saints if their faults are shown as well as

their virtues. But great harm is done to everybody by those hagi-
ographers who slur over their faults. . . . These writers commit
a wrong against the saints and against the whole of posterity."
John Paul wasn't a saint because he was perfect; he was a saint
because he was most fully himself. And that will make it easier
for me to say, some day, St. John Paul, pray for me.

—*Slate*, April 20, 2007

THE SAINT OF THE SOCK DRAWER

In this justly famous selection from My Life with the Saints, *Martin deftly obliterates the notion that the quest for holiness is out of reach for some of us and more natural for others. Rather, this passage about his own childhood spiritual yearnings suggests what St. Paul stated twenty centuries ago: that we all at first see as if through a glass darkly. Even in the simple and unsophisticated yearnings of a child (or the childlike) are the beginnings of a life dedicated to the slow and steady pursuit of holiness.*

When I was nine, my greatest pleasure was ordering things through the mail. The cereal boxes that filled our kitchen shelves all boasted small order forms on the back, which I would clip out, fill in with my address and send away, along with a dollar bill or two. A few weeks later a brown paper package addressed to me would arrive in our mailbox. Nothing filled me with more excitement.

While the most attractive offers typically appeared in comic books, these advertisements rarely represented what the postman eventually delivered. The "Terrifying Flying Ghost" on the inside back cover of a Spider-Man comic book turned out to be a cheap plastic ball, a rubber band, and a piece of white tissue paper. The "Fake Vomit" looked nothing like the real stuff, and the "Monster Tarantula" was not monstrous at all.

Worst of all were the "Sea Monkeys." The colorful advertisement depicted smiling aquatic figures (the largest one wearing a golden crown) happily cavorting in a sort of sea city.

Unfortunately, my six-week wait for them had a disappointing end: the Sea Monkeys turned out to be a packet of shrimp eggs. And while the Sea Monkeys did eventually hatch in a fishbowl on a chair in my bedroom, they were so small as to be nearly invisible, and none, as far as I could tell, wore a crown. (Sea Monkey City was nearly decimated when I accidentally sneezed on it during my annual winter cold.)

Other purchases were more successful. My Swimming Tony the Tiger toy, whose purchase required eating my way through several boxes of Sugar Frosted Flakes to earn sufficient box tops, amazed even my parents with his swimming skills. The orange and black plastic tiger had arms that rotated and legs that kicked maniacally, and he was able to churn his way through the choppy waters of the stopped up kitchen sink. One day, Tony, fresh from a dip, slipped from my fingers and fell on the linoleum floor. Both of his arms fell off, marking the end of his short swimming career. I put the armless tiger in the fishbowl with the Sea Monkeys, who seemed not to mind the company.

But even with my predilection for mail-order purchases, I would be hard-pressed to explain what led me to focus my childish desires on a plastic statue of St. Jude that I had spied in a magazine. I can't imagine what magazine this might have been, since my parents weren't in the habit of leaving Catholic publications lying around the house, but apparently the photo of the statue was sufficiently appealing to convince me to drop $3.50 into an envelope. That sum represented not only an excess of three weeks' allowance but also the forgoing of an Archie comic book—a real sacrifice at the time.

It certainly wasn't any interest on the part of my family, or any knowledge about St. Jude, that drew me to his statue. I knew nothing about him, other than what the magazine ad told me: he was the patron saint of hopeless causes. Even if I had been interested in reading about him, there would have been little to read; for all his current popularity, Jude remains a mysterious figure. Though he is named as one of the twelve apostles of Jesus, there are only three brief mentions of Jude in the entire New Testament. In fact, two lists of the apostles don't include him at all. Instead they mention a certain "Thaddeus," giving rise to the name "St. Jude Thaddeus." To confuse matters more, there is also a Jude listed as the brother of Jesus in the Gospel of Mark. And though some ancient legends mention his work in Mesopotamia, the *Encyclopedia of Catholicism* says candidly, "We have no reliable information about this obscure figure."

But Jude's story didn't concern me. What appealed to me most was that he was patron of hopeless causes. Who knew what help someone like that could give me? A tiger that could swim in the kitchen sink was one thing, but a saint who could help me get what I wanted was quite another. It was worth at least $3.50.

In a few weeks, I received a little package containing a nine-inch beige plastic statue, along with a booklet of prayers to be used for praying to my new patron. St. Jude the Beige, who held a staff and carried a sort of plate emblazoned with the image of a face (which I supposed was Jesus, though this was difficult to discern), was immediately given pride of place on top of the dresser in my bedroom.

At the time, I prayed to God only intermittently, and then mainly to ask for things, such as: "Please let me get an A on my next test." "Please let me do well in Little League this year." "Please let my skin clear up for the school picture." I used to envision God as the Great Problem Solver, the one who would fix everything if I just prayed hard enough, used the correct prayers, and prayed in precisely the right way. But when God couldn't fix things (which seemed more frequent than I would have liked), I would turn to St. Jude. I figured that if it was beyond the capacity of God to do something, then surely it must be a lost cause, and it was time to call on St. Jude.

Fortunately, the booklet that accompanied the St. Jude statue included plenty of good prayers and even featured one in Latin that began *"Tantum ergo sacramentum . . ."* I saved the Latin prayer for the most important hopeless causes—final exams and the like. When I really wanted something, I would say the "*Tantum ergo sacramentum*" prayer three times on my knees.

St. Jude stood patiently atop my dresser until high school. My high school friends, when visiting my house, often asked to see my bedroom (we were all inordinately curious about what each other's bedroom looked like). And though I was by now fond of St. Jude, I was afraid of what my friends would think if they spotted the strange plastic statue standing on my dresser. So St. Jude was relegated to inside my sock drawer and brought out only on special occasions.

My faith was another thing, you could say, that was relegated to the sock drawer for the next several years. During high school, I made it to Mass more or less weekly; but later, in college, I became just an occasional churchgoer (though I still prayed to the Great Problem Solver). And as my faith grew thinner and thinner, my affinity for St. Jude began to seem a little childish: silly, superstitious, and faintly embarrassing.

That changed for me at age twenty-six. Dissatisfied with my life in the business world, I began to consider doing something else, though at the time I had little idea of what that something else would be. All I knew was that after five years in corporate America, I was miserable and wanted out. From that rather banal sentiment, however, God was able to work. The Great Problem Solver was at work on a problem that I only dimly comprehended. In time, God would give me an answer to a question that I hadn't even asked.

One evening, after a long day's work, I came home and flipped on the television set. The local PBS station was airing a documentary about a Catholic priest named Thomas Merton. Though I had never heard of Merton, all sorts of famous talking heads appeared on-screen to testify to his enormous influence on their lives. In just a few minutes of watching the program I got the idea that Thomas Merton was bright, funny, holy, and altogether unique. The documentary was so interesting that it prompted me to track down, purchase, and read his autobiography, *The*

Seven Storey Mountain, which told the story of his journey from an aimless youth to a Trappist monk. It captivated me as few books ever have.

Over the next two years, whenever I thought seriously about the future, the only thing that seemed to make any sense was entering a religious order. There were, of course, some doubts, some false starts, some hesitations, and some worries about embarrassing myself, but eventually I decided to quit my job and, at age twenty-eight, enter the Society of Jesus, the religious order more commonly known as the Jesuits. It was certainly the best decision I've ever made.

Upon entering the Jesuit novitiate, I was surprised to learn that most of my fellow novices had strong "devotions," as they called them, to one or another saint. They spoke with obvious affection for their favorite saints—almost as if they knew them personally. One novice, for example, was especially fond of Dorothy Day, quoting her liberally during our weekly community meetings. Another talked a great deal about St. Therese of Lisieux. But though my brother novices were sincere in their devotions, and they patiently related the lives of their heroes and heroines to me, I now found the idea of praying to the saints wholly superstitious. What was the point? If God hears your prayers, why do you need the saints?

These questions were answered when I discovered the collection of saints' biographies that filled the creaky wooden bookcases in the novitiate library.

I pulled my first selection from the shelves as a result of some serious prompting from one novice: "You've got to read *The Story of a Soul,*" he kept telling me (badgering me was more like it). "Then you'll understand why I like Therese so much."

At this point, I knew little about the "Little Flower," as she is known, and imagined Therese of Lisieux as a sort of shrinking violet: timid, skittish, and dull. So I was astonished when her autobiography revealed instead a lively, intelligent, and strong-willed woman, someone I might like to have known. Reading her story led me to track down biographies of other saints—some well known, some obscure—in our library: St. Stanislaus Kostka, who, despite vigorous protests from his family, walked 450 miles to enter the Jesuit novitiate. St. Thomas More, whose fine intellect and love of country did not blind him to the centrality of God in his life. St. Teresa of Avila, who decided, to the surprise of most and the dismay of many, to overhaul her Carmelite Order. And Pope John XXIII, who, I was happy to discover, was not only compassionate and innovative but also witty.

Gradually I found myself growing fonder of these saints and developing a tenderness toward them. I began to see them as models of holiness relevant to contemporary believers, and to understand the remarkable ways that God works in the lives of individuals. Each saint was holy in his or her unique way, revealing how God celebrates individuality. As C. S. Lewis writes in *Mere Christianity*: "How monotonously alike all the great tyrants and conquerors have been: how gloriously different are the saints."

This gave me enormous consolation, for I realized that none of us are meant to be Therese of Lisieux or Pope John XXIII or Thomas More. We're meant to be ourselves, and meant to allow God to work in and through our own individuality, our own humanity. As St. Thomas Aquinas said, grace builds on nature.

Moreover, I found companions among the saints—friends to turn to when I needed a helping hand. My novice director told me that he thought of the saints as older brothers and sisters to whom one could look for advice and counsel. The Catholic theologian Lawrence S. Cunningham, in his book *The Meaning of Saints*, suggests that the saints also serve as our "prophetic witnesses," spurring us to live more fully as Christian disciples. Of course some might argue (and some do argue) that all you need is Jesus. And that's true: Jesus is everything, and the saints understood this more than anyone.

But God in his wisdom has also given us these companions of Jesus to accompany us along the way, so why not accept the gift of their friendship and encouragement? And there's no reason to feel as if devotion to the saints somehow takes away from your devotion to Jesus: everything the saints say and do is centered on Christ and points us in his direction. One day at Mass in the novitiate chapel, I heard—as if for the first time—a prayer of thanksgiving to God for the saints: "You renew the Church in every age by raising up men and women outstanding in holiness, living witnesses of your unchanging love. They inspire us by their heroic lives, and help us by their constant prayers to be the living sign of your saving power."

And I thought, Yes.

In reading the lives of the saints, I also discovered that I could easily recognize myself, or at least parts of myself, in their stories. This was the aspect of their lives that I most appreciated: they had struggled with the same human foibles that everyone does. Knowing this, in turn, encouraged me to pray to them for help during particular times and for particular needs. I knew that Thomas Merton had struggled greatly with pride and egotism, so when combating the same I would pray for his intercession. When sick I would pray to Therese of Lisieux; she understood what it was to battle self-pity and boredom during an illness. For courage, I prayed to Joan of Arc. For compassion, to Aloysius Gonzaga. For a better sense of humor and an appreciation of the absurdities of life, to Pope John XXIII.

Quite by surprise, then, I went from someone embarrassed by my affection for the saints to someone who counted it as one of the joys of my life. Even after the novitiate, as my Jesuit training continued, I read about the saints and took special pleasure in meeting new ones. You can never have too many friends.

Now I find myself introducing others to favorite saints and, likewise, being introduced. It's funny—the way you discover a new saint is often similar to the way in which you meet a new friend. Maybe you hear an admiring comment about someone and think, I'd like to get to know that person, such as when I started reading about English Catholic history and knew that I wanted to meet Thomas More. Perhaps you're introduced to a person by someone else who knows you'll enjoy that person's company, just as that novice introduced me to Therese.

Or perhaps you run across someone, totally by accident, during your day-to-day life. It wasn't until my philosophy studies as a Jesuit that I read St. Augustine's Confessions and fell in love with his writings and his way of speaking of God. . . .

At the beginning of this essay, I said that I wasn't sure what led me to my affinity to St. Jude. But as I think about it, I know it was God who did so. God works in some very weird ways, and moving a boy to begin a life of devotion to the saints through a magazine advertisement is just one of them. Yet grace is grace, and when I look back over my life, I give thanks that I've met so many wonderful saints—who pray for me, offer me comfort, give me examples of discipleship, and help me along the way.

All of this, I like to think, is thanks to St. Jude. For all those years stuck inside the sock drawer, he prayed for a boy who didn't even know that he was being prayed for.

—My Life with the Saints, 1–9

MODERN SPIRITUAL MASTERS
Robert Ellsberg, Series Editor

This series introduces the essential writing and vision of some of the great spiritual teachers of our time. While many of these figures are rooted in long-established traditions of spirituality, others have charted new, untested paths. In each case, however, they have engaged in a spiritual journey shaped by the challenges and concerns of our age. Together with the saints and witnesses of previous centuries, these modern spiritual masters may serve as guides and companions to a new generation of seekers.

Already published:
Modern Spiritual Masters (edited by Robert Ellsberg)
Swami Abhishiktananda (edited by Shirley du Boulay)
Metropolitan Anthony of Sourozh (edited by Gillian Crow)
Eberhard Arnold (edited by Johann Christoph Arnold)
Pedro Arrupe (edited by Kevin F. Burke, S.J.)
Daniel Berrigan (edited by John Dear)
Thomas Berry (edited by Mary EvelynTucker and John Grim)
Dietrich Bonhoeffer (edited by Robert Coles)
Robert McAfee Brown (edited by Paul Crowley)
Dom Helder Camara (edited by Francis McDonagh)
Carlo Carretto (edited by Robert Ellsberg)
G. K. Chesterton (edited by William Griffin)
Joan Chittister (edited by Mary Lou Kownacki and Mary
    Hembrow Snyder)
Yves Congar (edited by Paul Lakeland)
The Dalai Lama (edited by Thomas A. Forsthoefel)
Alfred Delp, S.J. (introduction by Thomas Merton)
Catherine de Hueck Dogerty (edited by David Meconi, S.J.)
Virgilio Elizondo (edited by Timothy Matovina)
Jacques Ellul (edited by Jacob E. Van Vleet)
Ralph Waldo Emerson (edited by Jon M. Sweeney)
Charles de Foucauld (edited by Robert Ellsberg)
Mohandas Gandhi (edited by John Dear)
Bede Griffiths (edited by Thomas Matus)
Romano Guardini (edited by Robert A. Krieg)
Gustavo Gutiérrez (edited by Daniel G. Groody)
Thich Nhat Hanh (edited by Robert Ellsberg)
Abraham Joshua Heschel (edited by Susannah Heschel)

Etty Hillesum (edited by Annemarie S. Kidder)
Caryll Houselander (edited by Wendy M. Wright)
Pope John XXIII (edited by Jean Maalouf)
Rufus Jones (edited by Kerry Walters)
Clarence Jordan (edited by Joyce Hollyday)
Walter Kasper (edited by Patricia C. Bellm and Robert A. Krieg)
John Main (edited by Laurence Freeman)
James Martin (edited by James T. Keane)
Anthony de Mello (edited by William Dych, S.J.)
Thomas Merton (edited by Christine M. Bochen)
John Muir (edited by Tim Flinders)
John Henry Newman (edited by John T. Ford, C.S.C.)
Henri Nouwen (edited by Robert A. Jonas)
Flannery O'Connor (edited by Robert Ellsberg)
Karl Rahner (edited by Philip Endean)
Brother Roger of Taizé (edited by Marcello Fidanzio)
Oscar Romero (by Marie Dennis, Rennie Golden, and
    Scott Wright)
Albert Schweitzer (edited by James Brabazon)
Frank Sheed and Maisie Ward (edited by David Meconi)
Sadhu Sundar Singh (edited by Charles E. Moore)
Mother Maria Skobtsova (introduction by Jim Forest)
Dorothee Soelle (edited by Dianne L. Oliver)
Edith Stein (edited by John Sullivan, O.C.D.)
David Steindl-Rast (edited by Clare Hallward)
William Stringfellow (edited by Bill Wylie-Kellerman)
Pierre Teilhard de Chardin (edited by Ursula King)
Mother Teresa (edited by Jean Maalouf)
St. Thérèse of Lisieux (edited by Mary Frohlich)
Phyllis Tickle (edited by Jon M. Sweeney)
Henry David Thoreau (edited by Tim Flinders)
Howard Thurman (edited by Mary Krohlich)
Leo Tolstoy (edited by Charles E. Moore)
Evelyn Underhill (edited by Emilie Griffin)
Vincent Van Gogh (by Carol Berry)
Jean Vanier (edited by Carolyn Whitney-Brown)
Swami Vivekananda (edited by Victor M. Parachin)
Simone Weil (edited by Eric O. Springsted)
John Howard Yoder (edited by Paul Martens and Jenny Howells)